FREUD AND JUNG ON RELIGION

D0002729

Michael Palmer

Routledge
Taylor & Francis Group

LONDON AND NEW YORK

First published 1997
by Routledge
11 New Fetter Lane, London EC4P 4EE

Reprinted 1999

Simultaneously published in the USA and Canada
by Routledge
29 West 35th Street, New York, NY 10001

Reprinted 2005
by Routledge
27 Church Road, Hove, East Sussex BN3 2FA
270 Madison Avenue, New York, NY 10016

Routledge is an imprint of the Taylor & Francis Group

The author has asserted the moral right to be identified as
the author of this work

Typeset in Garamond by
Ponting–Green Publishing Services,
Chesham, Buckinghamshire

Printed in Great Britain by
T.J. International Ltd, Padstow, Cornwall

This publication has been produced with paper manufactured
to strict environmental standards and with pulp derived
from sustainable forests.

British Library Cataloguing in Publication Data
A catalogue record for this book is available from the British Library

Library of Congress Cataloguing in Publication Data
Palmer, Michael F.
Freud and Jung on religion / Michael Palmer.
Includes bibliographical references and index.
1. Psychoanalysis and religion.   2. Freud, Sigmund,
1856–1939 – Religion.   3. Jung, C. G. (Carl Gustav),
1875–1961 – Religion.
I. Title.
BF175.4.R44P35   1997
200'.1'9–dc21   96–51720
ISBN 0–415–14746–8 (hbk)
ISBN 0–415–14747–6 (pbk)

CONTENTS

CONTENTS

FOREWORD

This book began life as a series of lectures delivered over a number of years in the Department of Theology and Religious Studies at the University of Bristol. Since the original title of the series was 'Darwin and Freud,' Jung made only a brief appearance; but gradually, and prompted by my students, this situation changed to the point where Jung had largely usurped Darwin's position. Not that this was entirely unexpected. If Freud's attack on religion is justly famous, then Jung's defence of it is no less celebrated. They remain, in this area at least, the two great protagonists.

This book is not, however, a comparative study between two different psychologies of religion. My primary intention has been to provide two separate accounts which will, I hope, stand on their own, and which will therefore be of use to those seeking fairly detailed information about either Freud or Jung. But here I should add a word of caution. Some comparisons between Freud and Jung are inevitable and helpful, and I shall often make them. One of these, however, should be stated at the beginning. This is between Freud's clarity and Jung's all too frequent lack of it. With that in mind, I have often used a summary of Freud's position to clarify Jung's. This has inevitably upset the balance between the two parts of this work: the shorter section on Freud contains next to nothing on Jung, but the longer section on Jung contains a good deal on Freud. This is not done to establish Freud's historical or conceptual priority – which Jungians would certainly protest about – but solely in order to overcome, or at least ameliorate, the notorious complexities of Jung's thought. In Jung's case, I have also taken the small liberty of highlighting important concepts by the use of a capital letter – hence Self, Persona, Anima, and so on. Again, there is no textual warrant for this, and it is done solely to aid comprehension.

Various other matters should be mentioned here. In attempting to cut the two sections of this book down to manageable size, I have had to make some omissions. I do not, for example, go into all the ramifications of Freud's account of the aetiology of hysteria and symptom-formation, and I have only made passing reference to Jung's theory of complexes and his analysis of attitude and function types. Nor do I go into details about the various editions and translations of the principal texts, but have, in each case, kept for the most part to the more accessible versions of the *Collected Works*.

Each of the two sections concludes with my own critical evaluation of the arguments presented. In the past, criticisms of Freud and Jung have often provoked the most violent reactions from their followers; and I must brace myself to the fact that mine, if noticed, may be no exception. All I can say at this point is that my own critique is in no way partisan – that I am neither neo-Freudian nor neo-Jungian – and that my overriding aim, notwithstanding my own serious objections, has been to reach some understanding of two important and quite remarkable theories of religion.

In conclusion, I should like to express my sincere thanks to three friends: to Professor John Heywood Thomas of the University of Nottingham; to Professor Denys Turner of the University of Birmingham; and to Dr Tom Scott of the University of Liverpool. I am also grateful to Edwina Welham of Routledge, who has made publication a painless and enjoyable process.

Michael Palmer

Sigmund Freud, Vienna c. 1936. In his study at Berggasse 19 with his chow Joti. Mary Evans/Sigmund Freud Copyrights.

Part I

SIGMUND FREUD: PSYCHOANALYSIS AND RELIGION

Of my own flashes of inspiration – I am quite well again and correspondingly unproductive – I can confide only one. It has occurred to me that the ultimate basis of man's need for religion is *infantile helplessness*, which is so much greater in man than in animals. After infancy he cannot conceive of a world without parents and makes for himself a just God and a kindly nature, the two worst anthropomorphic falsifications he could have imagined . . .

(Letter from Freud to Jung, 2 January 1910)

1

INTRODUCTION

A SHORT BIOGRAPHY

Sigmund Freud was born on 6 May 1856, in the Catholic town of Freiburg in Moravia, the eldest of eight children born to the wool merchant Jacob Freud and his second wife Amalia, both of whom were of Galician Jewish ancestry. In 1859 the family moved to Leipzig and then in 1860 to Vienna, where Freud was to remain until June 1938, when, following Hitler's invasion of Austria, he fled to England. He died in London on 23 September 1939.

The young Freud was intellectually precocious and the focus of parental ambition, a gifted linguist and extremely assiduous. In 1873, aged 17, he enrolled as a medical student at the University but did not graduate as a doctor until 1881. Most of this period was spent doing research on the anatomy of the central nervous system in the laboratory of Ernst Brücke (1819–1892), a renowned Viennese physiologist, whom Freud much admired. Although reluctant to go into general practice, his engagement to Martha Bernays in 1882 forced him to seek a more adequate livelihood, and accordingly he gave up his position under Brücke and began work in the Vienna General Hospital. In 1885 he was appointed to a lectureship in neuropathology at the University, and, in the same year, won a travelling bursary to study with Jean-Martin Charcot (1825–1893), the most renowned neurologist of the day, at the famous hospital for nervous disorders, the Salpêtrière in Paris. At this time Charcot was engaged in his research to distinguish traumatic and hysterical paralyses from organic ones – a distinction established by his ability to induce non-organic paralyses through the use of hypnosis. It was these dramatic demonstrations, coupled with others witnessed by Freud at Nancy in 1889, that convinced him 'of the possibility that there could be powerful mental processes which nevertheless remained hidden from the consciousness of men.'[1]

On his return to Vienna in April of 1886 Freud set up private practice as a consultant in nervous diseases, and on 13 September his long-delayed marriage took place. There were to be six children, the last being Anna Freud, who was herself to become a distinguished psychoanalyst. Freud continued with his neuropathological work but became increasingly interested in the neuroses, and in the application of hypnotism in their treatment. This led him to re-establish links with Josef Breuer (1842–1925), a highly cultivated physiologist, whom Freud had first met in the late 1870s, and who, after Charcot, was to exert the most profound influence on him. Seven years earlier Breuer had used hypnosis with remarkable success on a twenty-one-year-old girl, Fräulein Anna O. (Bertha Pappenheim), who showed signs of acute psychological disturbance, the immediate cause of which was mental and physical exhaustion after nursing her father through a terminal illness. While treating her Breuer made an important discovery: that if, under hypnosis, the girl recalled the precise moment at which a particular symptom had arisen (e.g., a paralysis of the right side of her body, a nervous cough, an aversion to nourishment), and if this moment was recalled with the re-experience of the accompanying emotions, the symptoms disappeared. Breuer told Freud of this new method of treatment – which he named 'catharsis' – but it was not until 1889 that Freud himself applied the technique on a highly hysterical woman, Frau Emmy von N. With Freud's repeated confirmation of Breuer's findings, the two men agreed on a joint publication, which first appeared in preliminary form in 1893, and then in the much-expanded *Studies on Hysteria* in 1895. The Breuer-Freud theory of hysteria may be summarized in their much-quoted 'Hysterics suffer mainly from reminiscences.'[2]

Although Freud was to modify both the procedure and theory set out in *Studies on Hysteria* – most notably in the increasing role he accorded to the role of sexuality in hysteria, which led to an estrangement from Breuer – the book is a landmark in the development of psychoanalysis; and James Strachey is correct in saying that 'from this moment onwards – from 1895, perhaps – to the very end of his life, the whole of Freud's intellectual existence revolved around this development, its far-reaching implications, and its theoretical and practical repercussions.'[3] With this in mind the rest of Freud's life, outwardly so uneventful, can be conveniently divided into three further periods:

1 the period of self-analysis, which extended from 1895–99;
2 the development of the system of psychology based on that self-analysis, which lasted until about 1914, and which included two books: *The Interpretation of Dreams* (1900) and the *Three Essays on Sexuality* (1905);
3 the final and further elaboration and revision of the main theories, particularly in relation to a variety of cultural phenomena, most notably religion (1914–39).

There are three aspects of this short biography that need to be highlighted. Each is invariably mentioned by commentators, and each has some relevance to his theories on religion. These have to do with Freud's religious background, his scientific background, and his own personality.

Freud's religious background

In his magisterial life of Freud, Ernest Jones comments that:

> He [Freud] grew up devoid of any belief in a God or Immortality, and does not appear to have felt the need of it. The emotional needs that usually manifest themselves in adolescence found expression, first in rather vague philosophical cogitations, and soon after, in an earnest adherence to the principles of science.[4]

This statement is supported by Freud himself in his most explicit reference to his religious background. In 1926, thanking the B'nai B'rith Lodge of Vienna for honouring him on his seventieth birthday, he writes: '... I was always an unbeliever, have been brought up without religion, but not without respect for the so-called "ethical" demands of human civilization.'[5]

These statements need to be qualified. I have already mentioned the fact that, on both sides of his family, Freud was of Jewish descent. His wife was also Jewish, coming from a family of distinguished orthodox scholars, and whose grandfather, Isaac Bernays, had been the renowned Chief Rabbi of Hamburg and an opponent of the Reform Movement.[6] It was her family that insisted on a Jewish wedding, much to Freud's disgust: he even toyed with the idea of converting to Protestantism to escape the ordeal. But although his writings and private correspondence generally confirm his own position as an atheist, this is not to say that he was indifferent to or even estranged from his own religious background. His father was a moderate Reform Jew, who diligently read both the Talmud and the Torah, and who saw to it that his son was instructed in the teachings of the faith. One of Freud's teachers, Samuel Hammerschlag, who was to become a life-long friend, specialized in the 'Israelite religion.' Hammerschlag's curriculum for 1868–69 has been published,[7] and, not surprisingly, the figure of Moses dominates – an interest that Freud was to retain in his study of Michelangelo's statue and in his book *Moses and Monotheism* (1939).[8] But despite Freud's formal instruction, the household as a whole ignored most of the Jewish feasts, and the festivals that were celebrated tended to be the traditional Christian ones, like Christmas and Easter. When Freud was a baby his parents even went so far as to employ a Catholic nanny, a Czech woman called Resi Wittek. Whenever Freud referred to her he called her 'that prehistoric old woman,' but he was clearly very fond of her, and she took him to church services and gave him ideas about heaven and hell. When Freud was about two and a half, the nanny was dismissed for theft. Much has been written of this event, and even Ernest Jones comments that '... perhaps her terrifying influence contributed to his later dislike of Christian beliefs and ceremonies'[9] but we shall never know whether this was, as some have claimed, the central traumatic event that set in motion all Freud's later antagonism towards religion, or whether his repudiation of religion can be inverted into some kind of unconscious longing for what he was rejecting.[10]

A more balanced view is, I think, that Freud's atheism was largely intellectual and formal: he repudiates both the arguments of religion and its ritual observances. But this is not to say that he disavowed his own Jewish identity. He still saw himself as a man standing within a specific cultural tradition – what he calls 'life-affirming Judaism,'[11] – and this tradition required a firm adherence to family values, to the highest moral standards and a concern for social justice, and a great tenacity in the face of persecution – this last quality tempered by his own painful experiences of anti-Semitism in Vienna. But above all he valued Jewish independence of thought and intellectual courage, characteristics which he correctly ascribes to himself:

> Nor is it perhaps entirely a matter of chance that the first advocate of psychoanalysis was a Jew. To profess belief in a new theory called for a certain degree of readiness to accept a position of solitary opposition . . . a position with which no one is more familiar than a Jew.[12]

Whether this means that psychoanalysis is a peculiarly 'Jewish science' is, however, a much more difficult question to answer, and one which I do not intend to go into here. Suffice to say, for Peter Gay, Freud's Jewish identity has no particular relevance for the creation of psychoanalysis. Much more important is his scientific and positivist orientation: 'In truth Freud could have developed his ideas in any city endowed with a first-rate medical school and an educated public large and affluent enough to furnish him with patients.'[13] For others, like Yosef Yerushalmi, this interpretation is far too restrictive, and in effect throws a *cordon sanitaire* around psychoanalysis, 'shielding it from any taint of historical or cultural conditioning.'[14] Commentators remain divided on this question, and a useful account of the debate has been provided by Justin Miller.[15]

Freud's scientific background

Gay's point is nevertheless an important one. Does Freud's intellectual independence stem from his own religious upbringing or does it in fact have far more to do with his general adherence to a specific scientific methodology? Certainly the relevance of Freud's scientific background to his views on religion is much more clear-cut. All his life Freud was a rigid determinist. That is, he held to the view that all phenomena, including all human actions and choices, operate according to the principle of universal causation, namely, that every event has a cause. Speaking psychoanalytically, this can be translated as follows: that it is the unconscious which determines what the conscious impulse and action will be; that there is, as in the case of Anna O., a strict correlation between the original trauma as cause and the ensuing symptoms as effects – to the point indeed where the recollection of the one will produce the disappearance of the other. Freud's adherence to determinism is often and correctly traced back to the influence of his teachers, and to the fact that he acquired his first scientific training among the medical materialists of the so-called 'Helmholtz school of medicine,' amongst whom were his own teacher Brücke and other physiologists like Émile du Bois-Reymond, Hermann Helmholtz and Carl Ludwig. Their aims were famously summarized in a letter written by Bois-Reymond in 1842: 'Brücke and I pledged a solemn oath to put into power this truth: no other forces than the common physical-chemical ones are active within the organism.'[16] Freud, of course, was to move far away from this attempt to reduce all phenomena to the explanatory categories of physics and chemistry; but at the same time he never departed from the assumptions underlying the programme, which were positivistic, deterministic and atheistic. Here Peter Gay is right when he remarks: 'They [the medical materialists] did not make him into an atheist; they did not awaken his hostility to religion. But they gave him the best possible grounds for both.'[17] It is therefore largely Freud's perception of psychoanalysis as falling within the main determinist-scientific tradition – a tradition which included his own teachers and which he extended out to include even greater luminaries like Copernicus, Kepler, Newton and Darwin – that leads him to maintain that religion and science are fundamentally incompatible. Indeed, such is the antagonism that he sees between them that the following rule applies: anyone who considers himself a medical man and an empiricist has to be an atheist. This was not a choice for Freud but more a matter of logical consistency.

All this is clearly expressed in his important lecture 'The Question of a Weltanschauung,' which is included in his *New Introductory Lectures on Psychoanalysis* (1933). Here Freud draws up the battle-lines between religion and science. A Weltanschauung, as he conceives it, is an 'intellectual construction which solves all the problems of our existence uniformly on the basis of one overriding hypothesis;'[18] and for an example of immense power and consistency we need look no further than religion. It provides its adherents with an account of the origin of the universe, it offers them protection and ultimate happiness through all the vicissitudes of life, and it directs their thoughts and actions through an ethical system of rewards and punishments. How does this compare with a scientific Weltanschauung? It compares in this crucial sense: science offers no overriding hypothesis, and indeed deliberately distances itself from the emotional demand to provide one. The motivation in science is thus much more restrictive: it asserts that there are no sources of knowledge other than those that proceed from verifiable observation and that no knowledge can be derived from such alternative sources as revelation, intuition or divination, all of which may be reckoned as the fulfilment of wishful impulses. Science, in other words, is content to investigate and to establish facts, and offers no hypotheses other than those that can be supported by critical observation of the natural processes:

> it is concerned carefully to avoid individual factors and affective influences; it examines more strictly the trustworthiness of the sense-perceptions on which it bases its conclusions; it provides itself with new perceptions which cannot be obtained by everyday means and it isolates the determinants of these new experiences in experiments which are deliberately varied. Its endeavour is to arrive at correspondence with reality – that is to say, with what exists outside us and independently of us and, as experience has taught us, is decisive for the fulfilment or disappointment of our wishes. This correspondence with the real external world we call 'truth'. It remains the aim of scientific work even if we leave the practical value of that work out of account.[19]

What, then, of psychoanalysis? Psychoanalysis, says Freud, 'is quite unfit to construct a *Weltanschauung* of its own: it must accept the scientific one,'[20] and to that extent it must proceed on the basis of the same objective and verificational techniques, and display the same concern to achieve a correspondence between its conclusions and reality. However, its peculiar service to science lies in the extension of research into the mental field, in its investigation of the intellectual and emotional functions of man. And herein lies its specific antagonism to religion. Religion, as we have seen, depends on specific forms of knowledge, and through these it presents an overarching explanation of the nature and purpose of things. What psychoanalysis can do – and indeed, with its special insights into mental functioning, is in a unique position to do – is explain why the human mind should *prefer* this body of knowledge and this particular explanation above all others: in that way it can expose the particular motivations behind religious belief. What emerges is a set of 'wishful impulses' that unmask religion as something of purely human origin, explicable solely in terms of the natural human desire for protection and happiness. These impulses, Freud argues, originate from the helplessness of childhood and survive into adulthood through the image of the father-god. The real father who once protected the helpless child is now reanimated as the god who protects the adult against all the dangers of the external world; and that the adult should desire to worship him is, for Freud, the clearest evidence of the infantile nature of his belief. For him religion is a return to the nursery.

At the heart of the religious Weltanschauung stands, therefore, the image of the father-god, and, by reducing this image to no more than an idealization of our real fathers, Freud divests religion of any claim to divinity and places it full square among other psychic phenomena, comparable for instance to the delusional obsessions of neurotics. To achieve and justify this reduction is in many ways the central preoccupation of Freud's entire account of religion, and we shall return to it many times; but that he should consider this at the same time to be a *scientific* reduction is absolutely central to his belief that religion, irrespective of how hard it fights, will eventually be defeated by the forces of reason. For no matter how many fears it may soothe or sufferings alleviate, no matter how many moral precepts it may offer for the better conduct of life, religion always operates from within a self-contained and inviolable system of doctrine and indeed invariably evades refutation by never submitting its hypotheses to the cold light of verifiable experience. In religion reality must conform to an idea; but in the science of psychoanalysis the reverse is true: here hypotheses are constructed and then confirmed or rejected only on the basis of experimental research. Where religion therefore draws its strength from the emotional consolations it offers, psychoanalysis derives its power from the criterion of truth, namely, the reality-principle that nothing can be held to be true unless it corresponds with the external world:

> Our best hope for the future is that intellect – the scientific spirit, reason – may in process of time establish a dictatorship in the mental life of man. The nature of reason is a guarantee that afterwards it will not fail to give man's emotional impulses and what is determined by them the position they deserve. But the common compulsion exercised by such a dominance of reason will prove to be the strongest uniting bond among men and lead the way to further unions. Whatever, like religion's prohibition against thought, opposes such a development, is a danger for the future of mankind.[21]

Freud's personality

Freud firmly believed that the force of his objections against religion lay in their scientific character; that the arguments he deployed against it were powerful because religion so exactly exhibited all those symptoms of neurosis that the science of psychoanalysis had discovered through the laborious process of experimental research. In this sense Freud's argument is analogical and inductive:

1 Psychoanalysis has discovered that Xs are the symptoms of neurosis;
2 Religion exhibits Xs;
3 Therefore religion is a neurosis.

This is straightforward enough, but it is nevertheless an argument that can be easily upset if the scientific objectivity sought by Freud cannot in fact be achieved; or rather, if it can be shown that, far from basing his critique of religion on verifiable evidence, Freud was far more inclined to ignore information unsuited to the picture he wished to paint and to uphold theories long since empirically invalidated. This is a criticism that Freud's detractors have made much of, and I shall return to it in some detail later on. But there is one aspect of this criticism that should be commented on immediately. It is sometimes held that the reason why Freud operated in this way was because he himself was psychologically incapable of doing otherwise. It is alleged, in other words, that Freud's whole enterprise is suspect because he himself suffered from the same neuroses and obsessions that he found in his patients; because, for instance, what he found neurotic in religion was what he found neurotic in himself. Freud was therefore predisposed to believe his own theories not for good scientific reasons but for reasons which had much more to do with his own personality.[22]

Now while it may be the case that knowing Freud was neurotic makes us suspicious of his claims that believers are neurotic, it does not for that reason invalidate them, any more indeed than would our knowledge that Collins was a thief immediately undermine his own statements about others being thieves. It might make us cautious about his evidence, but this in itself does not decide that his evidence is false. More than that, to suppose that it does is to commit what logicians call the 'genetic fallacy.' This fallacy is committed when one claims that the truth or falsity of X can be decided by specifying the origins of X. Thus the knowledge that Freud suffered from an Oedipus complex does not of itself invalidate Freud's conclusions about its universality, any more than does the discovery that Freud was obsessive in his conduct undermine his claim that all religious people are obsessive. Quite the reverse in fact. For if it is a central claim of Freud that the Oedipus complex is universal, then, as a matter of consistency, he must ascribe it both to himself and to everybody else, to believer and non-believer. But it is hardly a powerful criticism of Freud's case that he begins with a biographical warrant and does not make himself an exception to the rule. Indeed, as far as Freud is concerned, this is not merely to deny an important piece of empirical evidence but to deny the investigator access to the most immediate object of his enquiry, namely himself. Indeed, it is an oft-quoted aspect of Freud's greatness that he was relentless in turning the spotlight on himself.

The fact, therefore, that Freud's personality was of a certain type does not in itself constitute grounds for dismissing what he has to say about religion; but it does help explain why Freud should have been attracted to religion as an object of psychoanalytic investigation. We know, for example, that one aspect of religious behaviour that he discerned in himself and found worrying was the belief that reality could somehow be altered by a 'sacrificial act.' In his *The Psychopathology of Everyday Life* he reports that in 1905, during the illness of his eldest daughter and while passing through a room in his dressing-gown, he felt a sudden impulse to hurl one of his slippers at the wall, with the result that one of his antiquities, a little marble Venus, was shattered.

> This wild conduct and my calm acceptance of the damage are to be explained in terms of the situation at the time. One of my family was gravely ill, and secretly I had already given up hope of her recovery.

10

That morning I had learned that there had been a great improvement, and I know I had said to myself: 'So she's going to live after all!' My attack of destructive fury served therefore to express a feeling of gratitude to fate and allowed me to perform a '*sacrificial act*' – rather as if I had made a vow to sacrifice something or other as a thank-offering if she recovered her health![23]

Other examples of Freud's superstitions abound. We know, for example, that this high-minded rationalist was embarrassed by his own belief in omens and numerology. From 1900 he was convinced that he would die aged sixty-one or sixty-two – a calculation derived from the publication date of *The Interpretation of Dreams* and his new telephone number – and when that date passed he characteristically scoffed at his own credulity.[24] We also know from his short essay of 1919, 'The Uncanny,' that two of the superstitions he discusses there – belief in the return of the dead and the possibility of seeing one's double – were among those he also accepted.[25] And to this we should add a considerable interest in parapsychological phenomena – clairvoyance, telepathy and thought transference. But while it is probably true that Freud's own superstitions and his fascination for the paranormal fostered his interest in religion, it is still unlikely that they encouraged him to see much truth in religion. Indeed when Ernest Jones, in a midnight conversation with him, suggested that such interest in occult beliefs might lead to a belief in angels, Freud replied, 'Quite so, even *der liebe Gott*' – a remark that might otherwise be confusing if it had not been said, as Jones adds, 'in a jocular tone as if agreeing with my *reductio ad absurdam* and with a quizzical look as if he were pleased at shocking me.'[26] Other colleagues were treated less good-humouredly. He strongly condemned Jung's so-called 'mysticism,' which he associated with the latter's work on occult phenomena;[27] when A. A. Roback suggested that Freud too might have mystical inclinations, Freud was amazed by this 'reproach' and denied it absolutely;[28] and when Viktor von Weizsaecker confessed to being 'perhaps something of a mystic on the side,' Freud was clearly horrified and said: 'That is terrible.'[29] But the clearest evidence that Freud was not prepared to use paranormal activity as some covert justification for religious belief comes in his lecture 'Dreams and Occultism' (1933).[30] He admits from the beginning to a strong disinclination to proceed with any investigation of occultism if it is to be seen as assisting religion in its fight against science; that somehow this will justify religion in its claim that some sort of 'other world' exists. But even when this prejudice is overcome, the results are hardly helpful. Most occultist information can be discounted as the product of an unbridled imagination or, worse, of fraud; and even in those few cases where evidence is forthcoming – like the cases of telepathy or fortune-telling cited by Freud – it is never sufficient to confirm the experiences, and invariably alternative explanations, usually psycho-analytic, can be offered to account for them. Occultism, then, offers no reliable support for religion because, like religion itself, it too falls by the reality-principle of verification. Occultism, again like religion, is not *a priori* untrue but must be viewed with extreme scepticism on the basis of the evidence it presents. All that one can advance on its behalf is an occasional doubt about one's original scepticism, and admit that here we meet phenomena that the man of science cannot as yet account for.

RELIGION AS NEUROSIS: REPRESSION AND THE OEDIPUS COMPLEX

Whether compulsive or not, Freud's fascination with religion lasted for the greater part of his life. With one important exception, however, his major discussions on the subject belong to his last phase; that is, to the period 1914–39 when, having established the major elements of psychoanalysis, Freud set about summarizing and revising them. There are, of course, many scattered references to religion in Freud's early articles and letters.[31] One such is to be found in his *The Psychopathology of Everyday Life* (1901). Here he writes that

> a large part of the mythological view of the world, which extends a long way into the most modern religions, *is nothing but psychology projected into the eternal world*. The obscure recognition . . . of psychical factors and relations in the unconscious is involved – it is difficult to express it in other terms, and here the analogy with paranoia must come to our aid – in the construction of a *supernatural reality*, which is destined to be changed back once more by science into the psychology of the unconscious. One could venture to explain in this way the myths of paradise and the fall of man, of God, of good and evil, of immortality, and so on, and to transform metaphysics into metapsychology.[32]

Of these early writings on religion, the most important is undoubtedly Freud's short paper, 'Obsessive Acts and Religious Practices' (1907), which is rightly regarded as his first major essay in the psychology of religion. Here Freud introduces various themes, almost all of which he develops six years later in *Totem and Taboo*. But of these the most important is his view that obsessional neurosis may be taken as a pathological counterpart to religion, as a kind of individual religiosity, with religion functioning as *a universal obsessional neurosis*.[33] Freud reaches this conclusion by noting the striking resemblances between 'what are called obsessive actions in sufferers from nervous affections and the observances by means of which believers give expression to their piety.'[34] For example, both the religious worshipper and the obsessional neurotic spend hours in carrying out certain rituals, and in each case the omission of these acts excites feelings of acute apprehension. In neurotics these rituals take on ceremonial and compulsive importance (e.g., before going to bed, clothes must be folded in a particular order, the pillows arranged in a particular manner, and only then can one go to sleep), and any deviation from these apparently trivial formalities will result in intolerable anxieties, dominated by a sense of guilt if they are not performed. These ceremonies have indeed become 'sacred acts': no interruption of them will be tolerated and they are invariably performed in private. And much the same can be seen in religious practices. For while, by contrast, these have a public and communal character, we also find the same qualms of conscience when some ritual action is omitted, the same need to protect the ritual from external interruption, similar conscientiousness over detail, the same tendency of the ritual to become increasingly complex, and so on. For Freud the analogy seems complete: both types of action are designed to ward off certain temptations, usually unconscious, and to prevent the punishments that will come if one succumbs to them. In each case, in other words, the obsessional neurotic experiences both a profound sense of guilt and a lurking sense of expectant anxiety, an expectation of misfortune. Quite what motivates these feelings is, however, less easy to determine; but here Freud takes his first tentative steps in advancing an hypothesis that is to become increasingly dominant. As an obsessional neurosis, religion is formed through the suppression or renunciation of certain instinctual impulses, amongst which we must count the sexual instinct. Religion is thus *an expression of the instincts it has suppressed.*

Three years later, in his celebrated study of Leonardo da Vinci (1910), Freud re-emphasizes the role of sexual instinctual forces in the development of neurosis, but now traces religion's feeling of guilt and demand for protection back to a biological condition of childhood – 'to the small human child's long-drawn-out helplessness and need of help'[35] – and, more specifically, back to a parental complex, initiated primarily by the infant's awesome experience of his intimidating and authoritarian father.

> Psychoanalysis has made us familiar with the intimate connection between the father-complex and belief in God; it has shown us that a personal God is, psychologically, nothing other than an exalted father, and it brings us evidence every day of how young people lose their religious beliefs as soon as their father's authority breaks down. Thus we recognize that the roots of the need for religion are in the parental complex . . .[36]

In these early remarks, many of the main elements of Freud's theory of religion already make their appearance: the significance of a father complex for the origin of religion; the role of religion in the renunciation of instinctual pleasures and in the extent to which it provides security and protection; and in the degree to which religious behaviour mirrors the obsessional. For their detailed exposition, however, we must turn to four books. The first is *Totem and Taboo* of 1913. This is often regarded as Freud's greatest literary achievement – Freud agrees that its fourth essay is his best-written work – and I shall deal with it separately in Chapter 2. The three other books of importance are *The Future of an Illusion* of 1927, *Civilization and its Discontents* of 1930, and *Moses and Monotheism* of 1939. These I shall group together and discuss in Chapter 3.

Although it is true that each of these four books approaches the phenomenon of religion from a different angle, a constant theme nevertheless plays throughout. This is the association, already indicated in the earlier essays, between *religion and neurosis*. To repeat, for Freud religion is a universal neurosis of mankind, and nowhere does he depart from this thesis. Indeed, not only does neurosis explain the origin of religion, it also accounts for its continuing support. As a prologue to our discussion we must therefore ask the question: What is a neurosis? And to answer this we must turn, admittedly very briefly, to two of its primary components: repression and the Oedipus complex.

The most important assumption of all psychoanalytic theory is that there are unconscious mental processes, and that these processes are the cause of certain kinds of disorder which could not otherwise be explained as the result of organic disease. The disorder which first drew Freud's attention to this was hysterical paralysis: the absence of any physical cause of it, such as a dysfunction in the central nervous system, suggested that this was a mental disorder, 'neurotic' in origin. In collaboration with his early associate, Josef Breuer, Freud claimed, in the *Studies on Hysteria* of 1895, that such instances of hysteria were in fact the result of scenes in the past lives of the patient (traumas) – 'Hysterics,' we remember, 'suffer mainly from reminiscences'[37] – and further that the recollection or reproduction of these traumas under hypnosis resulted in the gradual disappearance of the hysterical symptoms. This surprising conclusion – which Freud and Breuer confirmed time and time again in their case-studies[38] – led Freud to postulate a further characteristic of the neuroses, which he was later to describe as 'the corner-stone on which the whole structure of psychoanalysis rests.'[39] This is the phenomenon known as *repression*.

Repression is the mechanism by which the mind prevents the traumatic past experience, or the emotions associated with it, from passing from the unconscious to the conscious. In this sense, repression is a form of forgetting, a kind of guardian or censor standing before the door of consciousness, disallowing the entry into memory of those reminiscences which it finds painful or shameful. Repression is therefore an active agent, sufficiently powerful to resist the impulses issuing from the unconscious, constantly on the alert. Thus, unknown to the individual, there is a perpetual conflict between the unconscious and conscious mind, and it is from this conflict that 'neurotic' disorders arise. The past emotion seeks to become discharged and conscious but, finding itself repudiated and disowned, channels itself into the production of neurotic symptoms. It becomes what Freud calls a 'comprom-ise formation,' a by-product of the interior antagonism, realized in the appearance of hysterias, obsessions, phobias and anxieties.

That neurosis is the result of repression is one axiom of psychotherapy from which Freud never departed. Another concerns the character of that which is repressed. As early as 1896 he presented the thesis that 'at the bottom of every case of hysteria there are *one or more occurrences of premature sexual experience*, occurrences which belong to the earliest years of childhood. . . .'[40] Freud's thinking on an individual's innate sexual instincts (to which he gave the generic name, 'libido') went through many permutations. His earliest theory, later abandoned in 1897, was that the primary cause of neurosis was the seduction of the child by an adult; but by 1905, with the appearance of his *Three Essays on Sexuality*, he was able to reinforce his view of sexuality by defining the nucleus of every case of neurosis in terms of *infantile* sexual impulses, and more particularly in a specific libidinal relation, which every individual passes through, between the child and its parents. This relation is characterized by an emotional attachment to the parent of the opposite sex and an attitude of rivalry to the parent of the same sex. To this situation, and to the whole mental structure associated with it, Freud gave the name *Oedipus complex* – so called after the Greek legend of King Oedipus, who killed his father and married his mother.

> When a boy (from the age of two or three) has entered the phallic phase of his libidinal development, is feeling pleasurable sensations in his sexual organ and has learnt to procure these at will by manual stimulation, he becomes his mother's lover. He wishes to possess her physically in such ways as he has divined from his observations and intuitions about sexual life, and he tries to seduce her by showing her the male organ which he is proud to own. In a word, his early awakened masculinity seeks to take his father's place with her; his father has hitherto in any case been an envied model to the boy, owing to the physical strength he perceives in him and the authority with which he finds him clothed. His father now becomes a rival who stands in his way and whom he would like to get rid of. If while his father is away he is allowed to share his mother's bed and if when his father returns he is once more banished from it, his satisfaction when his father disappears and his disappointment when he emerges again are deeply felt experiences. This is the subject of the Oedipus complex, which the Greek legend has translated from the world of a child's fantasy into pretended reality. Under the conditions of our civilization it is in-variably doomed to a frightening end.[41]

We can now be clearer about what a neurosis is. A neurosis results from repressed sexuality. More exactly, a neurotic illness is generated by the sexual component of the traumatic experience, and it is this element, and the memories associated with it, that the individual seeks to repress. We can be still more specific. What is repressed is not something unusual to sexual life but something which is a normal part of every childhood – the Oedipus complex – but which contains impulses that the neurotic finds shameful and threatening, namely, incest with the mother and hatred of the father. It is these two instinctual impulses that are overtaken by repression, debarred from being reproduced in memory, but which nevertheless break out and find discharge in the symptoms of neurosis. In this sense, therefore, neurosis results from an incomplete form of repression. Expelled from consciousness, the dammed-up libido nevertheless forces its way back into consciousness and finds an abnormal outlet in the symptoms of neurosis and the affects attaching to them.

At the risk of complicating matters, we should note that Freud's bipartite division of mind into conscious and unconscious had, by the early 1920s, given way to a tripartite division: the id, the ego, and the super-ego. I mention this now only because his later writings on religion reflect this change. In the id we find the unconscious drives and instincts which motivate the individual, the primary ones being the sexual drive (libido) and the demand for pleasure – a classification which was further revised into two general classes of instinct: the life-instinct (Eros) and the death-instinct (Thanatos). The ego, on the other hand, deals with reality, the first reality being our awareness of our bodily selves. Thereafter personality develops in relation to the ego and through the ego's encounter with the external world. The ego's primary task, therefore, is self-preservation, seeking to gain control not merely of the world outside itself but of the internal world of the id. Accordingly, the main aim of the id is pleasure and the main aim of the ego is safety. Similarly, if the mental processes of the id are subject to no logical laws and are unconscious, the processes of the ego, though sometimes unconscious, are generally conscious or preconscious, that is, capable of becoming conscious. Finally, there is the super-ego. The super-ego is primarily associated with the individual's attitude to parents. Parents bring with them family, racial and national traditions, together with the demands of the culture, reinforced by teachers and institutions. Like the id, then, the super-ego represents the past: the id containing the influences of heredity and the super-ego embodying the influences of other people; and in between stands the ego, which is determined by the individual's own exclusive experiences. According to Freud, all three are in conflict and this conflict is the major source of psychological disorder. The overwhelming instincts of the id are in conflict with the ego, which seeks to control those instincts as it comes to terms with the external world. The super-ego at the same time mediates between ego and id, and brings with it the standards and ideals learnt from parents and society in general. We are aware of it as our 'conscience,' often more rigorous in its demands than any parent. Thus the ego has to satisfy the instinctual demands of the id and the moral dictates of the super-ego.

16

Although Freud's notion of the super-ego is an important conceptual addition, it does not upset his theory of repression but supplements it. The core remains intact: neurosis is concerned with the patient's repressed sexuality or, to use the new terminology, with the repression by the ego of the instinctual impulses located in the id. Once again, the repressed material struggles against its fate, and creates for itself new avenues of expression over which the ego has no control, namely, symptoms. To this situation, however, we now add the new ingredient. The super-ego, acting within the unconscious and infused with the morality of family and culture, insists still more aggressively on the suppression of the instincts emanating from the id: it admonishes the ego, sets itself above it as both guardian and exemplar, and visits any infringements with the pangs of conscience. Invariably the ego obeys the moral demands of the super-ego, but sometimes the ego may react to an overly harsh super-ego by repressing part of the super-ego instead. Thus arises, says Freud, the unconscious sense of guilt so typical of neurotics.

All the categories introduced by Freud into his general account of neurosis reappear in his analysis of religion as a neurosis. Indeed, given the intimate connection already established between neurosis and sexual repression, it will come as no surprise to find that it is Freud's theory of sexuality that stands at the heart of his thinking about the origin and character of religious belief. In a word, *Freud sexualizes religion*. Traces of this argument have already been detected in earlier essays, most notably in the paper on religious practices of 1907; but by 1913, with the publication of *Totem and Taboo*, it had become quite dominant. This is Freud's first, and perhaps most successful, analysis of religion, in which he establishes the central principle of his theory: that the beginnings of religion can be explained in terms of the Oedipus complex.

2

TOTEM AND TABOO

TOTEM AND TABOO (1913)

We have already seen how, as early as 1907, Freud drew an analogy between the obsessive behaviour of neurotics and the behaviour of religious people. The intention of *Totem and Taboo* is to establish this link in much greater detail. Subtitled on its first appearance 'Some Points of Agreement between the Mental Lives of Savages and Neurotics,'[1] this is Freud's major contribution to social anthropology, although, as he admits, he wrote the book in a highly speculative manner. 'I am fully conscious,' he writes in the Preface, 'of the deficiencies of these studies,'[2] and time and time again Freud is almost apologetic for his lack of knowledge in certain areas. But while tentative, it remains one of his most provocative and influential books. Although initially stimulated by the work of Wilhelm Wundt and Carl Gustav Jung, Freud's principal sources are Darwin's *The Descent of Man* (1871), W. Robertson Smith's *Lectures on the Religion of the Semites* (1889), J. J. Atkinson's *Primal Law* (1903), and two volumes by Sir James Frazer, *The Golden Bough* (1890) and *Totemism and Exogamy* (1910). The book is divided up into four essays, and I shall examine each in turn.

The first essay is entitled 'The Horror of Incest.' It is, says Freud, one of the more surprising discoveries of anthropology that among primitive peoples, such as the aborigines of Australia, sexual relations, far from being unbridled, are in fact subject to the severest restrictions, and that, more particularly, incest is an even greater taboo among them than among more civilized communities. Indeed, the incest taboo is so extensive that it leads to a system known as 'exogamy,' which requires that sexual partners are sought outside the immediate social group or tribe. This prohibition, Freud claims, is itself linked to *totemism*. What is a totem? A totem is usually an animal – although sometimes a plant or natural phenomenon like rain or water – which is regarded by the clan as their guardian spirit and oracle, and for this reason its members are under a sacred obligation not to kill, destroy or eat their totem. Equally significantly, a totem is regarded as the clan's common ancestor, which therefore treats all members as if they were blood-relatives or one single family. It is this totem kinship which largely explains exogamy: it is not merely actual incestuous relations that are prohibited, but any sexual relations between members of the same totemic group.

In his second essay, entitled 'Taboo and Emotional Ambivalence,' Freud points to the remarkable similarity between the taboo prohibitions of totemic societies and the individual taboos to be found among obsessional neurotics. Indeed, so great are these similarities that it would be appropriate to describe obsessional patients as suffering from 'taboo sickness.'[3] The first, and most obvious similarity, is the belief that breaking the taboo will lead to disaster. No external threat of punishment is required, nor is the nature of injury specified, but the person concerned will have an undefined feeling that violation of the taboo will have disastrous consequences. There are other similarities as well: any object or person associated with what is taboo will become taboo itself; and taboos can be lifted through ceremonial acts like washing. But the most important similarity lies in what Freud calls the condition of 'ambivalence,' which is the desire to do that which is forbidden.

> But one thing would certainly follow from the persistence of the taboo, namely that the original desire to do the prohibited thing must also still persist among the tribes concerned. They must therefore have an ambivalent attitude towards their taboos. In their unconscious there is nothing they would like more than to violate them, but they are afraid to do so; they are afraid precisely because they would like to, and the fear is stronger than the desire. The desire is unconscious, however, in every individual member of the tribe just as it is in neurotics.[4]

This helps explain why anyone who violates the taboo becomes taboo himself: they possess the power to tempt others to follow their example, to arouse the forbidden desire in others. It is accordingly against the 'risk of imitation' that the community must protect itself. Any violation of the taboo must therefore be avenged quickly to prevent others from acting in the same way as the transgressor. This explains the contagious power inherent in the taboo-object: 'the power of reminding a man of his own prohibited wishes and the apparently more important one of inducing him to transgress the prohibition in obedience to those wishes.'[5] To impose a taboo is therefore to renounce something desirable. Why else, asks Freud, would such drastic prohibitions be required?[6] The fact, therefore, that the most ancient and important taboos are concerned with the two basic laws of totemism – not to kill the totem animal and to avoid sexual intercourse with members of the opposite sex within the totem clan – point to these as the oldest and most powerful of human *desires*, functioning also within the obsessional prohibitions of neurotics. This, we might say, is their point of contact, not merely as an historical inheritance from primitive times, but as an inherent characteristic of humankind. Here, then, history confirms an innate instinct.

In many ways Freud's third essay – 'Animism, Magic and the Omnipotence of Thoughts' – provides an unwelcome interruption to the flow of his argument about totemism. As its title suggests, it includes an extensive analysis of animism, which Freud, following Edward Tylor (1832–1917),[7] considers the 'groundwork' of all religions. The main purpose of this chapter is, however, to answer a question left begging from the previous one. Violation of a taboo, as we have just seen, brings disaster, its observance avoids it. The question now is: Why should one believe that a connection exists at all? What is it that makes people believe that doing or not doing something – something which, on the face of it, may appear trifling or even foolish – will have consequences of enormous importance, for good or ill? Why do some tribes believe that entering a King's house is fatal? Why do others believe that the slaughter of a bull will encourage crop growth? And are these beliefs really any different from a young girl's obsessional conviction that the constant washing of a basin will reduce the possibility of her sister's divorce? In all these cases, it is the distance between *action* and *result* which suggests that to believe that a causal connection exists between the two is psychogenetic.

How, then, to account for this connection? It is explained, says Freud, through the operation of the 'omnipotence of thoughts.' This phrase, he tells us, was first given to him by 'The Rat Man' (Ernst Lanzer), an obsessional neurotic of twenty-nine, first treated by Freud in 1907.[8] We need not go into all the details of the case here. Suffice to say, this patient's life was dominated by a whole host of premonitions, compulsions and rituals, and that his obsessions were intended to prevent harm coming to the two people he was most fond of: his father, who had died eight years before, and a lady whom he admired. For example, during thunderstorms he would count compulsively between flashes of lightning, thinking that somehow this would protect the girl; he felt compelled to remove a stone from a road because it might be dangerous for her carriage; at night he would indulge in a favourite fantasy that his father was still alive, and go through elaborate rituals intended to impress him with his industry, while at other times he feared that if he married his lady something dreadful would happen to his father in the next world. All this culminated in Lanzer's overwhelming horror of rats, which Freud traced to the young man's fear that a particularly nasty anal torture, which he had heard of from a Czech army captain whilst out on manoeuvres, would be applied to both his loved ones. What matters for us, however, is that Lanzer used the term 'omnipotence of thoughts' to describe the almost uncanny way in which his thoughts appeared to control reality.

> If he suddenly asked after the health of an acquaintance whom he had not seen for a long time, he would hear that he had just died, so that it would look as though a telepathic message had arrived from him. If, without any really serious intention, he swore at some stranger, he might be sure that the man would die soon afterwards, so that he would

feel responsible for his death. . . . All obsessional neurotics are super-
stitious in this way, usually against their better judgment.[9]

Omnipotence of thoughts, in other words, is a defiance of reality, or rather,
which amounts to the same thing, an overestimation of the powers of the
mind to control the external world. And this is most clearly visible among
obsessional neurotics. It is not merely that, in common with other neurotics,
their symptoms proceed from particular distortions of reality, but, more
specifically, that their obsessions are invariably designed to ward off those
expectations of disaster with which the neurosis usually starts. Omnipotence
of thoughts in this sense involves a loosening of the relation to reality, and is
part of the process by which neurotics both *defend* themselves against their
own repressed instinctual impulses, while simultaneously making *reparation*
for having them. This further suggests that, if omnipotence of thoughts is a
function of the neurosis, an analysis of its operation in any given case will
provide valuable evidence as to the nature of what is being repressed. And
what the outcome of such an analysis will be is not difficult to predict. For
the omnipotence of thoughts is another example of the power of ambivalence.
The mental action, in other words, which constructs a fantastical world
wherein thought controls reality is powered by the demand to prohibit that
which at the same time satisfies; and to that extent the belief, for example,
that a particular totemic object has the power both to protect and to punish,
originates from the same situation as all neuroses, namely, the necessity of
fending off the libidinal demands of the Oedipus complex.

We must now look to see how Freud connects the omnipotence of thoughts
to specific religious behaviour. The crucial factor here is his analysis of
animism. This is a primitive system of thought which, although not itself a
religion, 'contains the foundations on which religions are later built.'[10]
Animism is the doctrine of souls or, more precisely, the belief that all animate
and inanimate objects in the world are 'animated' by innumerable spiritual
beings, some benevolent, others malignant. Nor are human individuals
exempt: they too are inhabited by similar spirits, which have the capacity to
migrate from one human being to another. To the practical question of how
to obtain mastery over these spirits, primitive human beings answered by
devising a whole body of instructions, known as 'sorcery' or 'magic.' In
sorcery one influences the spirits in much the same way that one attempts to
influence people: one appeases them, one makes amends, one propitiates or
intimidates them, and so on. Magic is different: it is less concerned with the
control of spirits and more with the subjugation of natural phenomena and
with the need to give individuals the power to protect themselves from or
injuring their enemies. Here Freud follows Frazer in classifying magic into
two groups. First there is 'imitative' or 'homoeopathic' magic, where a
similarity is assumed between the act performed and the result expected (e.g.,
the use of an effigy to wound an enemy, the sprinkling of water to induce

rain, the act of intercourse to encourage crop fertility). In the second group we find 'contagious' magic, where an actual spatial connection, and not mere similarity, is assumed between act and result (e.g., the possession of an enemy's hair to injure him or the eating of his flesh to acquire some of his strength, the healing of a wound by treating the weapon). In both groups, says Freud, we see the underlying principle of magic at work. This is to mistake 'an ideal connection for a real one,'[11] a mistake which issues from primitive man's 'immense belief in the power of his wishes. The basic reason why what he sets about by magical means comes to pass is, after all, simply that he wills it. To begin with, therefore, the emphasis is only upon his wish.'[12]

It does not take much to see where this account of animism is leading. It leads to Freud's identification of the omnipotence of thoughts as the underlying *principle of magic* at work in animism. In animism, that is, we see precisely the same overvaluation of mental processes in their capacity to control or transform reality as we saw in obsessional neurosis: neither can believe that thoughts are free but rather that their mere expression will lead to their fulfilment. This allows Freud to define animism as the first *psychological theory* about the nature of human beings and their world. Animism is the first system of thought in which we see a shift away from an unsatisfying and ungovernable reality into an altogether more pleasurable world of fantasy, in which reality seems less alien because it can to an extent be controlled by the ceremonials of magic.

Herein lies animism's connection to religion. Religion contains this same movement away from the real world, and in the practices of religion we see much the same flight into fantasy. To call religion, therefore, a universal obsessional neurosis is to do more than ally it with certain mental disturbances: it is to reveal part of its own historical foundation, animism, and to conceive of it therefore as another example of how the omnipotence of thought – the primary mechanism of obsessional neurosis – operates. Religion is the child of animism, in other words, not merely because it inherits the belief that spiritual beings exist – an idea which, according to Freud, underlies all religious belief – but also because it too applies magical arts for the control of nature and the appeasement of spiritual powers, now externalized in the form of gods. Religion thus stands as a form of superstition, and obsessional religious acts as acts of magic: they become, as it were, the modern ritual equivalents of the ceremonials of animism, with their own prohibitions, precautions, expiations and substitutive satisfactions.

In the fourth essay of *Totem and Taboo*, entitled 'The Return of Totemism in Childhood,' Freud continues with his main argument. This is the historical section of the book and is, by Freud's own admission, its most successful chapter; it is also, we might add, its most notorious, containing as it does his reworking of Darwin's primal horde theory.

According to Darwin, the lives of primitive men mirrored those of the higher apes: they lived in small groups or 'hordes' ruled over by a powerful father, who had many wives and many children. To maintain his position, this dominant male drove the young males out of the tribe to find mates, and young females could expect to mate only with him. To this theory Freud added two further insights. The first was drawn from Atkinson: the practical consequence of the primal horde was exogamy for the young males. Owing to the leader's jealousy, there was a prohibition upon sexual intercourse, and this, following the development of totemism, became a rigorously enforced totemic regulation. The second insight was drawn from Robertson Smith. In his *Religion of the Semites*, Smith suggested that part of the totemic system involved a yearly ceremony known as the 'totem meal,' at which the totem animal was ritually sacrificed and consumed by the community. Once devoured, the totem animal was then mourned, this mourning being followed by a great festival. This ceremonial slaughter, which allowed the members of the totemic clan to do together what was forbidden individually, was justified on the grounds that it established a sacred bond between the worshippers and their god.

Freud utilizes the theories of Darwin, Atkinson and Smith to put forward the following reconstruction. The position of the dominant male within the primal horde was not unassailable. One day the sons collaborated to kill and devour their father, who had been both their enemy and their ideal, and thereby not only identified themselves with him and acquired a portion of his strength, but in so doing made an end of the patriarchal horde. Thereafter, however, the sons, overcome by guilt at what they had done, and failing individually to take over their father's position, banded together into a clan of brothers, turned to the practice of exogamy – thereby removing the original motive for killing their father – and created a father-substitute in the form of the totem. The yearly celebration of the totem meal was, accordingly, nothing less than the solemn commemoration of the original crime, the murder of the father.

Significantly, Freud finds psychoanalytic support for this identification of the totem with the father. He tells us that children suffering from the Oedipus complex commonly displace their fear of their fathers on to animals, and develop phobias to do with horses, dogs, cats, less often birds, but frequently very small creatures such as beetles and butterflies. Freud gives details of three cases, one given to him by his associate, Sándor Ferenczi (the case of little Árpád, a small boy who developed an obsession for chickens), another by Dr M. Wulff of Odessa (the case of a boy of nine suffering from a dog phobia), and the third his own: the case of Little Hans. This Freud published in 1909 under the title, 'Analysis of a Phobia in a Five-Year-Old Boy.'[13]

Little Hans (real name, Herbert) was the son of a psychoanalytically inclined father, the music critic Max Graf, who knew Freud. In January, 1908, the father wrote to Freud, saying that his son had developed a phobia of horses and refused to go out in the street. 'He expressed a fear,' Freud reports, 'that the horse would come into the room and bite him; and it turned out that this might be the punishment for a wish that the horse might fall down (that is, die).'[14] After much to-ing and fro-ing, which included a brief consultation with Freud, a diagnosis was presented. Little Hans was suffering from an Oedipus complex. He regarded his father as a competitor for the sexual favours of his mother, but at the same time could not dislodge his old-established feelings of affection and admiration. He therefore resolved this 'ambivalent' emotional attitude by *displacing* his hostile feelings on to an animal; the horse thereby becomes 'a *substitute* for his father.'[15] Displacement, however, does not resolve the problem because the feelings of ambivalence are now directed towards the animal: little Hans continued to be frightened of horses while simultaneously admiring them. What we have here, then, is a form of totemic ritual: a substitution of the father by an animal, and a displacement on to it of the child's love and hate towards him. This, according to Freud, tallies with the contradictory fact that, while the killing of the animal is generally forbidden, when it does occur it is a festive occasion: it is killed and yet mourned.

It is this psychoanalytic evidence which allows Freud to take his next step. The totemic system is a product of the conditions involved in the Oedipus complex. The totem meal is, says Freud, perhaps mankind's earliest festival; but more significantly, in its repetition and commemoration of the original criminal act, we discern the beginnings of religion itself. Its source has been traced by psychoanalysis to what Freud has already defined as the nucleus of every case of neurosis, namely, to the Oedipus complex. For if the totem animal is the father, then the two great taboos of totemism – the taboo against incest and the taboo against killing the totem animal – have here coincided with the two crimes of Oedipus: getting rid of the father and taking the mother to wife.

> ... we need only suppose that the tumultuous mob of brothers were filled with the same contradictory feelings which we can see at work in the ambivalent father-complexes of our children and of our neurotic patients. They hated their father, who presented such a formidable obstacle to their craving for power and their sexual desires; but they loved and admired him too. After they had got rid of him, had satisfied their hatred and had put into effect their wish to identify themselves with him, the affection which had all this time been pushed under was bound to make itself felt. It did so in the form of remorse. A sense of guilt made its appearance, which in this instance coincided with the remorse felt by the whole group. The dead father became stronger than the living one had been – for events took the course we so often follow in human affairs to this day. What had up to then been prevented by his actual existence was thenceforward prohibited by the sons themselves, in accordance with the psychological procedure so familiar to us in psychoanalysis under the name of 'deferred obedience'. They revoked

their deed by forbidding the killing of the totem, the substitute for their father; and they renounced its fruits by resigning their claim to the women who had now been set free. They thus created out of their filial sense of guilt the two fundamental taboos of totemism, which for that very reason inevitably corresponded to the two repressed wishes of the Oedipus complex. Whoever contravened those taboos became guilty of the only two crimes with which primitive society concerned itself.[16]

According to Freud, then, totemism's claim to be the first religion is based on the first of these taboos: taking the life of the totem animal. The totem was the first form of the father substitute, and by its veneration the sons could exhibit their remorse for the original crime, allay their burning sense of guilt, and so establish a new covenant with their father, in which they agreed not to repeat the murder of their real father in exchange for protection and care.

Features were thus brought into existence which continued thenceforward to have a determining influence on the nature of religion. Totemic religion arose from the filial sense of guilt, in an attempt to allay that feeling and to appease the father by deferred obedience to him. All later religions are seen to be attempts at solving the same problem. They vary according to the stage of civilization at which they arise and according to the methods which they adopt; but all have the same end in view and are reactions to the same great event with which civilization began and which, since it occurred, has not allowed mankind a moment's rest.[17]

Religion is therefore based on the sense of guilt and the remorse attaching to it. But how does totemic religion develop into the belief in a god? This, Freud suggests, was brought about by the inability of any single one of the brothers, who had collaborated in the killing of their father, to become like him, and this led to a desperate longing for the father-ideal, which increased as their original hostility towards their father decreased. This was expressed initially in the veneration of those individuals who had distinguished themselves above the rest and then in the creation of gods.

Thus after a long lapse of time their bitterness against their father, which had driven them to their deed, grew less, and their longing for him increased; and it became possible for an ideal to emerge which embodied the unlimited power of the primal father against whom they had once fought as well as their readiness to submit to him. As a result of decisive cultural changes, the original democratic equality that had prevailed among all the individual clansmen became untenable; and there developed at the same time an inclination, based on veneration felt for particular human individuals, to revive the ancient paternal ideal by creating gods. The notion of a man becoming a god or of a god dying strikes us to-day as shockingly presumptuous; but even in classical

25

antiquity there was nothing revolting in it. The elevation of the father who had once been murdered into a god from whom the clan claimed descent was a far more serious attempt at atonement than had been the ancient covenant with the totem.[18]

In this account the father is represented twice: first, as totemic animal victim, and second, as the god. But in either case, the ambivalence implicit in the father complex persists: triumph and remorse go hand in hand, the sacrifice of the animal now being duplicated in the theanthropic sacrifice of the god, the substitute for human sacrifice being now changed back into human form. And nowhere is this more apparent than in Christianity. In the Christian story the original sin is against God the Father – a crime so great indeed that it can only be atoned for by the self-sacrifice of the son. But even here the psychological law of ambivalence remains. The act by which the son atones for the murder of the father is the self-same act by which he achieves his victory over him. Thus a son-religion displaces the father-religion:

> As a sign of this substitution the ancient totem meal was revived in the form of communion, in which the company of brothers consumed the flesh and blood of the son – no longer the father – obtained sanctity thereby and identified themselves with him. Thus we can trace through the ages the identity of the totem meal with animal sacrifice, with theanthropic human sacrifice and with the Christian Eucharist, and we can recognize in all these rituals the effect of the crime by which men were so deeply weighed down but of which they must none the less feel so proud. The Christian communion, however, is essentially a fresh elimination of the father, a repetition of the guilty deed.[19]

A last question. Was the original murder an actual historical event? Freud's reply is ambivalent; but whether historical or not, the distinction between thought and deed is not essential. As he says, the mere existence 'of a wishful phantasy of killing and devouring (the father), would have been enough to produce the moral reaction that created totemism and taboo.'[20] The fact, however, that obsessional neurosis invariably originates in some actual traumatic experience suggests, if the comparison between primitive men and neurotics is to be pursued, that the remorse felt for the murder does have historical justification, and that, accordingly, 'in the beginning was the Deed.'[21]

THE PRIMAL HORDE THEORY: TWO ADDITIONS

Thus Freud concludes his theory of the primal horde, which may be regarded without dispute as one of the most imaginative and provocative constructions ever devised by him. To complete the picture, however, I should mention now two additions to the theory. The first is interesting rather than important, and arises from the discovery in 1983 of a previously unknown draft of a paper by Freud on metapsychology, written in 1915. The second is more significant but perhaps less interesting and involves Freud's application of his horde theory, in an article of 1921, to explain the social function of the Church.

Between November 1914 and the summer of 1915, Freud worked on a series of papers which he intended to publish under the title *Zur Vorbereitung einer Metapsychologie* (Preliminaries to a Metapsychology). There were to be twelve papers in all, but of these only five survive. However, in 1983, while preparing an edition of the correspondence between Freud and his Hungarian colleague, Sándor Ferenczi, the lost twelfth paper was found by Ilse Grubrich-Simitis. Entitled 'Übersicht der Übertragungsneurosen' ('Overview of the Transference Neuroses'), the first part of Freud's discussion of the neuroses is largely consistent with his previous work. Here, for example, he insists again that the constant factor is that the 'repressed instinctual impulse is always a libidinal one, belonging to sexual life. . . .'[22] In the second part, however, he revisits *Totem and Taboo* and considers again the primeval crime of the sons against the father. But now there is something new. Whereas before we had the theory that the neurotic duplicates within his own experience the anxieties felt originally by the sons towards their jealous primal father, we now have the suggestion that this was not the original situation but one which was itself generated by an even earlier stage of human development. Here Freud takes up the idea, first suggested to him by Fritz Wittels and elaborated by Ferenczi,[23] that 'the primal human animal passed its existence in a thoroughly rich milieu that satisfied all needs, echoes of which we have retained in the myth of the primeval paradise.'[24] This situation changed through the exigencies of the Ice Age. The outside world, hitherto friendly and providing, transformed itself into a mass of threatening perils for the primal humans. With insufficient food and without the ability to sustain so many helpless individuals, they 'must have been subjected to the conflict between self-preservation and desire to procreate. . . . Accordingly, it became a social obligation to limit reproduction.'[25]

> The subsequent evolution is easy to construct. It primarily affected the male. After he had learned to economize on his libido and by means of regression to degrade his sexual activity to an earlier phase, activating his intelligence became paramount to him. He learned how to investigate, how to understand the hostile world somewhat, and how by means of inventions to secure his first mastery over it. He developed himself under the sign of energy, forming the beginnings of language, and had to assign great significance to the new acquisitions. Language was magic to him, his thoughts seemed omnipotent to him, he understood the world according to his ego. It is the time of the animistic world view and its magical trappings. As a reward for his power to safeguard the

27

lives of so many other helpless ones he bestowed upon himself unrestrained dominance over them, and through his personality established the first two tenets that he was himself invulnerable and that his possession of women must not be challenged. At the end of this epoch the human race had disintegrated into individual hordes that were dominated by a strong and wise brutal man as father. *It is possible that the egoistically jealous and inconsiderate nature that we from ethno-psychological considerations attribute to the primal father of the human horde was not present from the beginning, but rather was developed in the course of the severe Ice Age as a result of adaptation to exigency.*[26]

This addition to the theory of the primal horde means that we now have a history of man's prehistoric ancestors, laid out in terms of a Darwinian struggle for survival, and moving through three stages instead of the original two. The first is the 'patriarchal stage of civilization' in which the threat to human existence comes from the geologic development of the earth: this is the period of Ice Age privations, of the suppression of the libidinal instinct for the survival of the few, and of the emergence of the dominant father of the horde. The second is the 'social stage of civilization,' and here the threat comes from the relation of the sons to their tyrannical father, from their fear of castration and the trauma of its reality. The sons avoid castration by fleeing, and this results in the creation of further alliances for the purposes of survival, the emergence of the brother-clan, and the consequent development of social feelings. The third stage marks the end of the horde and the victory of the brothers. In an historically momentous act, they overpower and kill their father, triumph over his death, but quickly mourn his loss when they realize that 'they all still revered him as a model.'[27]

Although interesting, this extension of the original theory should be viewed with extreme caution. In *Totem and Taboo* Freud has already pointed to the hypothetical and tentative character of his historical reconstructions, and it may well be that he considered these further additions about the emergence of the primal father after the Ice Age as simply unwarranted and the purest speculation. Certainly they do not appear again. Another reason for their exclusion may be this: that by setting this even earlier history within a geological context, Freud was to some extent drawing attention away from the central sexual theme of his horde theory and his concern to show how the relations between the father and his sons duplicate the familiar halves of the Oedipal complex, namely, the attraction to the mother and the death wishes against the rival father. Nothing could be allowed to obscure the fact that it is the sexual component which accounts for the emergence of religion, and that this is as true for the primitive savage within the horde as it is for modern man within the family unit.

Eight years after the publication of *Totem and Taboo*, Freud applied his theory of the primal horde in another direction and with much greater success. This time he uses it to explain the function of the Church as an organized social community. In his essay 'Group Psychology and the Analysis of the Ego' (1921),[28] he draws attention to the way in which the individual when placed within a group – for example, a member of a race, nation, caste, profession or institution – begins to act quite differently than when in isolation. Two new characteristics are particularly significant: first, the individual becomes altogether more credulous and open to influence: he suspends his critical faculty and is much more inclined to accept the 'illusions' fostered by the group; and second, he becomes naturally much more obedient to authority and submits instinctively to anyone who emerges as his master. These two characteristics are interconnected. A group is an obedient herd, which requires a master; but the master must be able to attract it not just by his personal qualities, by his strong and imposing will, but also by his ability to promulgate an 'idea' that will excite the group's emotions, fascinate it, and awaken its faith.

Significantly, these two characteristics form the basis of the Church as a group, and to a quite remarkable extent. The master of the group is Christ, and the illusion he fosters is the idea that he 'loves all the individuals in the group with an equal love' – an illusion upon which everything depends and without which the Church 'would dissolve.'[29] Equality before Christ's love is the 'democratic strain' which runs through the Church, and this explains why the Christian community is so frequently likened to a 'family' and why 'believers call themselves brothers in Christ, that is, brothers through the love which Christ has for them.'[30] Here, then, we are faced with a group of equal companions, submissive towards an individual of superior strength, who binds the community together by the illusion that he loves them equally and justly.

Of course, mention of a band of submissive brothers immediately reminds us of the primal horde. Indeed, according to Freud, *all* groups are revivals of this original scene, and the psychology of groups is 'the oldest human psychology,'[31] pointing back to the time when the dominant father, in directly thwarting his sons' sexual impulses, forced the band of brothers together. By his sexual jealousy and intolerance, the primal father thus *creates* group psychology. This being the case, we can now unravel the inner emotional need that creates the Church as a human group, and be more specific about the contents of the illusion that binds it together. The Christian community duplicates this archaic heritage, and, in the believer's response to Christ, reanimates each individual's relation to his primal father: in this sense, Christ has become the 'substitute father.'[32] At the same time, however, the Church binds the community together by promoting a particular 'idealistic remodelling of the state of affairs in the primal horde.'[33] Where once the sons knew that they were persecuted by their father, and feared him, the Church now fosters the illusion that the father-God loves and protects them. A religion of love is now introduced where none existed, and the figure of Christ is presented as a parent-ideal far removed from the terrifying and implacable original, the master of the horde.

SUMMARY

Many of the arguments that Freud has presented in *Totem and Taboo* reappear again, albeit in various guises, in the three other books devoted to religion. But before moving on to them, it is as well to have before us a brief summary of Freud's discussion so far. At least five essential ideas have been introduced, each crucial for the development of his general theory of religion and from which he does not depart in his later publications.

1 The first is that the origin of religion is to be found in the ambivalent relation of son to father, or, to speak psychoanalytically, in *the operation of the Oedipus complex*. In religion, the son's dependence on the dominant male, and the ambivalence of this filial relation, oscillating between love and hate, and which was first encountered within the primal horde, is projected anew onto the idealized object of religious worship, the father-god. Submission to this object is the first characteristic of belief and it is this above all else which binds believers into a community of faith.

2 For this theory to work a second idea must also be admitted, namely, that the sense of guilt engendered by the original murder must be able to persist through many thousands of years, even down to those generations which can have no knowledge of the original deed. This in turn suggests that there is a *mechanism of inheritance*, a kind of collective unconscious or mass psyche which accounts for this continuity. It is by means of this entity – whatever it is, because Freud is notoriously unspecific at this point – that man is able to inherit ideas (in this case, the memory of the primal horde), and, more particularly, to inherit a particular 'psychical disposition,' namely, the sense of guilt at the original killing of the father. It is this sense of collective guilt which is the second characteristic of belief, binding believers together in a religious community.

3 If guilt is to be inherited, then the original crime must, in some sense, be duplicated. We require, in other words, *a theory of recapitulation*. This the Oedipus complex also provides. Because it is an axiomatic truth for Freud that human beings pass through an Oedipal phase, it is a short step for him to conclude that what the original band of brothers experienced in relation to the dominant male of the primal horde is both inherited and re-experienced by all individuals in relation to their own fathers. This inheritance in consequence becomes doubly potent: it is both historical and constantly reaffirmed. Freud expresses this in the use of two terms, widely accepted at the time, first introduced by the German biologist Ernst Haeckel (1834–1919), and already employed by Frazer: *ontogeny* and *phylogeny*. Ontogeny is

concerned with the development of the individual organism, and phylogeny with the development of the species. In these terms, the Oedipus complex becomes the personal (and ontogenetic) repetition of something that is embedded within the unconscious, namely, the universal (and phylogenetic) experience of the killing of the father. In this sense, the unconscious acts as the custodian of an archaic image, of a birthright, if you will, acquired and accumulated far back, but constantly confirmed and reawakened by present experience.[34]

4   In the next strand of his argument Freud moves from an analysis of the causes of guilt to an account of its effect. This results in a *theory of religious behaviour*, which associates the practices of religion with those found among obsessional neurotics. Here the common denominator is the omnipotence of thoughts, in which magic properties are ascribed to the mind in its ability to control the external world. In religion this is seen primarily in the use of rituals both as a defence against the temptations arising from the instincts and as a protection against divine punishment for having them. In this sense, omnipotence of thoughts and the practices that arise from it betray an ambivalent emotional attitude – namely, the prohibition of a wish – and to that extent they too confirm the Oedipus complex as the nucleus of every neurosis and of every guilt. All religious rituals thus stand as expressions of remorse and attempts at atonement for the present re-experience of something that happened in the past.

5   The final strand of Freud's argument is less apparent in *Totem and Taboo* than it is elsewhere. What Freud is offering us here is an *evolutionary* history of how man views the universe, and indeed he specifies three stages: the animistic, the religious and the scientific. He further characterizes these three stages in terms of the omnipotence of thoughts. In the first, man ascribes omnipotence to himself, most notably in the practices of magic for the control of nature and the world of spirits; in the second, he transfers his omnipotence to the gods but still reserves some power for himself, thus enabling him to influence the gods according to his wishes; but in the third this omnipotence is for the most part given up because the 'scientific view of the universe no longer affords any room for human omnipotence; men have acknowledged their smallness and submitted resignedly to death and to the other necessities of nature.'[35] His next characterization of these three stages is even more revealing: the animistic stage corresponds to the auto-eroticism of earliest childhood; the religious to the slightly later stage in child sexual development, where the sexual instincts find an external object in the parent; and the scientific to the 'stage at which an individual has reached maturity, has renounced the pleasure principle, adjusted himself to reality and turned to the external world for the object of his desires.'[36] This leaves us with the distinct impression that a *decline in religion is coincident with human growth towards adulthood*. Religion is, in other words, an infantile obsession that

maturity will hopefully discard. This theme appears again in almost all Freud's subsequent writings on religion, but its appearance here, however slight, gives us a different slant on *Totem and Taboo*. The book now appears almost as an act of therapy. It is as if Freud, in unmasking the origin of religion, is deliberately following psychoanalytic procedure by seeking to effect a cure through unravelling the original repressed trauma. In his psychogenetic history of religion, the events of the primal horde, together with every individual's duplication of these events in their experience of the Oedipus complex, stand as the traumatic precipitating causes, now retrieved from memory and brought back into consciousness. This done, it is to be hoped that their effects – the guilts they generate, together with all the associated obsessional impulses constructed to deal with them – will disappear as well. And even if they do not disappear entirely, we have at least been enabled to see them for what they are – symptoms of neurosis and derivatives of repression – and so set on the path to maturity. Thus in *Totem and Taboo* historical and psychoanalytic research coincide with therapeutic effort.

3

RELIGION AND ILLUSION

We come now to the three books with which Freud completes his study of religion. These are, to repeat, *The Future of an Illusion, Civilization and Its Discontents* and *Moses and Monotheism*. These three represent an important shift in Freud's analysis, moving away from a discussion of the origins of religion, which we saw so provocatively presented in *Totem and Taboo*, and towards an examination of religion as a major cultural phenomenon. The central text here is his famous essay *The Future of an Illusion*,[1] in which Freud not only accounts for the emergence and role of religious ideas within our culture but provides reasons why such ideas are still accepted by believers. As we shall see, his argument turns on the classification of religion *as an aspect of human civilization* – to the point, indeed, where to explain the origin of civilization is, for all practical purposes, to explain the origin of religion.[2] *Civilization and its Discontents*,[3] written three years after *The Future of an Illusion*, is rightly regarded as its direct successor, and for that reason I shall treat them together. Here Freud again describes the origin and development of civilization, and thus by implication of religion, and once more does so in terms of the repression and restriction of instinctual wishes, but this time following the later conceptual framework of id, ego, and super-ego.

THE FUTURE OF AN ILLUSION (1927); CIVILIZATION AND ITS DISCONTENTS (1930)

As its title makes clear, the central claim of Freud's famous monograph is that *religion is an illusion*. What does Freud mean by an 'illusion'? We have already seen that an illusion is something necessary for the formation of a group like the Church: it binds believers together and forms of the content of their faith.[4] Now Freud is more specific. An illusion is not an 'error.' It was Aristotle's error to believe that vermin developed out of dung, but it was Columbus' illusion to believe that he had discovered a new sea route to the Indies. The difference between these two is that, while Aristotle presumably would not care one way or the other if his belief were proved false, Columbus would mind because he also wanted to believe in his discovery. The chief characteristic of illusions is therefore 'that they are derived from human wishes,' namely, that there is a motivation to believe.[5] This is not to say, however, that illusions are 'delusions.' A delusion is a false belief, a contradiction of reality, but an illusion is not necessarily erroneous. For example:

> a middle-class girl may have the illusion that a prince will come and marry her. This is possible; and a few such cases have occurred. That the Messiah will come and found a golden age is much less likely. Whether one classifies this belief as an illusion or as something analogous to a delusion will depend on one's personal attitude. Examples of illusions which have proved true are not easy to find, but the illusion of the alchemists that all metals can be turned into gold might be one of them. The wish to have a great deal of gold, as much gold as possible, has, it is true, been a good deal damped by our present-day knowledge of the determinants of wealth, but chemistry no longer regards the transmutation of metals into gold as impossible.[6]

This distinction between illusion and delusion is an important one. In calling religion an illusion Freud is not saying that religious beliefs are necessarily false but rather that they must satisfy the believer's wishes: they could be true, although this is unlikely. A further characteristic of an illusion follows on from this. Illusions set little store by verification. Unlike empirical assertions, therefore, the assertions of religion are not based on observations of the external world which can be either verified or falsified, but rather on inner convictions that neither seek nor require rational justification. Thus, when the question of corroborating evidence is raised, religious people appeal to the authority of their ancestors, to ancient texts which have been handed down to them, or even argue that it is wrong to raise questions of authenticity, punishing those that do. This last point, says Freud, is bound to rouse our deepest suspicions, because it can only mean that society is all too well aware that religious doctrines lack conviction or rational support, and that this is something that no appeal to our ignorant ancestors can allay.

> But these ancestors of ours were far more ignorant than we are. They believed in things we could not possibly accept today; and the possibility occurs to us that the doctrines of religion may belong to that class too. The proofs they have left us are set down in writings which themselves bear every mark of untrustworthiness. They are full of contradictions, revisions and falsifications, and where they speak of factual confirmations they are themselves unconfirmed. It does not help much to have it asserted that their wording, or even their content only, originates from divine revelation; for this assertion is itself one of the doctrines whose authenticity is under examination, and no proposition can be a proof of itself.[7]

34

These remarks, of course, only serve to highlight religion's peculiarity. If religion pays scant regard to rational justification, then it seems all the more strange that so many sensible men and women should continue to proclaim their religious beliefs. This alone suggests that the origin of religious ideas is a *psychical* one, rooted in the strength of the wishes they contain, wishes so urgent and powerful that they can obliterate all other concerns. Religion, it would seem, provides a unique set of satisfactions to certain demands inherent within the human experience – satisfactions so intense to the human psyche that it desires above all things to embrace them. What, then, are these demands? Freud isolates three: first, to come to terms with the external forces of nature which threaten to destroy humanity; second, to come to terms with the internal forces of nature – that is, the human instincts – which are no less threatening; and third, to satisfy mankind's universal longing for the father-figure.

The first demand is the most obvious. Men and women are born into a hostile world, and almost at every turn the forces of nature threaten to destroy them: there are earthquakes, floods, storms, diseases, and finally there is death itself. 'With these forces nature rises up against us, majestic, cruel and inexorable.'[8] The question is then: How to defend oneself against these superior powers? This is the principal task of civilization – its actual *raison d'être* – and its methods are various; but undoubtedly its most potent defence is through the creation of religious ideas. People *humanize* nature, *personalize* the forces that threaten them, turn them into gods, and thereby hope to gain some control over them.

> Impersonal forces and destinies cannot be approached; they remain eternally remote. But if the elements have passions that rage as they do in our own souls, if death itself is not something spontaneous but the violent act of an evil Will, if everywhere in nature there are Beings around us of a kind that we know in our own society, then we can breathe freely, can feel at home in the uncanny and can deal by psychical means with our senseless anxiety. We are still defenceless, perhaps, but we are no longer helplessly paralysed; we can at least react. Perhaps, indeed, we are not even defenceless. We can apply the same methods against these violent supermen outside that we employ in our own society; we can try to adjure them, to appease them, to bribe them, and, by so influencing them, we may rob them of a part of their power . . .[9]

This, then, is the first step in the creation of religion, a step so obvious to Freud that he is almost apologetic in mentioning it. To sum up, religion is a primary cultural method by which men and women attempt to deal with the suffering and helplessness they experience in relation to the external world. By our creation of gods, our happiness is increased by assuming some control over our unhappiness. The harsh facts of reality are, in this sense, moderated by our ability to communicate and placate the divine powers that control them. And in this process even death loses its sting:

> Everything that happens in this world is an expression of the intentions of an intelligence superior to us, which in the end, though its ways and byways are difficult to follow, orders everything for the best – that is, it makes it enjoyable for us. Over each one of us there watches a benevolent Providence which is only seemingly stern and which will not suffer us to become a plaything of the over-mighty and pitiless forces of nature. Death itself is not extinction, is not a return to inorganic lifelessness, but the beginning of a new kind of existence which lies on the path of development to something higher.... In the end all good is rewarded and all evil punished, if not actually in this form of life then in the later existences that begin after death. In this way all the terrors, the sufferings and the hardships of life are destined to be obliterated.[10]

The conclusion that religion provides a welcome answer to the problem of suffering owes nothing to the discoveries of psychoanalysis: it is for Freud almost a matter of common sense. The same cannot be said of the second step in the development of religion. Here we must utilize the discoveries of psychoanalysis. Civilization, to repeat, seeks to overcome the threat from *external* forces by the creation of gods, but it also serves to overcome the *internal* threat emanating from man's instinctual life. Religion emerges once again as an answer to suffering, but the suffering now encountered arises from the antagonism between civilization and instinct, or, more precisely, from the renunciation of instinct that civilization demands. If anything the pain engendered here is even more acute than that generated from the external environment, and it is one of the tasks of psychoanalysis to understand and, if possible, remedy it.

At one level, of course, human beings are grateful for the restrictions placed upon their instincts by civilization. We are by nature self-seeking and aggressive, with scant regard for our fellows; and without the rules and institutions of society, which coerce and suppress our instinctual wishes, we would rapidly find that social life had degenerated into a state of anarchy, of each against all. Amongst these instinctual wishes Freud counts incest, cannibalism and a lust for killing, and it is not difficult to imagine what would happen to our society if these wishes were unbridled. But however justified the moral demands of civilization may be, the fact remains, says Freud, that people feel an enormous hostility towards society for the impositions thus placed upon them. It is, therefore, the central paradox of cultural life that civilization creates a permanent measure of suffering amongst those it is seeking to protect.

In an article of 1908[11] Freud charts the course of this suffering in relation to the sexual instincts. According to the dominant so-called 'civilized' morality of Western society, and sanctioned by religion, sexual intercourse is prohibited except in monogamous marriage and restricted to the purposes of reproduction. This imposes on all individuals of either sex the demand of abstinence – abstinence until married, or, if unmarried, abstinence throughout life. However, given the strength of the libidinal impulse, and given that this impulse is directed primarily towards pleasurable satisfaction rather than reproduction (the primacy of the pleasure being only later put to the service of reproduction), this demand is almost impossible to fulfil and the result is repression and neurosis on a grand scale. It is true that in some cases this sexual force can, by the process known as sublimation, be redirected into some activity of social or ethical importance; but the overwhelming majority become neurotic or are harmed in some way or another. Even marriage provides no consolation for the sexual deprivations experienced before it. The promised satisfaction of sexual needs is rarely realized and disillusionment quickly follows.

The theme of this article – that the antagonism between civilization and the instinctual life causes acute human suffering – is developed still further in *Civilization and its Discontents*. Before coming on to it, however, Freud first tackles an argument suggested to him by an un-named friend who, in the 1931 edition, he identifies as the novelist Romain Rolland (1866–1944). On receipt of *The Future of an Illusion*, Rolland had protested that Freud 'had not properly appreciated the true source of religious sentiments.' This, he claims, may be traced back to a sense of eternity, to an 'oceanic feeling' in which the individual feels an indissoluble bond and sense of unity with the external world. One can, Rolland argues, 'rightly call oneself religious on the ground of this oceanic feeling alone, even if one rejects every belief and every illusion.'[12] Freud quickly disposes of this argument. He does not deny that these feelings exist in many people but interprets them as yet another example of the way in which the ego seeks consolation: its own impending annihilation is in part offset by this association with the universe. But even if these rather nebulous and rarified sensations become linked with religion later on, they do not and cannot displace the far more familiar way in which the 'common man' understands his religion. For him the object of worship is an enormously exalted father, who watches over him and who will compensate him in a future life for his sufferings on earth.

> The derivation of religious needs from the infant's helplessness and the longing for the father aroused by it seems to me incontrovertible. . . . I cannot think of any need in childhood as strong as the need for a father's protection. Thus the part played by the oceanic feeling, which might seek something like the restoration of limitless narcissism, is ousted from a place in the foreground. The origin of the religious attitude can be traced back in clear outlines as far as the feeling of infantile helplessness. There may be something further behind that, but for the present it is wrapped in obscurity.[13]

Rolland's argument dealt with, Freud returns to the main theme of his book. Even if we accept that religion is patently infantile and contrary to reality, it is still important to see the nature of the consolations it offers. Once again he refers to religion's ability to provide an answer to suffering, either through countering the forces of nature by personalizing them, or through overcoming the transitoriness of life by claims to an after-life. But when it comes to displacing the suffering produced by cultural restrictions on our instinctual life, matters are altogether more complicated, if only because the happiness when satisfying these instincts is so immediate and so intense. Of these the most powerful is, as we have seen already, the libidinal instinct, which provides such strong experiences of satisfaction that it becomes the 'prototype of all happiness.'[14] Here Freud reiterates his view that civilization, by imposing such restrictions on the erotic life, leads to repression, frustration, resentment and neurosis; but interestingly enough, and in contrast to his earlier position, Freud goes on to claim that the instinctual privation which is of even greater significance is that of *aggression*.[15] It is this inclination to aggression, this mutual hostility between human beings, that is the primary threat to civilized society; and it is because of the strength of this instinctual hostility that civilization expends so much energy in setting limits to it.

What methods, then, does culture, most notably in the form of religion, employ to eliminate or at least inhibit natural aggression? The first method is to impose some regulation upon our social relationships, to introduce a notion of justice, so that weaker citizens are protected from the stronger. By this means the power of the individual is replaced by the power of a 'community,' in which personal interest is sacrificed to the collective interest – a shift of focus that Freud calls 'the decisive step of civilization.'[16] This is formalized in the demand: 'Thou shalt love thy neighbour as thyself.' This law, which is older than Christianity, binds the community together not only in a *libidinal* way – namely, it diverts the sexual impulse away from genital satisfaction and redirects it towards the group – but also by countering the aggressive instinct by fostering the idea that my love of my neighbour implies that he or she is somehow deserving of it, and that they should not therefore be the object of my hostility. This, of course, is hard to do, particularly when the commandment to love is presented in its most extreme form: 'Love thine enemies.' In other words, the compulsion not to obey these, doubtless laudable, precepts is very strong, particularly when experience constantly confirms that it is those who ignore them who prosper. Accordingly, civilization adopts a second method for the control of the aggressive instinct, even more extraordinary than the first: it creates conscience (the super-ego):

What happens in him to render his desire for aggression innocuous? Something very remarkable, which we should never have guessed and which is nevertheless quite obvious. His aggressiveness is introjected, internalized; it is, in point of fact, sent back to where it came from –

that is, it is directed towards his own ego. There it is taken over by a portion of the ego, which sets itself over against the rest of the ego as super-ego, and which now, in the form of 'conscience', is ready to put into action against the ego the same harsh aggressiveness that the ego would have liked to satisfy upon other, extraneous individuals. The tension between the harsh super-ego and the ego that is subjected to it, is called by us the sense of guilt; it expresses itself as a need for punishment. Civilization, therefore, obtains mastery over the individual's dangerous desire for aggression by weakening and disarming it and by setting up an agency within him to watch over it, like a garrison in a conquered city.[17]

The important connection here is between conscience and guilt. The culture demands that instinctual satisfactions – notably, the libidinal and the aggressive – be renounced. Given the power of these instincts, this is more easily said than done, and these forbidden wishes persist – a fact that cannot be hidden from the super-ego and which accordingly creates a sense of guilt. Thus compliance with the demands of society does not have the liberating effect that is desired, for now fear of the external authority, of the punishments society will inflict on the individual for not complying with its demands, is replaced by fear of an internal authority, the fear of conscience. The super-ego, in other words, constructs a 'categorical imperative' of duty, an ideal of conduct, to counter the individual's persisting wish to satisfy the instinctual needs of the id; and the aggressive character of its disapproval, which causes a sense of guilt, is a further instance of the aggressive instinct at work. In this sense, the severity of conscience is the individual's aggression, previously turned upon others, now visited upon him or herself: it is an aggressiveness which has been displaced inwards. Thus, characteristically, a person who cannot express their aggression has a very harsh super-ego, while someone who finds an outlet for it may have a relatively mild one.

Pausing here for a moment, we can see that one of the major functions of religion is to defend civilization against human hostility. The sufferings that people endure externally from the forces of nature, and internally from the restrictions placed by society upon their instincts, are to an extent compensated for, on the one hand, by religion's personification of these inimical forces into gods not so very different from ourselves, and, on the other, by its transmutation of the libidinal and aggressive desires emanating from the id into the love of neighbour and the ethics of conscience. These ideas now coalesce into the final and most potent wish that religion satisfies: *the longing for the father-figure*.

This has already been pointed to by the function of conscience. The authority exercised over the ego by the super-ego, and the ambivalent feelings of dependence and apprehension that this engenders, are, according to Freud, reanimations of the relationship with the father. That is to say, the super-ego confronts the ego as a strict father confronts a child. But more than that: the sense of guilt which is apparent to the super-ego, and which is necessary for the construction of conscience, is not simply derived from the *individual's* inability to control the libidinal and aggressive instincts of their id: it stems also from an original and *collective* remorse for an original deed involving the father. We thus return to an old theme. Guilt is also an historical inheritance, a fundamental phenomenon of our emotional life acquired by the human race as a psychical bequest passed on from generation to generation.

By this route we return to the theory of the primal horde, and Freud once again brings religion within the circle of the father complex. The demand for a god as a father-figure follows an infantile prototype in the (ontogenetic) repetition of the helplessness felt by each of us before his own father; and this demand is at the same time a (phylogenetic) repetition of the relation of father to son in the primal horde. The situation is, accordingly, anything but new, and continues on into adulthood. As individuals turn from childhood to adulthood, they realize that they remain helpless, and in need of continued protection. Now, however, it is nature itself and the restrictions imposed by society which create the sense of helplessness. They therefore revert to the solution of childhood, and create a supreme being with all the attributes of a father:

> When the growing individual finds that he is destined to remain a child for ever, that he can never do without protection against strange superior powers, he lends those powers the features belonging to the figure of his father; he creates for himself the gods whom he dreads, whom he seeks to propitiate, and whom he nevertheless entrusts with his own protection. Thus his longing for a father is a motive identical with his need for protection against the consequences of his human weakness. The defence against childish helplessness is what lends its characteristic features to the adult's reaction to the helplessness which he has to acknowledge – a reaction which is precisely the formation of religion.[18]

It is worth spelling out the reason why the image of the father-god has such a particular *compulsive* character. It is, to repeat, a wish-fulfilment, and the fulfilment of a wish brings satisfaction; but the peculiar potency of the satisfaction achieved by religious belief consists in the fact that it feeds off those wishes and fantasies of the infantile mind derived from its repressed libidinal and aggressive instincts in relation to the father. In this sense, belief in the father-god duplicates the neuroses of children, and, like them, arises from the Oedipus complex. This complex, we remember, is essentially ambivalent in character: it comprises positive (affectionate) and negative (hostile) attitudes; on the one hand, there is reverence and love for the dominant male, and, on the other, fear and hatred of him because this dominance thwarts our own sexual impulses. In the first case, the father is what one would like to be; and in the second, the father prevents what one would like to have. This ambivalence is projected directly into the concept of God. On the one hand, God the father is the object of love and admiration, the ideal of manhood, who has the power to grant every desire; and, on the other, he is the negative authority, an all-seeing censor, who prohibits our desires and severely punishes those who transgress his commandments. In this projection the believer is thus re-experiencing the emotional relations originating in the repressed period of his childhood, and is transferring onto the divine father-figure attitudes and dispositions which are also part of the collective memory of humanity. God the father becomes the re-embodiment of the relationships that each of us has to his own father, and beyond that, to the ancestral father of the primal horde; and the force of the wish to believe in him derives from the force of the instinctual wishes and repressions involved in that relationship. Belief, as it were, draws into itself these repressed wishes and the guilt associated with them, and projects upon the world a figure to whose will and commandments we willingly submit, partly because of the security this brings and partly because we may thereby atone for the crimes committed against him and every father. Religion is therefore a fantasy born of a thirst for obedience, an obedience celebrated in obsessive rituals and pious practices. This obedience, hopefully, will avert the punishments which would otherwise be visited upon us for having the instincts we do, will reconcile father to son, and will thereby assuage our filial sense of guilt.

MOSES AND MONOTHEISM (1939)

In this, the last book that he was to complete before his death, Freud seeks to substantiate his account of the origin of religion through an analysis of the origins of Judaism and, something of an afterthought, of the beginnings of Christianity. *Moses and Monotheism*, it should be said, has not received a good press. Not only does it lack the formal construction typical of Freud's work, but it begins with the eccentric – although, as Freud presents it, highly plausible – hypothesis that Moses was not a Hebrew but an Egyptian. As we shall see, this theory has been largely discredited. But in a sense this hardly matters. Of much more importance is the psychological theory that Freud weaves around his historical data, a theory which he now requires to account for an aspect of religious experience previously omitted by him. In *The Future of an Illusion* Freud had been 'concerned much less with the deepest sources of religious feeling than with what the ordinary man understands by his religion'[19] and this understanding, as we have seen, Freud traces above all else to each individual's need for a father-figure. Freud accepted the criticism made immediately on publication that this analysis, while explaining the obsessive character of religion for the individual, did not explain why religion had developed its predominantly *monotheistic* form, and why, additionally,

41

this form had its own compulsive attraction. *Moses and Monotheism* is designed to remedy this omission.

So to begin: Moses was not a Hebrew but an Egyptian aristocrat associated with the monotheistic reforms of King Akhenaten in the 14th century BC. When the king died and the inevitable reaction set in, Moses, a convinced adherent of the new religion, decided to leave Egypt at the head of a new people, the Jews, who would remain true to its principles. Jewish monotheism thus originates in a particular monotheistic episode of Egyptian history, introduced through the influence of the powerful figure of Moses. However, whilst this was being achieved – and here Freud follows a suggestion made by Ernst Sellin in 1922 – the Jews rose up against their leader, killed him, and abandoned their new religion, symbolized in the story of the golden calf. There came a time, however, when the people began to regret the murder of Moses and sought to forget it. When therefore a century later another leader arose, the son-in-law of the Midianite Jethro, he was fused in tradition with his predecessor and given the name of Moses. We thus have two Moses: the Egyptian Moses and the Midianite Moses, and it was under the leadership of the latter that the original monotheism was transformed into the henotheistic worship of the volcano god Yahweh, a belief which was to dominate for many centuries. Gradually, however, the old faith, largely under the impact of the prophets, reasserted itself, and the original Mosaic monotheistic doctrine once again became the permanent content of the Jewish religion. The Jews' remorse for the killing did not however subside, but reasserted itself in the hope of another great leader, the Messiah, who was to return and lead his people to redemption and the promised world dominion. This guilt was finally clarified by the politico-religious agitator, Paul, who indeed went so far as to create a new religion out of it, Christianity. Jesus thus becomes the resurrected Moses, whose ritual sacrifice would atone for the original murder of his great predecessor. Thereafter, and as a result of Jesus' deification, Christianity became a religion of the son rather than the father.

Most of this hypothesis can be discounted.[20] While it is generally accepted that 'Moses' is an Egyptian name, this does not in itself suggest that the man Moses was Egyptian, let alone an aristocrat. Rather, it can be more confidently asserted that he was a Hebrew, albeit born in Egypt and strongly influenced by Egyptian culture. Equally, the suggestion that Moses belongs to the reign of Amenhotep IV (1377–1360 BC) – a Pharaoh, incidentally, whose age and physical health almost certainly disqualify him as the founder of the Aten cult – throws the whole Old Testament chronology into confusion by almost a century, since the Exodus is now generally dated no later than 1290 BC. It is also worth pointing out that, while the marriage of Moses to the daughter of the Midianite priest, Jethro, appears repeatedly in Israelite tradition, there is no evidence for his murder, nor of the existence of a second Midianite Moses.[21] With such historical inaccuracies, it is perhaps worth recalling, as others have done, the original title of the book: *The Man Moses, an Historical Novel.*

Turning now to the psychoanalytic argument, we find Freud on much surer ground. Why has religion developed monotheistically, and why does monotheism have such compulsive attraction? Freud's answer begins circuitously. He starts with an analysis of the phenomenon – well documented in the genesis of human neuroses – known as 'latency.' Latency we may describe as the dormant period between the experience of a trauma and the final onset of neurotic illness: it is that time, particularly evident in prepubertal children, when repression has been relatively successful and there are few signs of conflict. Suppose, therefore, to give Freud's own example, a young boy has the traumatic experience of observing his parents having sexual intercourse. This may result immediately in neurotic symptoms – for example, an identification with his father indicated by aggressive behaviour towards his mother, which she repels with threats of informing his father – but these may in turn subside, with the original experience apparently forgotten through the mechanism of repression. We then enter the latency period of undisturbed development: the little boy appears free from any disturbance, exemplary in behaviour and happy at school. The onset of puberty, however, triggers off the original neurosis and a more definite neurosis results as the belated effect of the original trauma. With the development of his own sexuality, the boy is filled with hate for his father, whose place he originally wished to usurp; and when, much later, he himself finds a wife, he turns into a despotic and brutal personality, thereby completing the copy of his father as he remembers him.[22]

Three factors are essential, therefore, in the development of neurotic illness: first, the original traumatic experience, which for Freud invariably occurs in early childhood and is of a sexual and aggressive nature; second, the latency period, in which the individual, suffering a kind of infantile amnesia, represses this experience, denies it entry into consciousness, and functions without apparent ill-effect; and third, the outbreak of neurotic illness – what Freud, in a memorable phrase, calls the 'return of the repressed' – when the defences of repression break down either because of the pubertal resurgence of the aggressive and sexual instincts or because another experience or impression occurs which so resembles the original trauma that it reawakens it. Neurotic disturbances are therefore, first and foremost, symptoms of the return of the repressed; but they have also this peculiarity: they have a compulsive quality, which governs the person's actions with obsessional impulses.

The turning-point of Freud's argument occurs when he associates the period of latency with that period in Jewish history, after the defection from the religion of Moses, when there was no sign of the monotheistic idea – an association which, following the account of neurosis just given, must also presuppose an original trauma and the eventual development of neurotic symptoms when this repressed experience returns. It will come as no surprise to learn that the original trauma is the killing of the father of the primal horde, but now *repeated* in the killing of Moses, who, by his strength, energy and independence, is 'a mighty prototype of a father.'[23] Such, however, is the collective remorse for this murder that we enter a latency period, where all memory of this crime is removed or 'repressed,' together with all ideas associated with the victim, namely, the monotheistic view of God. When, therefore, a second Moses emerged, so close to the original Moses that an identification took place, and when, still later, the prophets renewed the exacting demands made by Moses, the 'monotheistic idea returned like a boomerang to the land of its origin.'[24] Monotheism, in other words, is *a symptom of the return of the repressed*: it represents the re-emergence of the father, the re-elevation of the powerful male to the position of dominance, stimulated by the reawakened and overpowering sense of guilt for the original crime committed against him. Monotheism is therefore a reconciliation with God the Father, and the laws and commandments associated with it are no more than an act of atonement for what was done to him, obsessively held in order to assuage the overpowering sense of guilt. Nor does it come as a further surprise that these commandments should be primarily associated with the renunciation of those instincts which had operated so effectively in the original crime, the sexual and the aggressive. This explains the custom of circumcision: 'Circumcision is the symbolic substitute for the castration which the primal father once inflicted upon his sons in the plenitude of his absolute power, and whoever accepted that symbol was showing by it that he was prepared to submit to the father's will, even if it imposed the most painful sacrifice on him.'[25] This, however, is not the whole story. For its completion we must move outside Judaism. Remorse for the murder of Moses also provides the stimulus for the wishful fantasy of the Messiah, and it is hardly fortuitous that the violent killing of another great man should be the starting-point of Christianity. Indeed, what better atonement could there be for the killing of the father than that the Son should be killed in his turn?

> ... it was after all a Jewish man, Saul of Tarsus (who, as a Roman citizen, called himself Paul), in whose spirit the realization first emerged: 'the reason we are so unhappy is that we have killed God the father.' And it is entirely understandable that he could only grasp this piece of truth in the delusional guise of the glad tidings: 'we are freed from all guilt since one of us has sacrificed his life to absolve us.' In this formula the killing of God was of course not mentioned, but a crime that had to be atoned by the sacrifice of a victim could only have been a murder. And the intermediate step between the delusion and the historical truth was provided by the assurance that the victim of the sacrifice had been God's son. With the strength which it derived from the source of historical truth, this new faith overthrew every obstacle. The blissful sense of being chosen was replaced by the liberating sense of redemption. But the fact of the parricide, in returning to the memory of mankind, had to overcome greater resistances than the other fact, which

had constituted the subject-matter of monotheism (namely, the fact of the existence of the primal father); it was also obliged to submit to a more powerful distortion. The unnameable crime was replaced by the hypothesis of what must be described as a shadowy 'original sin'.[26]

Original sin and redemption through sacrifice thus became the foundation stones of the new religion founded by Paul. Neither was it merely by chance that this new religion called for anti-Semitism as its complement. To the reproach that the Jews had murdered God was added the charge that they had rejected the means of being cleansed of their crime, with the result that their guilt remains. Without this confession, concludes Freud, the Jewish people have taken on a tragic load of guilt, and 'been made to pay heavy penance for it.'[27]

We are now in a better position to understand the particular attraction of monotheistic religion and why it should be the focus of obsessional behaviour. Its attraction – to duplicate the argument already presented in *Totem and Taboo*, *The Future of an Illusion* and *Civilization and its Discontents* – lies in the fact that monotheism is a religion of the father. Monotheism, in other words, meets what appears to be a basic need of humanity as a whole, namely, to relate to an authority who can be admired, before whom one can bow down, by whom one is ruled and perhaps even ill-treated. But this fact alone would be insufficient to account for the *obsessional* character of monotheistic belief. For this to be explained we must realize also that monotheism

> must have undergone the fate of being repressed, the condition of lingering in the unconscious, before it is able to display such powerful effects on its return, to bring the masses under its spell, as we have seen with astonishment and hitherto without comprehension in the case of religion's tradition.[28]

In other words, monotheism stimulates obsessive and compulsive neuroses because it itself is a form of 'the return of the repressed,' because embedded within it are other feelings associated with the father, feelings so powerful indeed that they have required a defence against them in the form of repression. These feelings are feelings of guilt, and they originate from two memories: a memory arising from each individual's guilty relation to his own father, and a memory arising from mankind's remorse for the primal crime, the murder of the father by the primal horde. Consequently, monotheism is an attempt to resolve the unconscious individual and collective emotional repression created and reinforced by these two memories, its principal objective being to affect a reconciliation with the offended father. A sense of guilt thus becomes the most important factor in the development of religion generally and in monotheism particularly; and the rituals and ceremonies associated with them – rigorously upheld and producing an acute sense of anxiety when omitted – are revealed as obsessional activities designed to placate the father whom we have offended and, if possible, to avert the punishment that we have deserved. Thus in *Totem and Taboo* a history of guilt explains the emergence of the earliest form of religion, the totemic and its observances; and in *Moses and Monotheism* Freud adopts the same thesis, but now reconstructs another murder which would be for monotheism what the murder of the primal father had been for totemism. Accordingly, the deep impression of the monotheistic idea upon the Jews is based on a *repetition* of the primal murder of the father, but this time carried out on the father-substitute, Moses. This murder thus becomes the link between the repressed primal murder and its re-emergence in monotheism. It also serves, however, as the link between Judaism and the other religion that emerged out of it, Christianity. Guilt for the murder of Moses stimulated the wish for the Messiah, in such a way that Christ becomes a resurrected Moses, the son whose sacrifice redeems the company of brothers from the original primal sin. But the ambivalence towards the father remains: while guilt for the father's death is expiated, the son also replaces the father and becomes god himself. This is clearly expressed in the eucharistic revival of the totem meal: reconciliation occurs, but the son's flesh and blood have been substituted for that of the father.

In this remarkable account of the development of monotheism Freud repeats many of the ideas of his earlier books, most notably the theory of inheritance first promulgated in *Totem and Taboo*. The religious disposition is a compound of experiences: experiences that each of us has had of our own fathers (ontogenetic), and, more extraordinarily, experiences that we all share as part of our 'archaic heritage' in relation to the primal father (phylogenetic) – the first set of experiences recapitulating and reinforcing the 'memory-trace' of the second as it has been passed down through the generations, thereby enabling it to become 'a collectiv, universal property of mankind.'[29] Religion therefore contains an historical truth: there was once in primeval times 'a single person who was bound to appear huge at that time and who afterwards returned in men's memory elevated to divinity.'[30] But this historical truth cannot in any sense validate religion's claim that a god exists. This remains an illusion, but an illusion now at least explicable in terms of the strong emotional (and infantile) impulse to return to the past and to become once again the submissive son of the father of the horde.[31]

CONCLUSION: THE VALUE OF RELIGION

A final question remains: If religion has been unmasked as so much wishful-thinking, what value does it have for society? For a reply to this question we must return to the closing pages of *The Future of an Illusion*. Freud's answer is given in the form of a debate with an imaginary protagonist, who emphasizes both the human need for illusions in general and for the religious illusion in particular.[32] Freud's disputant makes two specific points. His first

is that civilization is built on the doctrines of religion, and that the mainten-
ance of human society is based on the great majority of people believing in
their truth.

> If men are taught that there is no almighty and all-just God, no divine
> world-order and no future life, they will feel exempt from all obligation
> to obey the precepts of civilization. Everyone will, without inhibition
> or fear, follow his asocial, egoistic instincts and seek to exercise his
> power; Chaos, which we have banished through many thousands of
> years of the work of civilization, will come again.[33]

The second point made by Freud's opponent is that to deprive men and
women of their religious beliefs would be a needless cruelty.

> Countless people find their one consolation in religious doctrines, and
> can only bear life with their help. You would rob them of their support,
> without having anything better to give them in exchange. It is admitted
> that so far science has not achieved much, but even if it had advanced
> much further it would not suffice for man. Man has imperative needs
> of another sort, which can never be satisfied by cold science; and it is
> very strange – indeed, it is the height of inconsistency – that a
> psychologist who has always insisted on what a minor part is played in
> human affairs by the intelligence as compared with the life of the
> instincts – that such a psychologist should now try to rob mankind of
> a precious wish-fulfilment and should propose to compensate them for
> it with intellectual nourishment.[34]

In replying to these accusations Freud admits that religion has performed
'great services for human civilization,' most notably in taming asocial
instincts. He is even willing to concede that if religion had succeeded in
making people happy, in comforting them and reconciling them to life, he for
one would not dream of replacing it. But what do we see instead? The great
majority remain unhappy, remain dissatisfied with civilization, indeed seek
to change it, particularly when it attempts to restrict their instincts. More than
that, the much-lauded morality of religion has often been cynically employed
by believers themselves to justify social immoralities of one kind or another.

> One sinned, and then one made a sacrifice or did penance and then one
> was free to sin once more.... It is no secret that the priests could
> only keep the masses submissive to religion by making such large
> concessions as these to the instinctual nature of man. Thus it was agreed:
> God alone is strong and good, man is weak and sinful. In every age
> immorality has found no less support in religion than morality has. If
> the achievements of religion in respect to man's happiness, suscept-
> ibility to culture and moral control are no better than this, the question
> cannot but arise whether we are not over-rating its necessity for

mankind, and whether we do wisely in basing our cultural demands upon it.[35]

Freud urges us, therefore, to replace a religious understanding of the precepts of civilization with a rational one, to see that our obedience to the rules, practices and institutions of civilization does not stem from the doctrines of religion but from social necessity: that, to give one example, the commandment against murder did not arise because God had forbidden it but because this rule was clearly in the interests of our communal existence. And once the purely human origin of these regulations is realized, Freud continues, people will become less antagonistically disposed towards them, and see that they are not imposed to rule us but to serve our own interests: 'they would adopt a more friendly attitude to them, and instead of aiming at their abolition, would aim only at their improvement. This would be an important advance along the road which leads to becoming reconciled to the burden of civilization.'[36] Freud admits, of course, that men and women are for the most part guided less by their intellect and more by their passions and instinctual demands – this, indeed, has been one of the great discoveries of psychoanalysis – but he expresses the hope that, although people are like this, there is no reason to suppose that they must be like this, and that if only they can be educated to see religion for what it is – an illusion – there might be some greater hope of social progress. He accepts that this hope may also be an illusion, and that human nature will remain much the same even without religion; but he believes that this experiment in 'irreligious education' is worth attempting and that there is some justification for believing that the results will be generally beneficial.

Freud does not therefore agree with his opponent that people are completely incapable of doing without the consolations of religion; but he does agree with him that the absence of this bitter-sweet poison, upon which we have been fed since childhood, will in all probability make life less easy to bear. After all, one cannot expect an insomniac to sleep well once deprived of his sleeping-pill.

> They will, it is true, find themselves in a difficult situation. They will have to admit to themselves the full extent of their helplessness and their insignificance in the machinery of the universe; they can no longer be the centre of creation, no longer the object of tender care on the part of a beneficent Providence. They will be in the same position as a child who has left the parental house where he was so warm and comfortable. But surely infantilism is destined to be surmounted. Men cannot remain children for ever; they must in the end go out into 'hostile life'. We may call this 'education to reality'.[37]

Thus, although life may be harder without the intoxicant of religion, the benefits are also worth fighting for. Having given up the fiction of another world, people will be thrown back on their own resources. They will now be able to concentrate their liberated energies into their life on earth, thereby hopefully achieving 'a state of things in which life will become tolerable for everyone and civilization no longer oppressive to anyone.'[38]

Freud's concluding remarks on the role of religion in civilization are presented in terms of an analogy between the development of the child into adulthood and the development of the human race into maturity. As we have seen, the path from the infant at the breast to the responsible adult is a long and tortuous one: driven by instinct and weak in intellect, it must pass through a period of neurosis in which its instinctual wishes are repressed, develop into infantile neuroses, become latent, and are eventually overcome in the course of growing up. Much the same occurs with humanity as a whole. It too falls into states akin to the neurotic, most notably when, in its infancy, it was not intellectually strong enough to bring about the instinctual renunciations indispensable for man's communal existence. Religion is the primary neurosis to emerge in this period, one which, like the other neuroses of childhood, will be discarded as humanity matures:

> Religion would thus be the universal obsessional neurosis of humanity; like the obsessional neurosis of children, it arose out of the Oedipus complex, out of the relation to the father. If this view is right, it is to be supposed that a turning-away from religion is bound to occur with the fatal inevitability of a process of growth, and that we find ourselves at this very juncture in the middle of that phase of development. Our behaviour should therefore be modelled on that of a sensible teacher who does not oppose an impending new development but seeks to ease its path and mitigate the violence of its irruption.[39]

4

FORMS OF RELIGIOUS
NEUROSIS

Thus far Freud has presented various arguments to unmask religion as an obsessional and incapacitating neurosis. In *The Future of an Illusion* he has made clear that religion hinders both the individual and society in the process towards maturity; and to those who might object that he leaves nothing in its place – that in depriving human beings of religion he is depriving them of any sense of purpose in their lives – he could reply that such a complaint is rather like a patient deploring the cure because he is now without a disease. It is not, in other words, for Freud to find a substitute but rather to provide evidence against a particular form of belief, a belief which, once removed, will allow people to find meaning for themselves within the world and not outside it, within the world of reality and not illusion. This indeed is the essential therapeutic value of his psychoanalytic account of religion. Having once observed the repressive role of religion within their own lives, individuals can, so Freud claims, take a first step towards recovery from an infantile and obsessional illness.

This is all very well, but what we need to know now is how Freud's general theory of religion is validated in its specific application: not why religion is neurotic but whether or not specific cases exemplify the particular behaviour that has been identified as neurotic, and, further, whether the form of therapy indicated by the theory is or is not applicable in these instances. Now it has to be said that, thus far at least, Freud often paints with a very broad brush, his description of particular religious practices frequently lacking detail, as if the detail would detract from the argument. To be sure, he has given us broad indications of how he would treat, say, the eucharist or acts of contrition; but, frankly, this is not quite what we want if we are to be convinced by his arguments. If it is true that believers are unaware of the motives that impel them to adopt certain practices, then it is all the more important for us to see how a psychoanalytic technique can uncover the source of these compulsions not just in the general but in the particular. To fill this gap I want to turn to two sources. The first is provided by Freud's distinguished disciple, Theodor Reik. The second is provided by Freud himself in two of his famous case-studies.

THEODOR REIK: COUVADE AND THE FEAR OF RETALIATION

Theodor Reik's little-known book, *Ritual: Psycho-Analytic Studies* (1919),[1] is often and understandably overlooked. In fact however, it provides one of the most ingenious and important supplements to Freud's argument – in this case, given its date, to the argument presented in *Totem and Taboo*. Freud was sufficiently impressed by it to write a Preface. Here he repeats his view that the 'ceremonials and prohibitions of obsessional patients force us to conclude that they have created a private religion for themselves,' and goes on to commend his pupil for making this abundantly clear in his analysis of particular religious rituals. And no wonder. Reik accepts Freud's thesis without equivocation, and calls *Totem and Taboo* the most important work of its kind in establishing 'the trains of feelings to which religion owes its origin.'[2] Indeed, so absolute is Reik's adherence to Freud's argument – with complete acceptance of the primal horde theory, the Oedipus complex, the role of magic, the nature of ambivalence, and the omnipotence of thoughts – that one gets the distinct impression that this is the kind of book that Freud would have been pleased to write himself; that, in a word, it bears the *imprimatur* of the master and that one can, without much ado, take Reik's work as an important extension of the main argument. Like Freud, Reik argues that the symptoms of obsessional neurosis 'show the essential characteristics of religion in an exaggerated and pathologically crude form'[3] and, that established, he feels free to equate the origin of religious ceremonial with the function of repression. Reik deals with four examples of religious ceremonial: the practice known as 'couvade,' the puberty rites of savages, the singing of Kol Nidre, and the use of the Shofar in Jewish festivals. In the first of these we find his most ingenious explanation, and the clearest example of how psychoanalysis can expose a religious ritual as a neurotic obsession.

The term 'couvade' refers to 'male childbed.' This is the custom in which, after the birth of a child, it is the father who remains in bed, while the mother carries on with her normal duties. This practice is an ancient one and widespread, particularly in South America and south-east Asia, and usually involves various abstinences imposed on the father, which, if broken, will bring harm or even death to the new-born infant. Thus he must not eat certain foods, he must not kill certain animals, he must do no work. Nor is it just a question of restricting diet and movement. Among the Caribs, for example, the father must express no pain while his shoulders are bled with an agouti tooth or while his wounds are being treated with large grains of pimento or Indian pepper – for the more unflinching the father the more courageous the child.

Reik reviews various attempts to solve the riddle of couvade. In 1773 the missionary, Josef Lafitau, thought it a sign of repentance for man's original sin; others thought it a means of establishing the father's rights over his child in a matriarchy; or a method of eluding the devil of puerperal fever; or an invention of the women to reduce their work-load; or a means by which the father could publicly recognize the child as his. The most important theory, however, is that advanced by Frazer in his *Totemism and Exogamy*, and here, like Freud before him, Reik borrows Frazer's distinction between the two forms of magic. Thus the post-natal and dietetic couvade is an example of 'contagious' magic, because the regimen observed by the father is thought to further the development of a healthy infant; and the pre-natal and pseudo-maternal couvade is an example of 'homœpathic or imitative' magic, because here the simulation of childbirth is thought to relieve the mother of her pain.[4]

Again following Freud, Reik believes that each form of magic, and the instances of each in the couvade, are examples of the omnipotence of thoughts commonly encountered in the mental life of neurotics. Thus in the pre-natal and pseudo-maternal couvade we again find the belief that thought alone – here expressed in the imitation of a process – can change reality. So, just as a male Californian Indian will groan in labour to reduce the pain of an actual delivery, a neurotic man will have a fictitious pregnancy for the same reason. And the same is true of the post-natal and dietetic couvade. Here the omnipotence of thoughts operates by assuming that two apparently un-associated actions can be linked together by a wish. So one abstains from eating turtle because otherwise the child will become as deaf and brainless as the animal; and, as Reik points out, this is not so very different from the Rat Man's neurotic obsession that 'If I marry Fräulein X. something will happen to my father (in the next world).'[5]

But this is by no means the end of the story. Freud has also taught us that where we find the omnipotence of thoughts we also find ambivalence – the desire to do what is forbidden – and that it is this which, in generating contradictory feelings of hostility and tenderness towards the same object, requires a prohibition as powerful as a taboo. This, for Reik, unravels the mystery of couvade still further. In both types we find unconscious motives at work, in which a pregnant woman and new-born infant are exposed defenceless to the sexual and hostile impulses of the savage man. Thus behind the husband's desire to remove his wife's pain in the pseudo-maternal couvade, we find 'the hidden unconscious wish to increase her pains.'[6] Why this should be results primarily from the man's thwarted libidinal instincts: sexual intercourse is forbidden in advanced pregnancy and accordingly the masochistic punishments he exacts upon himself are symptoms of his repressed sadistic attitude towards her for being unavailable. Consequently the pains he suffers are the pains that he wishes for his wife because she is taboo. Similarly, behind the father's desire to protect the child in the dietetic couvade we find its exact opposite: a repression of malevolent instincts against the child, in which 'the increased tenderness is to be attributed to the intense repression of these impulses.'[7] But from whence arise these aggressive instincts towards the son?

For an explanation Reik reactivates Freud's theory of the father's murder in the primal horde – which he calls 'the most important event of primitive development, perhaps of human development'⁸ – a state of affairs duplicated in every subsequent Oedipal relation between father and son. Psychoanalytic investigation shows

> that the situation of the man who has become a father signifies the fulfilment of an old desire originated in the infantile Oedipus complex. The son, who in childhood had wished the death of the father in order to take his place with the mother, has now himself become a man and a father. A fundamental change in the mental life of the man now sets in. We know that the welling-up of the fear of retaliation starts from this point. The new-made father fears that his son's attitude towards him will be the same as his own once was towards his father.⁹

In other words, the dietetic couvade – the desire to protect the son – is an indication of the victory of the father's conscious and tender feelings towards his son over the hostile and repressed feelings that he otherwise has towards him; and in that sense it is a reanimation of the ambivalent Oedipal impulses that every father experiences, first manifested in the primal horde. With the birth of the child, the father not only experiences the reawakening of his own infantile, malevolent and incestuous impulses against his own father, but sees in his son the repeat of those impulses and thus, in a sense, the revenge of his own father upon him. In desiring the death of his child, the father can therefore achieve two ambitions: he can thwart his own murder but also, through this sacrifice, appease his own father for the hostile wishes that he once entertained against him. All the precautions and abstinences of the dietetic couvade may therefore be taken as obsessional and neurotic reactions against the temptation lurking and repressed within the father's mind, and the tortures to his flesh as a just punishment for what he unconsciously desires to do. All these ordeals and deprivations by which the father seeks to change reality for his son, all these omnipotent and magical activities of thought, thus become deferred signs of obedience towards his own father, and forms of penance to which his guilty conscience impels him on account of the wishes he once held. Lafitau's theory concerning the origins of the couvade is therefore justified, albeit in a way that he could not have anticipated. It does proceed from the memory of original sin and the desire for repentance; but the sin is that of the original parricide in the horde, and the repentance is for an Oedipal guilt reanimated in the repressed and ambivalent relations between every father and every son.

TWO CASE-STUDIES: THE WOLF MAN; JUDGE SCHREBER

Following on from Reik's analysis of a religious ritual, let us now turn to Freud himself and see how his psychoanalysis of particular patients incorporates many of his arguments about religion. Freud refers in all to 133 cases, but only six are the subject of full histories.[10] Of these, four were analysed by Freud himself: 'Dora,' who was treated for a few weeks in 1900; the 'Rat Man,' who was treated for eleven months from October 1907; a young homosexual girl of 18, whose treatment was discontinued; and the 'Wolf Man,' whose case history was written down shortly after the completion of the analysis in the winter of 1914–15. In two other cases Freud was not directly involved: the case of Judge Schreber is based on the judge's own *Memoirs*, and the case of 'Little Hans' depends on information obtained from the boy's father. Of these six, two stand out for their religious content. In the 'Wolf Man' we find a specific 'totemic' identification of the patient's father with an animal – an identification which leads on to a belief that the patient is Christ himself; and in 'Schreber' we come across a still more bizarre theology, in which the judge appears as the saviour of the world. In both cases, as we shall see, Freud traces the religious delusions suffered by each man back to an Oedipus complex, thereby confirming his general theory about the origin and neurotic effects of religious belief.

The Wolf Man

The Wolf Man is Freud's most famous and elaborate case.[11] His followers regarded it as one of his greatest successes, as did Freud himself. In 1910 a wealthy young man (Sergei Pankejeff) came to him suffering from severe and recurrent bouts of depression, which had first manifested itself when he was about four and had taken the form of an animal phobia: he was afraid of wolves. This fear, which first expressed itself in his terror of fairy-stories like 'Little Red Riding-Hood' and 'The Wolf and the Seven Little Goats,' further manifested itself in a nightmare:

> I dreamt that it was night and that I was lying in my bed. (My bed stood with its feet towards the window; in front of the window there was a row of old walnut trees. I know it was winter when I had the dream, and night-time.) Suddenly the window opened of its own accord, and I was terrified to see that some white wolves were sitting on the big walnut tree in front of the window. There were six or seven of them. The wolves were quite white, and looked more like foxes or sheep-dogs, for they had big tails like foxes and they had their ears pricked like dogs when they pay attention to something. In great terror, evidently of being eaten up by the wolves, I screamed and woke up.[12]

From this dream Freud derived the causes of his patient's infantile neurosis. He concluded, after many years of careful analysis, that behind the nightmare lay a long-forgotten memory of a 'primal scene.' When eighteen months old Pankejeff had fallen ill with malaria, and, instead of sleeping with his nanny, had been taken into his parents' bedroom. On one hot summer's afternoon, 'he witnessed a coitus *a tergo* [from behind], three times repeated; he was able to see his mother's genitals as well as his father's organ.'[13] According to Freud, this experience explained both the dream and the boy's rapidly deteriorating relations with his father. The dream revived a powerful wish to obtain sexual satisfaction from his father, whose observed position during intercourse identified him as an animal. The primal scene had also shown him the cost of such satisfaction: he had observed his mother's 'castrated' state, and had thus become convinced of the reality of castration if his own wish should be fulfilled. 'If you want to be sexually satisfied by Father . . . you must allow yourself to be castrated like Mother.'[14] Thus his fear of his father became embodied not just in an animal phobia but more particularly in a wolf phobia: his mother became the castrated wolf, his father the castrating wolf, striking terror in those whom he satisfied sexually. Small wonder, then, that the small boy should be horrified at the possible fulfilment of his wish and that he should immediately repress his homosexual inclinations in light of the violence that would be done to him. His fear of his father was thus revealed as the strongest motive for his falling ill.

Significantly, Pankejeff's wolf-phobia was followed by a period of religious fervour. Hoping to distract him from his nightmares, his mother introduced him to the Bible story. This had the desired effect of reducing his anxiety symptoms, but it stimulated others, obsessional in character. Now the boy was obliged to pray for a long time before going to sleep, to make endless series of signs of the cross upon himself and his bed, and to kiss all the holy pictures that hung in his bedroom. These devotions were also accompanied by blasphemous thoughts. God had used his own son cruelly, and was no better disposed towards men: he had sacrificed his own son but had ordered Abraham to do the same. At other times he would unaccountably think 'God – swine' or 'God – shit,' and once, on a journey to a health-resort, 'was tormented by the obsession of having to think of the Holy Trinity whenever he saw three heaps of horse-dung or other excrement lying in the road.'[15] Similar blasphemies attached to the figure of Christ. One of his first questions to his nanny was whether Christ had had a behind, and this had led to the further question of whether Christ used to shit too. This last question he resolved for himself. 'Since Christ had made wine *out* of nothing, he could also have made food *into* nothing and in this way have avoided defaecating.'[16]

Freud's interpretation of the Wolf Man's religious obsessions turns on the Oedipal and ambivalent feelings that every son has towards his father, and which Freud here calls 'an underlying factor in all religions. . . .'[17] Both the wolf that Pankejeff feared and the God that he feared were transferred images of his father. Both his fear of being eaten by the wolf and his fear of divine punishment were anxieties generated by his wish to be copulated with by his father, and by his repudiation of that wish because of what would happen to him if he did. Each fear thus emanated from the repression of an infantile impulse, which being repressed, was not reproduced by Pankejeff as a recollection but had become present to his consciousness in the shape of phantasies or dreams, these being now regarded as substitutes for un-performed actions. What became conscious, in other words, was terror of the wolf; but the wolf was a substitute for the father, and the terror that was repressed was a fear of castration by him. On this reading, the obsessive religious rituals performed by the Wolf Man before going to bed stand as ritualized defence mechanisms against this possibility. They become the necessary precautions undertaken by him to avoid being placed in a situation of acute jeopardy.

There are two important points that stand out in this analysis. The first is that Pankejeff's transition from wolf-phobia to religious piety reflects a similar transition, already charted by Freud in *Totem and Taboo*, from totem animal to deity. Properly speaking, however, this is not a development away from the totem, since both the idea of a totem and the idea of a God have their origin in the image of the father. Each, in other words, has the same Oedipal root: it is just that the 'totem was the first father-surrogate, and the god was a later one, in which the father had regained his human shape.'[18] The Wolf Man's fear of wolves and his fear of God are, in this sense, not original reactions but impulses bearing the same prototype. This is equally true of his later identification with the figure of Christ. For if Christ is God's son, then the appalling question remains whether he too was used by his father like a woman – or rather like Pankejeff's own mother in the primal scene – a question which explains his agonized question about whether Christ too had a behind. Did the divine son engage in the same sexual relationship to his father that Pankejeff had to his, but which he had repressed in his un-conscious? His horrified rejection of such a blasphemous thought is, accord-ing to Freud, a further indication of the boy's inability to come to terms with his own fixation upon his father and his feminine attitude towards him.

If animal phobias are totemic in form, then the second point to note is how easy it is to revive a totemic system of thought, particularly in childhood. Both Pankejeff's replacement of his father by a wolf, and indeed Little Hans' replacement of his by a horse, are returns to totemism, the nucleus of each being, as with all totemic replacements, the repression of certain Oedipal impulses – the repression indeed requiring a totemic and animal disguise. But why should a totemic system be so simple to activate? Freud gives three reasons. First, the substitution of a man by an animal is a comparatively simple thing to do in childhood because children do not distinguish so easily between the human and animal world. 'In their eyes the grown man, the object of their fear and admiration, still belongs to the same category as the big animal who has so many enviable attributes but against whom they have been warned because he may become dangerous.'[19] Second, if the father is replaced by an animal then the child can more easily overcome the danger associated with him by simply removing the totemic object. So Little Hans can avoid horses by not leaving the house, and the Wolf Man can avoid seeing particular story-books. Third – and much more significantly – a totemic system is, according to Freud, part of every child's *phylogenetic inheritance*. Pankejeff's wolf-phobia was fuelled, in other words, not just by his long-forgotten memory of a scene that terrified him, but by something much more ancient: by a scene of a parental intercourse and threats of castration which form 'an ancestral pre-history' or 'prehistoric truth,' namely, *the memory of the primal horde*.[20] In the Wolf Man we find an example, therefore, of the way in which an ontogenetic and personal experience can reanimate a phylogenetic and universal one. Thus Pankejeff's story is that of a double inheritance: immediate through his repression of an individual experience of his actual father, and historical through his repression of an inherited experience of his primal father. In this sense, the child and the primitive savage have united in their image of the father as a castrator. 'I cannot feel surprised,' Freud concludes,

> that what was originally produced by certain circumstances in pre-historic times and was then transmitted in the shape of a predisposition to its re-acquirement should, since the same circumstances persist, emerge once more as a concrete event in the experience of the individual.[21]

Judge Schreber

Although a much shorter and less celebrated case than the Wolf Man, the story of Judge Schreber is equally interesting. This is partly due to the fact that it results in an altogether more complex concept of God, which is hardly surprising given that we are dealing here not with the animal phobia of a child but with the delusions of a man aged fifty-one at the time of his first illness. As I mentioned earlier, the case is unique in Freud's experience because it is the only one not based on direct analysis but on the patient's own *Memoirs*.[22] These were published in 1903 and were widely discussed among psychoanalysts. Freud's attention was drawn to them as late as the summer of 1910, but letters to Abraham and Ferenczi indicate that his analysis was completed sometime before December of that year. Publication was delayed until the summer of 1911, with a 'Postscript' being added some months later.

Daniel Paul Schreber was a Judge of an Appeal Court Division (*Oberlandesgericht*), whose various delusions had a mystical and religious character: he believed he was in direct communication with God, that he was the plaything of devils, that he saw 'miraculous apparitions' and heard 'holy music.' These delusions culminated in his belief that he was the most remarkable man in history, with a mission to redeem the world. This mission, however, could only be accomplished by a unique event: by *his transformation into a woman*. Schreber's attitude towards God was equally singular. God was composed of nothing but 'nerves,' and these had the creative power of turning themselves into anything whatever. Having completed his creation, God withdrew to an immense distance, resigned the world to its own laws and dealt only with the souls of the dead. It appears that, although this distance was initially maintained for God's own protection – the nerves of living men could attract the nerves of God to such an extent that even God's existence was threatened – it had equally unfortunate results: God could learn nothing from experience, could derive no lessons for the future, and so had become faintly ridiculous in his unimaginative and repetitive use of certain ordeals, miracles and voices. For these reasons it was therefore only in exceptional cases that he entered into relations with outstanding individuals – an experience which, in Schreber's case, was accompanied by feelings of intense sexual voluptuousness during which his body, through penetration by the divine nerves (which he likened to male semen), was transformed into that of a female, even down to the acquisition of female breasts and genitals.

Freud's deciphering of this complicated theology holds few surprises. As with the Wolf Man, the origin of Schreber's delusional phantasies lies in the repression of his homosexual impulses. His initial resistance to these, which took the form of an extreme antagonism towards their first object (his doctor, Dr Flechsig), was resolved when this object became God himself. If it was impossible for Schreber to become reconciled to playing the part of a female towards his doctor, then there was no such inhibition if the object of his desire was the Almighty, if his emasculation could be seen as a form of service to a power of the greatest might and by means of which a new race of men could be born. This legitimated his homosexuality: the sexual excitement he experiences is demanded of him by God.

Again not surprisingly, the 'unmistakable prototype' of Schreber's relation to God is his previous relation to his father.[23] This was Dr Daniel Gottlob Schreber, a highly distinguished physician, famous for his introduction of therapeutic gymnastics throughout Germany. Freud argues that almost all the characteristics of Schreber's God emanate from the son's ambivalent attitude towards this dominant male. What, after all, could be more dismissive of a doctor than to declare that he knows nothing of the living but only deals with corpses? Or that the miracles he performs are in fact ridiculous? Or that, more generally, he knows nothing of experience? Here, then, we have a concept of God proceeding directly from a father-complex. The infantile ambivalence Schreber felt towards his father is duplicated in his image of God – to the point indeed where God has become his transfigured father, where the infantile conflict that Schreber had with his actual father has become the content of his delusions. Schreber's delusions about God represent in fact a victory over his repressed homosexuality, in which his father's punishment for having them (castration) is transmuted into the mechanism by which they can be obtained: namely, his wishful phantasy of being transformed into a woman.

The Wolf Man and Schreber cases dramatically indicate the quite precise way in which a father-complex can determine a concept of God. The God feared is the father feared; and the nature of the experience that produced that fear will be directly projected into the God worshipped.[24] Freud's thesis is not therefore some general argument about the transference of internal and infantile impulses upon an external and divine reality, but is quite specific in claiming that the nature of the God conceived will bear direct and concrete witness to what has been effaced from consciousness. In this sense, there is a strict correlation between the Wolf Man's history and his God, and Schreber's history and his God. Both these cases, of course, are intended to corroborate Freud's general thesis that the roots of religion, like all the neuroses, lie in the Oedipus complex; but behind this lies a much more specific concern. Both reveal that the form of religion, as a symptom of neurosis, will provide important information about its precipitating cause. If God himself is nothing more than an exaltation of the image of the father presented initially to the mind of a child, then within the image is embedded a replay of childhood, individually unique. In this sense, the whole history of religion can be read as a catalogue of innumerable and distinct instances of infantile obeisance before the father.

5

A CRITICAL APPRAISAL

Freud, who had a fair estimate of his own worth, placed his criticisms of religion very highly. This is best indicated by a famous remark first made in 1917 but subsequently repeated. He concluded that the dominating position acquired by man over his fellow-creatures in the animal kingdom – a superiority indicated in the Genesis stories – had suffered three 'death blows.' The first two he called the *cosmological* blow and the *biological* blow. The first was dealt by Copernicus (1473–1543) in putting to an end a geocentric view of the world; and the second by Darwin (1809–1882), in establishing the animal descent of man. The third blow, he claimed, had been dealt by psychoanalysis, and thus in effect by himself as its creator.[1] Freud was not, it must be admitted, always consistent in naming his intellectual heroes. Sometimes he replaced Copernicus with Newton or Kepler, and once, astonishingly, substituted the sixteenth-century physician Johannes Weier for psychoanalysis; but there is little doubt that for Freud himself, and certainly for the great majority of his followers, the discoveries of psychoanalysis provided not just a devastating critique of religion but a terminal one. We must now consider whether this claim is justified.

The idea that men and women have peopled the world with creatures of their own imagining, and that these creatures should be formalized into representations of good and evil powers, is hardly something new. As Bruno Bettelheim has observed, this process stands at the heart of the fairy-story and extends far back through the millennia.[2] Nor is it a great discovery to suppose that this projective process is the source of religious objects. In *The Natural History of Religion* (1757) Hume presented much the same idea – arguing that it was not refined speculation that first prompted human beings to suppose that there was a god but rather 'the ordinary affections of human life,' such as a concern for happiness, the dread of misery, and the terror of death.[3] Later still, Ludwig Feuerbach in his *The Essence of Christianity* (1841) described religion as the childlike condition of humanity, an illusion fashioned out of man's alienation from himself and his world, following which he projects onto a god all the qualities that he himself lacks. 'The divine being,' he writes, 'is nothing else than the human being, or, rather, the human nature purified, freed from the limits of the individual man, made objective – *i.e.*, contemplated and revered as another, a distinct being. All the attributes of the divine nature are, therefore, attributes of the human nature.'[4] Freud himself, of course, was well aware of his distinguished pedigree: 'I have said nothing which other and better men have not said before me in a much more complete, forcible and impressive manner.' But Freud was equally aware of his own special contribution in 'giving psychological foundation to the criticisms of my great predecessors.'[5] Freud's unique contribution lies, then, not in saying that religion is an illusion but in locating the *motivation* for that illusion in the repressed history of early childhood. Thus it is not his general theory that is original – that religion is the transmutation of wishes into belief is a well-worn reductionist argument – but rather the wealth of evidence Freud brings to bear in its support.

SOME GENERAL CRITICISMS

This evidence, as we have seen, is of various types: anthropological, in its account of the development of totemism and the ceremonial killing of the totem god; historical, in its presentation of the origins of Judaism and Christianity; genetic, in its thesis that past experiences may be inherited; and, most important of all, psychological, in its central claim that religion is an obsessional symptom of repression. It would be churlish to deny that Freud pulls all these various strands of evidence together in a quite remarkable way, and that his central preoccupation is always held firmly in view: to uncover the connection between belief in God and the image of the father.

The problem is that almost all the evidence that Freud presents has been discredited in one way or another. I have already referred to the unreliability of Freud's historical reconstruction of how monotheism developed;[6] but much the same can be said of his anthropological speculations, most of which have been rejected by modern ethnologists. Freud's first critic, A. L. Kroeber, accused him of indulging in 'the old expedient of pyramiding hypotheses,' while Evans-Pritchard, more unkindly and more recently, dismissed *Totem and Taboo* as a 'just-so story.'[7] Not surprisingly, criticism has tended to focus on Freud's two main propositions: first, that the pretotemic family was a horde, wherein the dominant male possesses all the females and drives out all the young males; and second, that the subsequent totemic identification of human beings with plants and animals, culminating in the commemoration of the original parricide in the eating of the totem-father, is the beginning of religion. These criticisms can be summarized as follows:

1 Freud's primal horde theory is an unsubstantiated hypothesis, based on Darwin's own speculations, which were themselves written at a time when no reliable data was available. Subsequent research[8] has revealed, however, a wide variation in the social groupings of primates, with one author, Paul

Simonds, indicating organizations based on solitary individuals, mated pairs, isolated one-male groups, and troops of adult males and females plus offspring.[9] Admittedly gorillas possess a social structure similar to a primal horde; but as Zuckerman reminds us, 'the fact that apes live in family groups is in itself no proof that the first men did the same . . . there is no clear reason why the social behaviour of the "pre-humans" should be considered to have been like that of apes rather than like that of monkeys.'[10]

2   The sexual aggression required by Freud (and Atkinson) to explain the primal crime of murder, while certainly present among primates, is not as constant as he supposes, with Zuckerman again observing that he could find no single instance of a male baboon dying as a result of sexual rivalry. Admittedly Jane Goodall found greater evidence of aggression among male chimps, including cannibalism and even systematic extermination, but even these are isolated examples within a particular species and not held to be a general characteristic among primates.[11] Freud could of course reply that the primal horde is a *hominid* and not a subhuman primate grouping, but even then palaeoanthropology does not provide conclusive support to his theory. There is some evidence that Peking Man practised cannibalism and that Australopithecines murdered each other, but again this is hardly sufficient evidence to support the hypothesis of an original crime or universal pre-disposition to commit it. One of Freud's early critics, W. Schmidt, is particularly dismissive: 'As to patricide, the authority of the father is firmly rooted, among the oldest peoples, in their social organization, their morals and their affections; and the murder of anyone, especially within their own clan, is something so rare that the thought of murdering a father could simply never enter these people's heads at all.'[12]

3   Criticism of Freud's theory about the genesis of religion has been equally damaging. Here the primary objection is that totemism is a variable phenomenon, and that accordingly it cannot be used as the initial stage of all religions. In the first place, we know of many peoples, ethnologically the oldest, who did not practise totemism: the south-east Australians, the Ainu, the primitive Eskimos, to name a few. In the second place, totemism is now generally considered to be not merely a later stage of development but one which not all peoples have passed through. Here it is interesting to note that Frazer, upon whom Freud otherwise depends, rejects totemism as a religion – 'for the totems as such are not worshipped, they are in no sense deities, they are not propitiated with prayer and sacrifice'[13] – and clearly indicates that the three great ruling races (the Indo-Europeans, the Hamito-Semites and the Ural-Altaics) originally had no totemism but rather acquired it later on their travels.

4   The weakest of all Freud's speculations is that derived from Robertson Smith: his idea of the totemic meal and sacrifice among the Semites. In fact,

however, Smith supports his theory by only one historical example – the eating of camels by the Sinai bedouin – and Frazer could only find four cases of totemic sacrifice but none of totemic communion, although subsequently one instance of it has been found among the Australian aboriginals. 'All one can say of the theory as a whole,' concludes Evans-Pritchard, 'the argument of which is in the main both tortuous and tenuous, is that, whilst eating of the totem animal could have been the earliest form of sacrifice, and the origin of religion, there is no evidence that it was.'[14] Remarkably, these criticisms, many of which Freud was well aware of even before the publication of *Totem and Taboo* in 1913, seem to have disconcerted him not at all. Twenty-six years later, he remained unrepentant – 'I have not been convinced . . . of Robertson Smith's errors' – excusing himself on the grounds that 'I am not an ethnologist but a psychoanalyst. I had a right to take out of ethnological literature what I might need for the work of analysis.'[15]

Given these remarks, it will come as no surprise that Freud adopted much the same cavalier attitude towards his bio-genetic theory that past experiences could be passed on from one generation to the other. For him the Oedipus complex was, as we have seen, the ontogenetic repetition of the phylogenetic experience of Darwin's primal horde in killing the father. The fact, however, that this theory requires a belief in the discredited Lamarckian thesis that acquired characteristics may be inherited did not trouble Freud. His daughter, Anna, testifies to the fact that to the end of his life Freud remained a staunch believer in Lamarck, and he insisted on retaining his neo-Lamarckian statements in his last book, *Moses and Monotheism*, despite Ernest Jones' objections that they contradicted the biologists in their own field.[16] And once again his justification was the priority of his researches in psychology. So, while admitting that biological science now rejected a theory which he had previously thought 'established beyond question,' he nevertheless doggedly persists in upholding it because he 'cannot do without this factor in biological evolution.'[17] This is a strange position to be adopted by one who so frequently proclaimed the priority of evidence over theory.

As is to be expected, Freud achieves much greater success with the psychoanalytic foundations of his argument, but even here there are significant amendments to be made. Freud maintains that religion emerges out of an Oedipal father complex, and that its compulsive-obsessional character can be accounted for by the need first to repress and then to atone for the overwhelming sense of guilt that this complex initiates. Now while there is ample clinical evidence to demonstrate the existence of repression as a defence mechanism, as a function of keeping something out of consciousness, the evidence in support of the Oedipus complex is much less satisfactory. Freud himself regarded its discovery as his supreme achievement, on a par with the discovery of electricity and the wheel. It is all the more ironic, therefore, that four years after Freud's death, R. R. Sears, in his *Survey of Objective Studies of Psychoanalytic Concepts*, should conclude that the Oedipus complex was a grotesquerie of Freud's imagination.[18] This is perhaps going too far, since other studies – notably those by Friedman in 1952 and Hall in 1963[19] – have indicated much greater support for the theory. A more judicious summary is provided by Paul Kline. While admitting that research does indicate that young children often do have sexual feelings towards their parents, and that the study of dreams does indicate that the Oedipal situation is often a source of psychological conflict:

> it does not establish the Oedipus complex as the central conflict of mental life or show it to be the kernel of neurosis. . . . This, therefore, is an example of where the objective evidence so far confirms the Freudian theory but suggests that Freud may have attached too much importance to it.[20]

Needless to say, such conclusions also have serious implications for Freud's already vulnerable theory of the primal horde. This theory, to repeat, describes how the Oedipus complex becomes a fateful inheritance for all humanity. In this sense, then, the original action taken by the parricidal sons is elevated to the position of something absolute, the primordial source of culture itself: it not only accounts for the two fundamental taboos of totemism – those against incest and the killing of the father-substitute, the totem animal – but, through the process of 'psychic inheritance,' sets in motion a chain-reaction of associated Oedipal guilts, which in turn explains the subsequent creation of all cultural phenomena, including religion. But Freud's speculations about the phylogenetic implications of the primal horde – his view that the unconscious memory and guilt associated with the original crime could be genetically transmitted from generation to generation – are not only extremely doubtful, given their neo-Lamarckian presuppositions, but are doubly so because they also require a *uniformity of experience* between past and present which the Oedipus complex cannot support. For this reason it is fair to say that very few anthropologists – with one or two notable exceptions[21] – have ever offered any confirmation of it as a universal characteristic. It is also worth mentioning that even within Freud's own circle, the claim that the Oedipus complex was the nucleus of every neurosis was rejected by those otherwise indebted to him. Alfred Adler (1870–1937) analysed non-sexual factors in the causation of neurosis, particularly the feeling of inferiority; Otto Rank (1884–1939) proposed that the cause of neurosis lay in the trauma of birth; and, most famously of all, Carl Gustav Jung (1876–1961) rejected the infantile-sexual component in neuroses in favour of inborn dispositions or 'archetypes' common to the human race.[22]

MALINOWSKI'S CRITICISM OF FREUD

It is important to see, however, not merely that the Oedipal complex has historically been challenged as a general theory but also how other essentially *non-Freudian* reasons can be given for its existence. For this I want to turn to the work of Bronislaw Malinowski, following his anthropological fieldwork among the Trobriand islanders of north-eastern New Guinea, and published in his *Sex and Repression in Savage Society* (1927).[23] Although strongly influenced by Freud, Malinowski nevertheless attacks him on many fronts, primarily in contesting the view, *not* that the Oedipus complex is valid – Freud's observations as to its nature are held to be correct – but that it is a *universal* phenomenon: this cannot be the case because the family complex in which it is said to arise is not the same in all human societies. So, while the Oedipus complex is undoubtedly to be found in the patrilineal family of our Western civilization, it is not to be found among the *matrilineal* families of the Trobriands. In our Western type of family the father is seen as authoritative and powerful, the bread-winner upon whom the family depends; but among the Trobriands he is assumed to have had nothing to do with the procreation of the children, is regarded more as their benevolent friend and conscientious nurse, his place as the source of discipline and authority being taken by the mother's brother. Nor indeed does the husband have sexual rights over his wife: these he has to deserve and pay for. Accordingly the children 'never see their mother subjugated or brutalized or in abject dependence upon her husband, not even when she is a commoner married to a chief.'[24]

This reduction of the sexual bond between husband and wife does not, however, mean a heightening of the sexual attraction between mother and son. Quite the reverse in fact. From puberty onwards, the mother never thwarts her son's sexual independence, never regards sexual activity as in any way reprehensible, and even encourages him during adolescence to leave home to live in special houses where sexual activity may be freely indulged in. This early detachment from the mother largely accounts for the almost total absence of cases of mother–son incest. Certainly a taboo against incest exists and is rigorously upheld; but, interestingly, it is not the mother who is its chief focus but the sister. Thus, concludes Malinowski, if we are to speak at all of repressed desires among the Trobriands, they cannot follow the formula of the Oedipus complex: it is not the father to be killed, but the maternal uncle; and it is not the mother to be married, but the sister.[25]

Malinowski's research explodes the theory that repressed Oedipal desires are our common inheritance. If it is an inheritance, it cannot be a universal one since no traces of it, conscious or unconscious, can be found among the Trobriander islanders. But Malinowski goes further. If the universal consequences of the original crime may be questioned, then so too may their historical origin, the crime itself. He begins by noting that Freud, like Darwin before him, makes no distinction between precultural family life among the anthropoid apes and subsequent human family life in a cultural environment. This means, in effect, that if the original parricidal crime is to be regarded as the origin of culture – as the first cause of it – then it must have occurred before culture, namely, within the prehuman anthropoid family. The trouble with this, however, is that in animal conditions we find a complete absence of any motive for such a crime. Family life is here determined by a chain of linked instincts – courtship, mating, common life, tenderness towards infants and the mutual help of the parents – a union which is dissolved only when the offspring is capable of fending for itself, there being now no need to keep the family together. Not only, therefore, do male and female children naturally leave the horde on becoming independent, but we find that the old male, when past his prime, does so as well, thereby making room for a younger guardian. Malinowski's conclusion is, therefore, that the conditions necessary for the primal crime did not exist within the prehuman anthropoid family; and that indeed those conditions that would be required 'would constitute a lethal endowment for any animal species.... It is easy to perceive that the primeval horde has been equipped with all the bias, maladjustments and ill-tempers of a middle-class European family, and then let loose in a prehistoric jungle to run riot in a most attractive but fantastic hypothesis.'[26]

> Why should the father have to expel the sons if they naturally and instinctively are inclined to leave the family as soon as they have no need of parental protection? Why should they lack females if from other groups, as well as from their own, adult children of the other sex have also to come out? Why should the young males remain hanging around the parental horde, why should they hate the father and desire his death? As we know they are glad to be free and they have no wish to return to the parental horde. Why should they finally even attempt or accomplish the cumbersome and unpleasant act of killing the old male, while by merely waiting for his retirement they might gain a free access to the horde should they so desire?[27]

But even if we accept, for purposes of argument, that an original crime was committed, this still leaves another objection. It is vital for Freud's theory that the memory of this murder should be transmitted to later generations. But how is this to be achieved? Family life among the anthropoids is instinctive, is governed by innate emotional attitudes and biological needs, and is uninfluenced by tradition, for animals have no language, no laws and no institutions. Even if we supposed, therefore, that the horde did contain the necessary conflicts for the crime to take place, how could the memory of it be passed on? We are thus faced with a dilemma: Either the sons of the horde did have the forms to hand by which the memory of the crime could be transmitted – in which case the raw material of culture existed *prior* to the great event which is said to have created culture; or the sons did not possess the mechanisms for transmission, in which case no memory of it exists to haunt later generations. How can one speak of remorse for a crime among animals, when, as far as we can tell, animals have no conscience? This, of course, still leaves us with the possibility that the transition from a state of nature into that of culture was done in one leap, that all the first elements of culture – speech, tradition, material inventions, conceptual thought – suddenly sprang into being fully armed as a direct result of the sons' rebellion; but this, concludes Malinowski, is an absurd hypothesis. For although the origin of culture cannot be reconstructed in detail, we have to assume that it was 'a very laborious and very slow process achieved in a cumulative manner by infinitely small steps integrated over enormous stretches of time.'[28]

In the final part of his criticism, Malinowski reverses Freud's hypothesis: it is not the Oedipus complex which creates culture but culture which creates the complex. This is the most elaborate section of *Sex and Repression*, and I can here only give an outline of what it contains. Briefly put, Malinowski contends that the family unit is the only type of grouping which humans have taken over from the animals: here too we find the instinctual bonds of parents and children, the maternal tie, the relation of father to offspring. In humans, however, these regulative instincts are gradually transformed; and transformed, moreover, under the conditions of culture. For example, in animals the selection of a mate begins with the rutting season, with the onset of ovulation in the female which releases a sexual response in the male, and outside this season all sexual interest is held in abeyance. In humans, by contrast, there is no biological release mechanism, sexual intercourse is not seasonal, and selection is restricted by well-defined taboos which exclude from mating members of the same family (hence the law of exogamy). The sexual tendencies with which we are endowed are thereby moulded by regulations which vary from one society to another. Similarly, in animals the matrimonial response is largely dependent on the act of sexual union, on the mutual attachment which results, and the tendency of the male to guard and protect the female; but in human society marriage is not so constituted but is something over and above the biological bond, something which sanctions that bond, which imposes numerous obligations upon the couple, and which is maintained through a system of developing emotions and social pressure. With the appearance of offspring further contrasts appear. While the human mother shares with the animal mother the anatomical equipment necessary for the rearing of the child, human society, whether patrilineal or matrilineal, imposes additional obligations and rites on both parents which cement and endorse the new relationship and which welcome the young infant into the community (e.g., ceremonies of purification, baptismal rites). Amongst animals the family unit lasts until the children are sufficiently independent to leave their parents, but among humans this unit continues almost indefinitely, largely because the parents have to see to the cultural education of their children, to equip them with the necessary technical and intellectual tools for survival within society. What we have here, then, is a cultural overlay to human instinctual life. Our emotional lives can be, and are, trained, adjusted and organized into complex cultural systems, which are themselves artificial rather than innate, imposed from without, but which enable us to master our surroundings and co-operate with our neighbours.

It is against this background that Malinowski repudiates Freud's thesis that the primal horde encapsulates the two primary instincts associated with the Oedipus complex: the first to do with the mother (incest), the second to do with the father (murder). According to Freud, it is precisely because we are dealing here with *instinctual* wishes or desires that a system of taboos must be imposed to prevent them becoming reality. Now, to repeat, Malinowski does not contest the existence of the complex, but what he does do is replace its instinctual origins by cultural ones.

Mother-incest

Malinowski rejects the Freudian claim that infantile attachment to the mother is essentially sexual in character. This follows from the account he has already given of the differences between the animal and the human family unit. The instincts which exist between mother and child are initially designed to satisfy definite organic wants, most notably nutrition and protection; later on, this relationship changes as the infant develops, and the human mother's function (in contrast to her animal counterpart) now consists in meeting certain cultural requirements: to educate her offspring so that he can take his place in civilized society, and for this to be achieved the infant must respond with attitudes of submission and reverence. If, however, we are to suppose, with Freud, that this connection is essentially sexual – where the instinct exists to serve sexual union and the production of new offspring – then this would introduce a 'destructive element' into this otherwise carefully constructed relationship. We would have to suppose a desire for courtship and mating totally incompatible with submission, dependence and reverence. We would have to replace the otherwise harmonious relationship with the protecting father with an active hostile rivalry for the affections of the mother. Incest, therefore, is not prohibited because it is an inherent desire but because it is *incompatible with the foundation of culture*; because if it were not forbidden the family unit would disintegrate, because there would be social chaos, and because there could be no continuing cultural tradition:

> Incest would mean the upsetting of age distinctions, the mixing up of generations, the disorganization of sentiments and a violent exchange of roles at a time when the family is the most important educational medium. No society could exist under such conditions. The alternative type of culture under which incest is excluded, is the only one consistent with the existence of social organization and culture.[29]

Father-murder

Like the mother–son relation, the father–son relation is, as we have seen, an instinctive one, this biological need being expressed in the demand for a caring protector of the family. Amongst animals the paternal role is temporary – the offspring leave him when he ceases to be useful; but among humans it continues over the long period of cultural training. Whereas initially, therefore, the father was guardian and nurse – the solicitous male willingly subordinating himself to the demands of wife and infant – this gradually gives way to a more authoritarian approach, which is necessary for the instruction of the child into society. Thus the tender and loving guardian of infancy is gradually transformed into the representative of law and enforcement, at times indeed into the dreaded autocrat. The inevitable tension that this change of roles creates does not therefore arise from an innate sexual jealousy between father and son, but depends rather on the father's two principal tasks: the first, to propagate and protect his offspring, and the second, to oversee their education into culture. There is, accordingly, no need to construct an Oedipus complex to account for the ambivalent tenderness and repulsion between father and son because we can see these features 'emerging from the very constitution of the family.'[30] When the Oedipus complex occurs, this is not therefore due to innate biological drives but rather to the necessary preparation and conditioning of the child for cultural life. Malinowski, in other words, *desexualizes its origins*; it is not innate to human beings but is more the result of the social-familial forces at work within the typical patriarchal and authoritarian families of the West – an argument reinforced by the absence of the complex in matriarchal societies.[31]

These conclusions, although they do not destroy the psychoanalytic theory of an Oedipus complex, do destroy Freud's hypothesis, central to his account of religion, that this complex is universal and that it originates in a phylogenetic memory of the patricide of the primal horde. This has the further consequence of undermining Freud's account of the role of guilt in instigating obsessional behaviour among believers. Again, whilst it can scarcely be doubted that some religious behaviour is obsessional and motivated by feelings of guilt, it is difficult now to substantiate Freud's claim that this guilt is *of a particular type*. Why should we credit religious guilt with a common history and so define it as an archaic inheritance issuing from an original patricide? Why should we suppose that our guilt is transmitted through some kind of collective mind, and that the guilt generated by this initial crime is constantly repeated and reinforced in our own relations with our fathers? Undoubtedly some guilt is Oedipal in form, and this could indeed account for some of the demand for a protective father-god; but this is not to say that *all* guilt is Oedipal and that *every* religious orientation towards a father-image is a 'return of the repressed.' The relationship of child to father may well be a fraught one, and may even contain sexual-aggressive tendencies; but this does not mean, as Freud clearly suggests, that it is a relationship which must be outgrown, that its continuance, even in the religious context, is a sign of immaturity. What we have to consider is Malinowski's alternative: that the need for a father-relation is not the equivalent of psychosis but rather a creative and revitalizing cultural requirement, necessary for the entrance of the individual into society.[32]

FREUD'S MALE CONCEPT OF GOD

This is the appropriate point at which to mention another area of criticism, made much of in recent years. Malinowski has given us the plan of a matriarchal society; but Freud's account of the origins of religion is presented exclusively in terms of fathers and sons: the Mosaic religion is father-obsessed, and Christianity is son-obsessed. In this androcentric scheme of things, women function primarily as acquisitions, as prizes to be fought over. In the primal horde, the sons rebel and kill their father in order to possess the available females; and, as we have noted many times, the Oedipus complex revivifies this ancient drama by repeating it on the individual level: to acquire the mother one must murder one's father. Either way, the female is booty, an object to be won by force. It is scarcely surprising, therefore, that feminist theologians, when rejecting more generally the dominance of the male model of God, should also reject this aspect of Freud's theory. As Sallie McFague has written: 'Freudianism, in its complete neglect of women as *subjects*, is impressive witness to the thoroughness with which the patriarchal model has pervaded Western culture.'[33]

Whether or not feminists are justified in their critique of male models of God, it is not my business to decide here. What cannot be denied, however, is that such models do predominate in the Western religious tradition, and that Freud was totally uncritical of this fact. What makes this strange is that Freud was not only well aware of the prevalence of female personifications of deity – one thinks of the early goddess cults such as the Greek Demeter, the Egyptian Isis, the Mesopotamian Ishtar, and the Canaanite Anath – but also alert to those dissenting voices from within the psychoanalytic movement which pointed to an implicit male bias within Freudian orthodoxy. One such was Otto Rank, whose *Trauma of Birth* (1924) elevated the maternal role at the expense of the paternal by arguing that the birth trauma, and not the Oedipus complex, was the decisive psychological event – a conclusion which divided the early psychoanalysts and led to an acrimonious split with Freud. Two years before, at a meeting in Berlin chaired by Freud, the young German psychoanalyst Karen Horney had described psychoanalysis as an example of 'masculine narcissism' and sought to redress the balance with a revision of penis envy – a position further defended in 1935 by no less a figure than Ernest Jones, Freud's invariably fair-minded biographer.[34]

How, then, are we to account for Freud's almost exclusive use of masculine imagery in his concept of God? There are, I think, three factors to be borne in mind. The first is that Freud, in Peter Gay's words, was 'an unreconstructed nineteenth-century gentleman.'[35] This meant that, more often than not, he follows the Victorian stereotyping of women as domestic, dependent and sexually passive, and men as self-willed, independent and sexually aggressive. It is hardly unexpected, therefore, that the origin of religion – located as it is within the murderous relations of the primal horde and Oedipus complex – should be characterized in male terms. There was, of course, more to it than this. Freud also pondered on the origin of these differences, and concluded, not surprisingly, that it lay in the anatomical distinction between the sexes. The boy, having a penis and seeing that girls do not have them, develops a castration complex. In the Oedipal situation this gives to the father the powerful threat of removing from the son something that he already has. The girl, however, having no penis – or rather, in the clitoris, having a poor substitute for one – feels an acute loss of self-esteem (and incidentally develops an unrivalled capacity for jealousy) as she accepts her identity as someone already castrated. She does not fear the loss of what she does not have but looks rather to its acquisition from someone else. Thus she too enters into an Oedipal relation to her father, and turns to him passively and receptively as the one individual who can make good her loss, replacing her wish for a penis with that for a baby. In one case, therefore, the father is seen as thwarting the son's libidinal desires, and in the other as providing the daughter with the only means of achieving them. Logic dictates therefore that the first criminals were male. For if the original murder is of a father, then it is the sons who have more to gain by their success and more to lose by their failure. This also explains why the primal horde theory does not easily admit of any alteration of gender-terms, in such a way that female deities could still be accommodated as representations of authority and power. Indeed Freud adamantly refuses to make any such adjustments when he could easily have done so. The primal horde theory, we should finally remember, is an *historical* reconstruction – in the beginning was *the act* – and the 'memorable criminal act' it enshrines is a crime perpetrated by sons against their father. It is therefore no accident that all subsequent images of God are masculine: indeed, if anything, they provide Freud with further justification for his theory. These 'phallocentric' images bear witness to the fact that religion arose from the helplessness of one group of males before one dominant male; and their persistence within the culture is testimony to the force of guilt engendered by the murder of the father by his sons. The feminist writer, Mary Daly, has put her case succinctly: 'If God is male, then the male is God.' For Freud the truth of the matter is slightly different and less hypothetical: 'God is male because the male is God.'[36]

ILLUSION AND OBJECT-RELATIONS THEORY

I want now to turn to another important feature of Freud's argument: the role of illusion. Freud's account of its function is particularly important because it stands at the heart of a recent development in psychoanalysis, known as 'object-relations' theory. First, however, let us remind ourselves that Freud's attack on religion is but one aspect of his unrelenting attack upon the role of all illusions in human affairs. To destroy illusions he considered part of his life's work, not merely because the arguments which supported them invariably insult the intelligence, but more precisely because they contradicted reality – because they allow men and women to devalue their lives, so making them almost incapable of changing society for the better. Freud in fact vacillates between calling religion an 'illusion' or a 'delusion.' The former, we remember, is not necessarily false: it derives from wishes which might come true. But we have to allow, I think, that for Freud the chance of this happening was so remote that, for all practical purposes, religion belongs to the 'mass-delusions' of mankind – something which must be eliminated if we are to mature beyond a state of psychical infantilism.[37]

It is Freud's negative assessment of illusion that object-relations theory vehemently opposes. The outstanding figure in this new development within psychoanalysis is Donald Winnicott, with his analysis of what he calls 'transitional objects.'[38] As a paediatrician Winnicott observed that young children rapidly become attached and even addicted to some special object, for example, a teddy bear or blanket. This attachment follows from the infant's gradual separation from the mother, who had previously provided not merely sustenance but a sense of unity and security: the chosen object thereby becomes a substitute for her, and continues to evoke the maternal experience of soothing and nurturance. The sensitive parent invariably allows this to happen, but gradually over a period of time the hallowed object, by now worn and tattered, is used less and less, not so much forgotten as now without meaning. The significant point to note, however, is that such 'transitional phenomena' transcend, or occupy an intermediate area between, objective and subjective experiences: they are neither related solely to the world of objects nor solely to the inner life of the individual. For the object selected by the child, while clearly separate from him, is also endowed with a vitality and reality of its own: the teddy bear is therefore neither purely an external object nor yet an hallucination, but rather both at the same time. Winnicott therefore contends:

> [that a] third part of the life of a human being, a part that we cannot ignore, is an intermediate area of experiencing, to which inner reality and external life both contribute. It is an area that is not challenged because no claim is made on its behalf except that it shall exist as a resting-place for the individual engaged in the perpetual human task of keeping inner and outer reality separate yet interrelated.[39]

Winnicott is here redefining the concept of illusion. For Freud an illusion is something to be rejected because it contradicts the reality-principle; but for Winnicott an illusion operates within the intermediate psychological space occupied by transitional objects. We have already seen it at work in the capacity of young children for play, where they invest external objects with meanings and feelings derived from their own private subjective worlds. Illusion, in this sense, is the vehicle by which the infant creates a realm of meaning for itself, by which it begins to move into the external world and to establish a relationship with objects outside itself. For Freud, illusion is something to be outgrown; but for Winnicott the illusions of childhood, as our earliest creative impulses, point in the direction of all our subsequent cultural experiences. What was previously regarded as the infantile area of play now expands into the phenomenon of culture itself. Here too humans occupy the transitional space and play with reality, transfiguring their environment and its objects by endowing them with subjective meaning. So art is the creation of poetic illusion, enabling the artist to fashion and communicate an inner world of his own devising. What Freud sees as a contradiction of reality thus becomes for Winnicott the vehicle for human creativity. This crucial difference is admirably summarized by the Jesuit psychoanalyst, William Meissner:

> Illusion, therefore, becomes in Winnicott's view a developmental form of transition to reality, in the sense that without the capacity to utilize transitional objects and to generate transitional forms of experience the child's attempts to gain a foothold in reality will inevitably be frustrated. Illusion in this view is not an abstraction to experiencing reality but a vehicle for gaining access to it. If Freud wished to rule out illusion and to destroy it, Winnicott wishes to foster it and to increase man's capacity for creatively experiencing it. Winnicott sees that illusion is an important part of human experience precisely because it is not by bread alone that man lives. Man needs to create, to shape and transform his environment, find vehicles for expressing his inner life, or rather the constant commerce between the ongoing worlds of his external experience and his inner psychic reality. Winnicott's standard of psychic health is not the separation of the real and the wishful, as Freud might have had it, but rather their constant intermingling and exchange. It is through illusion, then, that the human spirit is nourished. Freud would have man live in the harsh world of cold facts and realities, ruled by reason. Reason has its place for Winnicott, of course – and its place is not a small one. But the life of the imagination, the life of creative expression, whether wishful or not, is an important, even vital, part of human experience. The man without imagination, without the capacity for play or for creative illusion, is condemned to a sterile world of harsh facts without color or variety, without the continual enrichment of man's creative capacities . . .[40]

What, then, of the so-called illusion of God's existence? Is Freud right to admonish believers for preferring to remain children forever? Winnicott only deals with religion peripherally; but an important extension of his work into this area has been undertaken by Ana-Maria Rizzuto, in her pioneering study

The Birth of the Living God (1979). For Rizzuto God is an object representation, occupying the same kind of intermediate space already created by the child when investing other transitional objects – toys, blankets etc. – with powerfully real illusory lives. Like them, therefore, God is neither an hallucination nor yet totally subjective, but stands, to use Winnicott's phrase, 'outside, inside, at the border.'[41] But God is also a unique object representation. First, unlike the teddy bear, God is not immediately evident to the senses, and is accordingly created out of the individual's experience of other objects: not merely the father (as Freud supposed), but the mother as well, grandparents, siblings, the wider family unit, the social class to which the individual belongs, organized religion and particular subcultures. 'All these experiences,' Rizzuto argues, 'contribute a background to the shape, significance, potential use, and meaning which the child or the adult may bestow on their God representations.'[42] Second, again unlike the teddy bear and all other transitional objects, God is not eventually outgrown and put away. Quite the reverse in fact. God is not forgotten or relegated to a psychic limbo but remains always available for further adaptation, constantly accepted or rejected according to a person's needs. 'God, like a forlorn teddy bear, is left in a corner of the attic, to all appearances forgotten. A death, great pain or intense joy may bring him back for an occasional hug or for further mistreatment and rejection, and then he is forgotten again.'[43] This process continues throughout life. As the person develops, so he or she brings fresh experiences to their inner representational world; and whether one becomes an atheist or believer will be governed by the extent to which the image of God satisfies one's requirements at any given developmental stage. As Rizzuto explains:

> *belief in God* or its absence depends upon whether or not a *conscious 'identity of experience'* can be established between the God representation of a given developmental moment and the object and self-representations needed to maintain a sense of self which provides at least a minimum of relatedness and hope.[44]

Religion is thus located, together with art and culture, within Winnicott's transitional space, the so-called illusion of God now being redefined as a representation uniquely connected with, and reflecting, our encounter with the world and the beings within it. In this sense, religion is not an illusion in the Freudian sense – it is not contrary to reality nor is it infantile – but is an integral part of being human, not least in our capacity to create, like the child at play, 'fictive realities' which are uniquely connected with both our sense of ourselves and our relations with others. Rizzuto concludes:

> I have arrived at the point where my departure from Freud is inevitable. Freud considers God and religion a wishful childish illusion . . . I must disagree. Reality and illusion are not contradictory terms. Psychic

reality – whose depth Freud so brilliantly unveiled – cannot occur without that specifically human transitional space for play and illusion. To ask a man to renounce a God he believes in may be as cruel and as meaningless as wrenching a child from his teddy bear so that he can grow up. We know nowadays that teddy bears are not toys for spoiled children but part of the illusory substance of growing up. Each developmental stage has transitional objects appropriate for the age and level of maturity of the individual. After the oedipal resolution God is a potentially suitable object, and if updated during each crisis of development, may remain so through maturity and the rest of life. Asking a mature, functioning individual to renounce his God would be like asking Freud to renounce his own creation, psychoanalysis, and the 'illusory' promise of what scientific knowledge can do. This is, in fact, the point. Men cannot be men without illusions. The type of illusion we select – science, religion, or something else – reveals our personal history and the transitional space each of us has created between his objects and himself to find 'a resting place' to live in.[45]

FREUD ON SCIENCE AND RELIGION

In these last remarks, Rizzuto refers to a more general philosophical criticism that may be levelled against Freud's account of religion. Freud's case is fashioned on the basis that a radical opposition exists between natural science and religion – the primary cause for religion's decline being its inability to submit itself to a scientific methodology. To the question, 'Why has religious influence waned?', Freud answers by pointing immediately to the 'deplorable effect of the advances of science,'[46] an effect which, as his argument develops, he associates increasingly with science's particular *methods of verification*. The most graphic instance of this occurs in *The Future of an Illusion*, with his famous 'Constance-test.' The statement that 'The town of Constance lies on the Bodensee' makes sense, is convincing, precisely because we can check its truth against our experience; but when we turn to the assertions of religion we find no such possibility; indeed what we do find is something altogether more deplorable: a concerted effort to prevent such checks being made. I think there is little doubt that Freud would subscribe to the view of some twentieth-century linguistic philosophers that religious statements are 'pseudo-propositions' – that they are assertions only masquerading as factually significant – and that, in the final analysis, they are only informative of the particular subjective disposition of those who utter them. Here it is worth recalling that A.J. Ayer, who gave classic expression to this position in his *Language, Truth and Logic* (1936), consigns those who persist in upholding religious claims to the psychoanalyst's couch,[47] and it is tempting to think that he had Freud in mind. *For it is precisely because Freud believes that scientific language is the paradigm language that he also believes that religious language is psychoanalytically interesting.* How else are we to explain the continued allegiance of so many educated men and women to doctrines and claims that have no evidential value? The remedy, as we have seen, is to replace religion with science – a painful process, admittedly, for those still submissive to religious ways of life, but a necessary one nonetheless for the maturing and betterment of the individual and society. In this sense, Freud's 'education to reality' is a postulate of human reason, of people's capacity to think for themselves, free from the burden of religious teaching. Is this belief in science – 'our god Logos,'[48] as he calls it – an illusion? Freud admits that it could be, but denies that it is. Again the test is an empirical one. Religion has proved itself to be untrustworthy and oppressive; but science, by its discoveries and openness to correction, has shown itself time after time to be a genuine vehicle of knowledge. 'No, our science is no illusion. But an illusion it would be to suppose that what science cannot give us we can get elsewhere.'[49]

Criticism of Freud at this point raises the whole vexed question of the relation between science and religion; and I do not want to go into this in any detail here.[50] But a few remarks cannot be avoided. The first thing to say is that even Freud's first critic, Oskar Pfister, saw the dogmatic assumptions behind these conclusions. It is not merely that Freud's account is a caricature of religion – are we really to suppose that theologians, apologists and biblical critics are unaware of the need to verify their conclusions? – but that Freud's own account of the inevitability of scientific progress is illusory. What, Pfister asks prophetically, 'will become of the greatest achievements of technology if they are put at the disposal of human greed, cruelty, and an infrahuman lust for pleasure?'[51] Similarly, natural science appears incapable of forming ethical concepts. If science is a purely factual enterprise, then it is difficult to see how, from a mere description of what is, one can derive any conclusions about what ought to be. In this respect, religion, he says, 'is an educator that science with its theories certainly cannot replace.'[52]

If Freud's belief in scientific progress is illusory, he is equally wrong, says Pfister, about the nature of science itself. In a letter to Freud, dated 24 December 1927, he writes:

'Pure' experience is in my view a fiction in any event, and if we look at the history of the sciences we see how doubtful is the reality hidden behind our so-called experience. . . . Conceptions such as causality, the aether, the atom, etc., are certainly saturated with much bigger contradictions than those of the theologians, and you know better than I do how natural laws have been uprooted by present-day physics. In my view there can be no such thing as a pure empiricist, and a man who sticks rigidly to the data is like a heart specialist who ignores the organism as a whole and its invisible laws, divisions of function, etc. . . .[53]

Pfister's point is an important one. Freud's contrast between religion and science – between two alien Weltanschauungen – is intended to reveal the difference between the untrustworthy and subjective claims of the one, in which the illusional component is decisive, and the verifiable and objective claims of the other, in which the possibility of any wishful-thinking is restricted by the close connection between the claims of science and its data. But to talk of the 'objectivity of science' in these terms is to misrepresent what a scientific theory is actually intended to do. A scientific theory is not merely a collection of data or the report of experimental results, but is more accurately an attempt to make sense of such information through a process of reordering, reclassification or redescription. In this sense, then, a scientific theory is a re-presentation not a literal description of phenomena, the value of which does not lie in its supposed truthfulness but in the degree to which it is helpful in making our world intelligible to us. To every scientific theory, therefore, we bring a process of selection based on our own prior commitments and tacit beliefs about what is required for this theory to be *useful*.

To this, of course, Freud could answer: Whilst I accept that scientific results are not always accurate – or, as Hume would have it, that there is no deductive step between observation and theory – I can at least verify these results in a way that I cannot verify theological conclusions. So much is evident from the fact that one feature of religious thinking, and indeed of metaphysics in general, is the introduction of non-empirical entities to explain what is actually experienced – one thinks, for example, of the Platonic Forms or the Leibnizian Monads or the Aristotelian Unmoved Mover. But if this difference is the substance of Freud's objection, then Pfister is again correct to point out that it is not as wide as Freud supposes, and that even in scientific explanations we not infrequently find the introduction of unverifiable objects – or at least objects that no one at the time could in practice consider verifiable – as part of a scientific hypothesis, as was the case with genes, chromosomes, molecules, atoms and neutrinos, to give just a few examples. We might add to this list many of Freud's own constructions – what about id, ego and super-ego? – but presumably Freud would not wish these excluded because of their non-observability. His reply, of course, would be that, although not immediately verifiable themselves, these can be admitted by science because of their ability to explain what is in fact experienceable; that, for example, the reason why we no longer believe in the existence of 'phlogiston,' 'caloric fluid' and the 'ether' is precisely because they have lost their power to explain what does exist. But once this is accepted, much of Freud's initial objection loses its force, since most metaphysicians would also accept, indeed emphasize, the non-verifiable nature of certain entities but also insist that, although not experienced, such entities are essential to any explanation of what is experienced. So, most famously, while the existence of a Form of Justice can explain the existence of just acts, it is not an existence perceivable by any of the senses; and it was precisely this conclusion that led Plato to a belief in a super-sensible world.

The question is therefore this: If the truth of a religious explanation is not even intended to be established empirically, is it a fair objection to say, with Freud, that such an explanation is not justified because it does not fulfil the criterion of verifiability? Or rather: If a scientific explanation is of a particular type, contrasted as we have just seen with a metaphysical explanation, why should we conclude that it is only scientific explanations that can explain anything, and that accepting these explanations will be tantamount to eliminating God as an explanation? Quite apart from the fact that it appears doubtful whether science can ever plausibly justify such a monopoly – hence, for example, Ayer's problems over the verification of the principle of verification – there is additionally an important ambiguity at work here, which Freud has not observed. An explanation may be unscientific because it contradicts or conflicts with the findings of science; but it may also be unscientific by not being a scientific explanation but an explanation *of a different type*, such as a religious explanation. On this reading, claiming that any explanation which introduces the unobserved entity called 'God' is unscientific, is in fact saying that this explanation is not scientific but something else. This ambiguity can be better explained by an example suggested by Richard Purtill.[54] A court case may be stopped not for legal reasons but for medical ones: the judge has had a heart attack. But the fact that this was a *non-legal* reason does not mean that it was an *illegal* reason, that is, against the law. In much the same way, a non-scientific explanation is not necessarily anti-scientific: this confusion arises from our unfortunate association of 'unscientific' with 'anti-scientific' rather than with 'not scientific but something else.' Freud, I think, is guilty of not perceiving this ambiguity. For him, a religious explanation is not so much non-scientific as anti-scientific, something which must be eschewed if we are to come to terms with reality. This, however, gets suspiciously close to the view, for which there is no obvious warrant, that reality is something which can only be apprehended through the application of a scientific-experimental method; and that whenever two theories compete, the non-scientific explanation must always give way to the scientific. It may, of course, be the case that the scientific explanation is preferred; but for Freud to allege that the only reason for rejecting it would be a psychological inability to face up to reality is to miss the point. To reject what science considers requisite for an explanation to be valid is not necessarily a flight from reality since it may result from a different view of what is necessary for reality to be explained.

I am sure I do not have to repeat in detail the lesson learned from Wittgenstein, when he speaks of the function of language not in terms of its verification but in terms of its use, of the 'game' it plays within a particular 'form of life.'[55] One form of life cannot judge another: certainly it cannot judge it by its own terms. The rules of one game do not apply to another, and for one game to say that the rules of the other are meaningless is a form of trespass. So empiricists should seek to understand the language of belief, not condemn it because it does not express their own form of life. When therefore Freud characterizes religion as an illusion, he may be accused, as Winnicott would surely do, of using illusion in one sense only; of using it within the context of a tradition which says that an illusion is a flight into fantasy. But this may not be the only meaning of illusion. When the child plays with her teddy bear, to take Rizzuto's example, she constructs an illusional world which is hers alone, a world which is real and crucial to her for her own maturity. This is not something to be lightly dismissed as a regression into infantilism. Yet in doing so, Freud betrays his own wishful thought that there is only one form of life, and a materialist one at that. What is operating here may, in fact, be something rather different: a conflict between two systems of play, between two functioning myths if you will, the story of Oedipus on the one hand, and the story of Adam on the other. The Oedipus myth, for Freud, is the demythologized history of the Fall, of man's acquisition of universal guilt; but to say that this myth is more true than its biblical counterpart because it is psychoanalytically verifiable is to set up a false comparison. The story of Adam, after all, is not there to be tested, but derives its validity from within the community of beliefs and practices associated with a religious form of life.

FREUD AND THE GENETIC FALLACY

One final question remains. Freud's critique of religion is fundamentally an exposé of its Oedipal origins, which as far as he is concerned explains both its first emergence and its continuing attraction. The question is whether, in pointing out to the believer the fallacy of wishful thinking, he has not inadvertently fallen into a fallacy of his own – what logicians call the 'genetic fallacy.' This fallacy is committed when one infers the truth or falsity of a belief on the basis of its causal origin. Often, of course, the cause of a belief does bear upon its acceptance or rejection: for example, 'What caused me to believe that Roger was a thief was that I saw him steal the books.' This belief would not, however, be justified if its cause was 'Mrs Gossip told me so.' To specify the origin of a belief is not therefore to determine whether a belief is true or false, and to suppose otherwise is to commit the genetic fallacy.

Has Freud committed it? I think not. First, we should remember that an illusion is not necessarily false, and that therefore to categorize religion as an illusion is not to establish its untruth. And second, we should also note how quick Freud is to repudiate any suggestion that psychoanalysis can legislate on such matters. 'To assess the truth-value of religious doctrines does not lie within the scope of the present inquiry. It is enough for us that we have recognized them as being, in the psychological nature, illusions.'[56] Thus, even if we accept Freud's theories as true, this does not imply that religious belief is false. But then Freud continues:

> But we do not have to conceal the fact that this discovery also strongly influences our attitude to the question which must appear to many to be the most important of all. We know approximately at what periods and by what kind of men religious doctrines were created. If in addition we discover the motives which led to this, our attitude to the problem of religion will undergo a marked displacement. We shall tell ourselves that it would be very nice if there were a God who created the world and was a benevolent Providence, and if there were a moral order in the universe and an after-life; but it is a very striking fact that all this is exactly as we are bound to wish it to be. And it would be more remarkable still if our wretched, ignorant and down-trodden ancestors had succeeded in solving all these difficult riddles of the universe.[57]

This is a different kind of argument, but one which still does not fall foul of the genetic fallacy. The 'all-important question' is, of course, the question of whether religion is true or false, of whether a God actually exists or whether he exists only as a projection of Oedipal desires. In a sense Freud is conceding the logical possibility of God's existence, but arguing on evidential grounds that this is highly unlikely. His argument, indeed, is inductive in form:

1 Beliefs which are held to be true because they satisfy some deep psychological need are invariably found to be false.
2 Religious beliefs are held to be true because they satisfy some deep psychological need.
3 Therefore religious beliefs are invariably found to be false.

It is on these grounds that Freud, while conceding that strictly speaking his position proves nothing, justifies his conclusion that the believer is 'defending a lost cause.'[58] It also explains why Freud sometimes lapses into the language of 'delusion' rather than 'illusion.' The claims of religion – that there is a benevolent Creator, that there is a moral order in the universe, that there is an after-life – are admittedly weak already in the light of the kind of evidence presented in their favour; but when we consider their *origin* – when we discover that these claims are not rationally supported but solely motivated by a *will to believe* – then the possibility of their ever being confirmed becomes still more remote, to the point indeed where calling them delusory is not entirely inaccurate. For it is precisely this desperate need to believe which highlights both the extraordinary character of the faith and the extreme poverty of its justification.

This argument does little to strengthen Freud's case. Even if we set aside the question of whether he is right to characterize illusion as an escape from reality, and right to define religion in these terms, it will hardly come as a surprise to believers that their beliefs should be considered extraordinary and contrary to what one might expect from past experience. This of itself does not therefore decide for the existence or non-existence of the object to which the belief refers. The fact that Freud has defined religion as wishful-thinking does not mean that God is only a wish and not a reality because, after all, a real God might exist who corresponds to that wish. Equally, to exclude rational reasons for a belief in God, and thus to accuse it of irrationality, is hardly to do justice to a theological tradition which includes thinkers like Anselm and Aquinas, whose main concern was to secure faith's rational foundation. Freud, we may conclude, gives many reasons why religion should not be believed in – not least because it has a compulsive quality usually associated with neurotics – but he has not given any good reasons why religion should be believed in, and has never considered the evidence given in its favour, except in the most general and pejorative way. Even if we admit that religion is compulsive, this does not of itself reduce its claims to truth since it may equally be a feature of the evidence provided that it has this effect. That is, the compulsive wish to believe may characterize not what the believer perceives, but the result of his perceiving it, and in this sense a religious belief may derive its strength not from a series of verifiable propositions but from some kind of personal experience in which their truth is revealed.

Carl Gustav Jung. Mary Evans Picture Library

Part II

CARL GUSTAV JUNG: ANALYTICAL PSYCHOLOGY AND RELIGION

... the outlook for me is very gloomy if you too get into the psychology of religion. You are a dangerous rival – if one has to speak of rivalry. Yet I think it has to be this way, for a natural development cannot be halted, nor should one try to halt it. Our personal differences will make our work different. You dig up the precious stones, but I have the 'degree of extension'. As you know, I always have to proceed from the outside to the inside and from the whole to the part. I would find it too upsetting to let large tracts of human knowledge lie there neglected.

(Letter from Jung to Freud, 14 November 1911)

6

INTRODUCTION

A SHORT BIOGRAPHY

Carl Gustav Jung was born on 26 July 1875 in Kesswil, a small town on Lake Constance in Switzerland. Six months later the family moved to Laufen, close to the Falls of the Rhine where his father was the vicar, and then in 1879 to Klein-Hüningen, a small village close to Basel. He was educated at the Gymnasium in Basel, and from there went on to study medicine at the University of Basel (1895–1900). In 1900 he became assistant to Eugen Bleuler at the Burghölzli Mental Hospital in Zurich, with one term at the Salpêtrière in Paris studying psychopathology with Pierre Janet. In 1903 Jung married Emma Rauschenbach, the daughter of a rich industrialist, with whom he had fallen in love seven years before, and at first sight, when she was a young girl of fourteen. Together they built a house at Küsnacht on the Lake of Zurich – in 1923 they were to build a country retreat, the Tower at Bollingen – and from here Jung established a private practice so extensive that he left the Burghölzli in 1909. Meantime, in 1906, Jung had sent Freud his publication on word association, and then in 1907 his important book, *The Psychology of Dementia Praecox*. This brought an invitation from Freud to visit him in Vienna in the same year. Their first conversation lasted without interruption for thirteen hours. In 1908, at Freud's instigation, Jung became chief editor of the first psychoanalytic periodical, the *Jahrbuch für psychoanalytische und psychopathologische Forschungen* (with Freud and Bleuler as directors); in 1909 they travelled together to the USA, where both received honorary degrees from Clark University, Massachusetts; and in 1910 Jung became the first president of the International Psychoanalytic Association. However, in 1911 Jung published the first part of his *The Psychology of the Unconscious* (later translated as *Symbols of Transformation*) in which he made clear that he did not agree with Freud's views on sexuality and the Oedipus complex. In September 1912 Jung travelled again to the USA, and there openly criticized Freud and psychoanalysis. Their association became increasingly difficult on both a personal and academic level, and came to an acrimonious end in 1913. With the outbreak of war in 1914 Jung was called upon for military service and was in charge of camps for interned officers and other ranks of the British and Indian Armies. Jung's international reputation largely depends on work completed after this period, most notably *Psychological Types* (1921), which is his principal contribution to the psychology of the unconscious mind, and in which he distinguishes between two attitudes to life, the introverted and the extraverted. This study of the structure and activity of the unconscious led to an extensive analysis of other activities of the unconscious, most notably that of the 'collective unconscious,' 'archetypes' and the 'individuation process,' together with their associated phenomena: mythology, gnosis, kabbala and alchemy. Specific theological problems also fascinated Jung, as is clear from his Terry lectures of 1938, *Psychology and Religion*, and his highly controversial *Answer to Job* of 1952. Jung's research was also greatly enriched by his interest in other cultures, particularly those of the East, and by several trips abroad, to Kenya, India and to the Pueblo Indians of Arizona and New Mexico. He died on 6 June 1961.

This, then, is the outline of Jung's life. Let us now retrace our steps and take more detailed note of two important elements: his family background and his dispute with Freud.

Family background

Jung's family background was predominantly academic and religious. His father Paul Achilles Jung (1842–1896) was an impecunious and undistinguished minister of the Reformed Church – two uncles were also clergymen – but his paternal grandfather, also named Carl Gustav (1795–1864), had been a much-respected professor of medicine in Basel. Rumoured to be the natural son of Goethe, to whom he bore an uncanny resemblance, he had also become Rector of the University and Grandmaster of the Freemasons of Switzerland, had written several plays, and had shown an early and compassionate interest in the treatment of mental illness, founding the Institute of Good Hope, a home for retarded children. Jung's mother, Emilie, was the youngest daughter of the vicar of Kesswil, Samuel Preiswerk (1799–1871), later *Antistes* of Basel, an enthusiastic spiritualist, Zionist and linguist of distinction, whose devotion to Hebrew was prompted by the belief that this was the language of heaven. Of his sons, six became theologians. Small wonder, then, that as a child at school and in the village, Jung should be known as 'parsons's Carl,' a nickname he disliked.[1]

This overtly religious background also goes some way towards explaining three important experiences that Jung had between the ages of four and twelve. The first was a dream, the earliest he could remember, one which was to preoccupy him all his life. In it Jung discovered a stone-lined hole in the ground, with a stairway leading down. This led to a large room, at the end of which was a magnificent throne with a red cushion. Upon it stood something that Jung thought at first was a tree trunk twelve to fifteen feet high and about one and a half to two feet thick. It was a huge thing, reaching almost to the ceiling. But it was of a curious composition: it was made of skin and naked flesh, and on top there was something like a rounded head with a single eye, gazing motionlessly upwards.[2]

Jung was paralysed with fear; but his terror intensified as he heard from outside his mother's voice calling out, 'Yes, just look at him. That is the man-eater!' Jung did not mention this dream until he was sixty-five years of age, and then only to his wife. In his autobiography he frankly admits that it haunted him for years, and that it was only much later that he began to appreciate its momentous significance. Expecting to see God and the Lord Jesus enthroned in glory he had seen instead a monstrous phallus, a 'sub-terranean God,' un-nameable, fascinating, and terrible. Thereafter 'Lord Jesus never became quite real for me, never quite acceptable, never quite lovable, for again and again I would think of his underground counterpart, a frightful revelation which had been accorded me without my seeking it.'[3]

Jung associated this dream with an event which occurred at about the same time and which he calls 'my first conscious trauma.'[4] One hot summer day he saw a strange figure walking up the road: it looked like a man wearing women's clothes. As the figure approached, however, Jung saw that it was a man wearing a broad hat and a kind of black robe that reached down to the ground. His fear grew into terror as he realized that this was a Jesuit! He had recently heard his father talking about their sinister activities, and he assumed that this man had evil designs on him. 'Terrified, I ran helter-skelter into the house, rushed up the stairs, and hid under a beam in the darkest corner of the attic. . . . For days afterwards the hellish fright clung to my limbs and kept me in the house.'[5] This experience became fused with Jung's earlier dream. In his mind *Jesuit* became *Jesus*, the dark Lord, the subterranean phallus, the man-eater, whose flapping black coat cast its shadow over the comforting Christianity he had been taught.

Eight years later Jung had another vision, perhaps the most momentous of his whole life. He found himself standing in the courtyard of the Gymnasium at Basel on a bright summer's day. From here he could see the Cathedral, and above it God sat upon his throne. Then something terrible happened, a thing so awful that even to think of it would damn him for all eternity. For two days Jung resisted the forbidden thought, becoming so overwrought that his mother became alarmed. On the third night, just as his torment was becoming unbearable, he began to consider that perhaps God was putting him to the test, that this was a trial of courage, and that he would receive grace and illumination through 'the unusual task of doing something against my own moral judgment and against the teachings of my religion . . .':

I gathered all my courage, as though I were about to leap forthwith into hell-fire, and let the thought come. I saw before me the cathedral, the blue sky. God sits on His golden throne, high above the world – and from under the throne an enormous turd falls upon the sparkling new roof, shatters it, and breaks the walls of the cathedral asunder.

So that was it! I felt an enormous, an indescribable relief. Instead of the expected damnation, grace had come upon me, and with it an unutterable bliss such as I had never known .[6]

These early experiences are, of course, susceptible to a straightforward Freudian interpretation. What we have here are images expressive of a young boy's burgeoning but repressed sexuality, set within an atmosphere of sexual puritanism and thus forced underground, culminating in the adolescent's fear of and eventual capitulation before something obscene but blissful – perhaps, as Anthony Stevens suggests,[7] his first non-productive orgasm. But, as both Stevens and Laurens van der Post further remind us,[8] this was not how Jung himself interpreted his vision, nor was it in this wise that he considered it central to his whole life's work. For Jung this was a direct experience of God, and through it two truths had been revealed: first, that the traditional teachings of religion no longer provided sustenance and that even God himself regarded them as waste-products; and second, that illumination would follow through obedience to God's will, no matter how terrible or incomprehensible the command placed upon him. It is small wonder, then, that Jung found himself increasingly estranged from the conventions of religion. His first communion proved a hollow experience, he found even entering a Church increasingly difficult, and, most painful of all, he witnessed his father's faith disintegrating before his eyes. He found himself 'cut off from the Church and from my father's and everybody else's faith. In so far as they all represented the Christian religion, I was an outsider. This knowledge filled me with a sadness which was to overshadow all the years until the time I entered the university.'[9]

Jung entered the University of Basel in 1895. At first he joined the classes on natural science but soon changed to medicine. He was an exemplary student and completed his studies quickly. In his autobiography Jung refers to two events which drew him towards psychiatry. In his fourth year he attended the séances of his fifteen-year-old cousin, Hélène Preiswerk. Jung was particularly struck by the fact that, when in a trance, this young girl lost her Basel accent and spoke in high German, and that she claimed to be controlled by a variety of spirits, some serious, others frivolous. Jung's copious notes, taken over a period of two years, formed the basis for his first published work: his degree dissertation, 'On the Psychology and Pathology of so-called Occult Phenomena' (1902).[10] Shortly after this, and with still no thought of taking up psychiatry as a career, Jung read Krafft-Ebing's Lehrbuch der Psychiatrie (1890). As he records, his excitement was intense and it became clear to him 'in a flash of illumination, that for me the only possible goal was psychiatry.'[11] He immediately turned down his tutor's offer to become his assistant in internal medicine at Munich, moved instead to Zürich, and shortly after, on 10 December 1900, took up a position there as an assistant to Eugen Bleuler (1857–1939) at the Burghölzli Mental Hospital. Bleuler was one of the outstanding psychiatrists of his day – it was he who introduced the terms 'autism' and 'ambivalence' into the psychiatric vocabulary and who replaced the outmoded and inaccurate 'dementia praecox' with the more appropriate 'schizophrenia' – and with his support Jung's career advanced rapidly, becoming his deputy in 1905 and in the same year lecturer in psychiatry at the University of Zurich. Jung was to call his nine years at Burghölzli 'my years of apprenticeship.'[12]

The dispute with Freud

Jung's dispute with Freud – in itself one of the most significant moments in the whole history of psychoanalysis – has generated an extensive literature and is still the subject of heated debate between the two schools of thought.[13] Initially Freud regarded Jung not merely as his ablest but as his most important pupil, his crown prince, the man destined to carry his work forward into the future. As Freud often said, Jung was Joshua to his Moses. And from the first Freud was quick to see the practical advantages of this relationship. Not only had Jung proved himself a formidable champion of Freud's theories, not only had his own researches at Burghölzli independently supported them at a time when Freud was still generally reviled within the academic community, but the fact that Jung was not Jewish and not Austrian meant that psychoanalysis could more easily defend itself against charges of intellectual and sectarian élitism and so enlist the sympathetic interest of a much wider audience. As Jones records, 'Freud himself perceived the advantage of establishing a broader basis for the work than could be provided by Viennese Jewry,' and that it was largely this consideration which explains why Freud was so determined that Jung should be appointed the first president of the Psychoanalytic Association.[14]

For his part Jung reciprocated with feelings of awed respect and filial devotion. What had been lacking in the relationship with his own ineffectual father was more than compensated for in Freud's dominant personality, and Jung was happy to fall in with the emotional demands of a surrogate father–son relationship. Shortly after their first meeting in 1907, Jung expressed the hope that their friendship would not be 'as one between equals but as that of father and son.'[15] This hope, however, was short-lived and it soon became clear that the psychological need that they undoubtedly had for one another contained disturbing and disruptive elements. For Freud it became apparent that their relationship was increasingly Oedipal: that the son harboured parricidal feelings towards the father and wished to replace him – to the point indeed that Freud fainted on two occasions (at Bremen in 1909 and again at Munich in 1912) when Jung spoke of death. For Jung, it was equally clear that Freud's authority was robbing him of his own intellectual independence; that the fantasy of father-murder also required the emasculation of the son. Matters came to a head during the seven-week trip to the USA in 1909. Freud and Jung began analysing each other's dreams. Apparently Freud had little success interpreting Jung's, although Jung still 'regarded Freud as an older, more mature and experienced personality, and felt like a son in that respect.' But then something happened, continues Jung, 'which proved to be a severe blow to the whole relationship.'

> Freud had a dream – I would not think it right to air the problem it involved. I interpreted it as best I could, but added that a great deal more could be said about it if he would supply me with some additional details from his private life. Freud's response to these words was a curious look – a look of the utmost suspicion. Then he said, 'But I cannot risk my authority!' At that moment he lost it altogether. That sentence burned itself into my memory; and in it the end of our relationship was already foreshadowed. Freud was placing personal authority above truth.[16]

Whatever it was that Jung discovered about Freud – and to the end of his life Jung refused to divulge more on the grounds of professional confidentiality[17] – it was not until the following year (1910) that Jung became aware of the exact areas in which Freud would brook no opposition; where, as Jung saw it, Freud would employ the full force of his authority to stave off criticism and indeed regard any deviation from his views as an act of apostasy. *These were the areas of sexuality and religion.* From the outset of their friendship Jung began to suspect that Freud's own latent religious feeling had been projected into his theory of sexuality. He knew, as did all Freud's associates, that Freud considered himself an irreligious man; but he became increasingly uneasy the more Freud himself became obsessed with sexual matters, the more he employed his sexual theory to denounce religion and culture generally as the morbid consequences of repression, the more indeed the dogma of sexuality appeared to replace the dogmas of religion. Jung comments:

> There was no mistaking the fact that Freud was emotionally involved in his sexual theory to an extraordinary degree. When he spoke of it, his tone became urgent, almost anxious, and all signs of his normally critical and sceptical manner vanished. A strange, deeply moved expression came over his face, the cause of which I was at a loss to understand. I had a strong intuition that for him sexuality was a sort of *numinosum*.[18]

Jung then goes on to record a conversation in 1910, which seemed to have confirmed his suspicions. I have mentioned this in the previous chapter, but it is worth repeating.[19] 'My dear Jung,' Freud said, 'promise me never to abandon the sexual theory. That is the most essential thing of all. You see, we must make a dogma of it, an unshakable bulwark ... against the black tide of mud ... of occultism.' Jung reports that he was both alarmed and amazed at these remarks. By 'occultism' he took Freud to mean virtually everything that philosophy and religion, including the new science of parapsychology, had learned about the psyche; and, as far as he could see, a dogma was 'an indisputable confession of faith' set up in order to 'suppress doubts once and for all. But that no longer has anything to do with scientific judgment; only with a personal power drive.'[20] This was an attitude entirely alien to Jung, and he frankly admits that it was this 'that struck at the heart of our friendship.'[21] It was some time, however, before Jung fully appreciated what had been revealed to him. What he had observed in Freud was 'the eruption of unconscious religious factors.' Freud, in other words, who had always made so much of his lack of religion, had now constructed another: the jealous God, whom he had lost, had now been replaced by another compelling image, that of sexuality.

> The advantage of this transformation for Freud was, apparently, that he was able to regard the numinous principle as scientifically irreproach-able and free from all religious taint. At bottom, however, the numin-osity, that is, the psychological qualities of the two rationally in-commensurable opposites – Yahweh and sexuality – remained the same. The name alone had changed, and with it, of course, the point of view: the lost god had now to be sought below, not above. But what difference does it make, ultimately, to the stronger agency if it is called now by one name and now by another?[22]

In itself this criticism of Freud is nothing new, and I have already mentioned other critics of Freud who have said much the same thing.[23] There are, however, two important points to note in Jung's comments. The first is a matter of methodology. Jung is claiming here that what Freud has to say about religion is conditioned by Freud's own psychology. In itself this is not an error because, as Jung remarks, 'every psychology – my own included – has the character of a subjective confession. ... Even when I deal with empirical data I am necessarily speaking about myself.'[24] Freud's mistake, rather, was to construct a general theory on the basis of his personal preferences – to succumb to a kind of 'metaphysical' arrogance by going beyond the available data and by deliberately ignoring evidence which did not conform to the hypothesis he was advancing. For Jung, therefore, intellectual honesty requires the undogmatic inclusion of information ex-cluded by Freud, and demands an understanding of psychic reality altogether more extensive. Thus, for example, while Freud's positivistic and determin-istic approach – most notable in his biological preoccupation with the sexual origin of neurosis – leads to a reductive account of mental phenomena like religious belief, Jung adopts a much more open-ended approach, holding that there is more to the universe than scientific materialism will allow; that in this sense psychic reality is not a secondary product or an epiphenomenon but *sui generis*; and that accordingly ideas as ancient and persistent as the idea of God must be accorded a degree of 'psychological truth' as an *empirically evident psychic reality*, and not dismissed as aberrant because reducible to a father complex. Jung, we should add, no less than Freud, believes in the *vis medicatrix naturae* – that is, in the healing power of nature, by which man has the capacity, through his discovery of his unconscious life, to heal himself; but whereas Freud sees this as involving the elimination of the religious neurosis in the life of the maturing individual, Jung sees the process as requiring a reorientation of the consciousness towards religion, towards those psychic processes generic to the human species which religion embodies and which are thus expressive of the deepest and innermost processes of the psyche. For Jung, then, *it is not the presence of religion which is a symptom of neurosis but its absence.* And this conclusion is not merely the result of a temperamental difference between Freud and Jung. It is also the logical outcome of the difference between them over what counts as psychological data and how it is to be assessed, over what embodies the therapeutic ideal and how it is to be achieved. This difference is crucial to the development of Jung's thinking on religion, and I shall return to it in some detail in a later chapter.

The second point I want to mention raises still more complicated matters, and brings us at last to the details of Jung's own analytical psychology. This concerns Jung's claim that Freud's rejection of religion is a consequence of his sexual theory. Again, this is hardly an original thing to say – and Freud himself would accept its accuracy, so far as it goes. Jung's conclusion, however, tells us almost as much about Jung as it does about Freud, allowing us our first entry into a very different account of religion. We might say, in fact, that Jung's revaluation of religion, and thus departure from the Freudian line, first requires a rejection of Freud's pan-sexual theory. With that in mind, let us now turn to Jung's own theory of the libido, as the necessary prologue to his assessment of religious belief.

7

THE STRUCTURE OF THE PSYCHE

A fundamental principle of Freudian psychology is that men and women always carry within themselves the marks of certain infantile sexual experiences, and that the later development of neuroses will largely depend on their reaction to those experiences: whether, for instance, they react by 'repression' or not. In this sense, neuroses are not just expressions of libidinal disturbance but also represent an historical and retrospective account of each person's infantile sexual activity – the particular form taken by an illness being linked to the particular stage to which the libido has regressed. This being the case, the neurotic appears wedded to his or her infantile past, and whatever symptoms may later develop will stem from the powerful libidinal impulses generated during those early years.

Although Jung's relations with Freud were very close between 1907 and 1912, it is worth recording that even during that period Jung had expressed some reservations about Freud's theory of neurosis and the role it assigned to the sexual instinct.[1] The first indication of this comes in a letter to Freud dated 5 October 1906, in which Jung, commenting on the criticisms levelled against Freud by the Cologne professor of criminology Gustav Aschaffenburg, writes that 'it seems to me that though the genesis of hysteria is predominantly, it is not exclusively, sexual.' Replying two days later, Freud acknowledges that Jung's 'appreciation of my psychology does not extend to all my views on hysteria and the problem of sexuality,' but adds optimistically: 'I venture to hope that in the course of the years you will come much closer to me than you now think possible.'[2] However, a month later, in a formal reply to Aschaffenburg, Jung repeats his reservations about Freud's theory becoming 'somewhat one-sided' and cautiously modifies it to read: 'An indefinitely large number of cases of hysteria derive from sexual roots.'[3] Two years later the same criticism appears, with Jung this time noting that 'no one knows whether Freud's (sexual) schema is applicable to all forms of hysteria,' and adding that 'my own experience, which is considerably less than his, has yielded nothing that would argue against this assertion.'[4] Even Jung's most important work of this period – his study of schizophrenia in *The Psychology of Dementia Praecox* (1907), which he had sent to Freud and which had led to their first meeting – contains a similar reluctance to go all the way with this aspect of Freudian theory. So while he admits that 'even a superficial glance at my work will show how much I am indebted to the brilliant discoveries of Freud,' he nevertheless feels impelled to add the following qualification:

> Fairness to Freud, however, does not imply, as many fear, unqualified submission to a dogma; one can very well maintain an independent judgment. If I, for instance, acknowledge the complex mechanisms of dreams and hysteria, this does not mean that I attribute to the infantile sexual trauma the exclusive importance that Freud apparently does. Still less does it mean that I place sexuality so predominantly in the foreground, or that I grant it the psychological universality which Freud, it seems, postulates in view of the admittedly enormous role which sexuality plays in the psyche. As for Freud's therapy, it is at best but one of several possible methods, and perhaps does not always offer in practice what one expects from it in theory.[5]

According to Jung, the decisive break from Freud came with the two-part publication in 1911 and 1912 of his *Wandlungen und Symbole der Libido*, subsequently translated as *Symbols of Transformation*.[6] Freud in fact received the first part with some pleasure – in a letter to Jung, dated 12 November 1911, he writes light-heartedly that 'it is the best thing this promising author has written, up to now, though he will do better'[7] – but Jung himself was well aware that the second part, in which he decisively repudiates Freud's theory of the libido, 'would cost me my friendship with Freud.'[8] Indeed, so great was Jung's fear of this happening that for two months he could write nothing, notwithstanding his wife's reassurances that 'Freud would magnanimously raise no objections.'[9] Jung was less optimistic, and Jung was right. Thereafter the correspondence between the two men, previously so friendly, takes a decisive, downward turn. Nor were matters improved by Jung's tactless letter to Freud, dated 11 November 1912, in which he reports on his recent lectures at Fordham University in New York and claims that his new version of the libido theory had 'won over many people who until now had been put off by the problem of sexuality in neurosis.'[10] Freud refers to this letter in his 'On the History of the Psychoanalytic Movement' (1914). To sacrifice one of the 'hard-won truths of psychoanalysis' is nothing to boast of and betrays a 'total incompatibility' with the movement as a whole. 'Some people,' he continues, 'may be inclined to fear that this secession is bound to have more momentous consequences for analysis than would another ... I do not share this apprehension.'[11] And here Freud was wrong. *Symbols of Transformation* is in many ways the decisive work in the development of Jungian psychology and thus in a new understanding of the unconscious mind. This point is worth underlining. For Freud the unconscious is, as it were, the underside of consciousness: it is that extensive and dynamic field of mental life in which repose ideas and memories censored from the conscious mind through the powerful mechanisms of repression. Jung now radically alters this definition and broadens it to the point where the Freudian unconscious becomes a comparatively insignificant part of the total unconscious material available; where indeed the most significant psychological factors are said to exist independently of the individual's experience, to be incapable of personal acquisition, and to owe their existence exclusively to heredity. This, then, is a still deeper layer beneath the personal unconscious, in which is to be found the primordial and universal images common to all mankind. Jung calls it the *collective unconscious*. This third dimension upsets the Freudian order of priority. Whereas for Freud the unconscious arises out of consciousness, for Jung consciousness arises out of the unconscious, the unconscious mind in this sense 'pre-dating' the conscious mind.

THE PRIMORDIAL IMAGES OF THE COLLECTIVE UNCONSCIOUS

Symbols of Transformation is a study of the schizoid fantasies of a young American woman, pseudonymously known as Miss Frank Miller, originally collected and published in 1906 by Jung's friend, Théodore Flournoy of Geneva.[12] Miss Miller was clearly a lady of singular suggestibility and possessed of an extraordinary capacity for identification and empathy. When attending a performance of *Cyrano de Bergerac*, such is her identification with the romantic hero, Christian de Neuvillette, that she feels 'a real, piercing pain in my own breast' when he is mortally wounded. On another occasion, when wrapping a towel round her head before taking a shower, she suddenly sees herself 'with an almost breath-taking clarity' on a pedestal, 'a veritable Egyptian statue with all its details; stiff-limbed, one foot forward, holding insignia in my hand....'[13] More important fantasies were to follow while travelling through Europe. Sailing from Naples to Leghorn she dreams a 'Hymn of Creation,' and so vivid is her recollection of it that she is able to write it down almost at once. A similar thing happens travelling by train from Geneva to Paris. In her compartment she sees a tiny butterfly or moth fluttering towards the light and, on falling asleep, dreams another poem, again so vividly recalled that she writes it down immediately, calling it 'The Song of the Moth.' Miss Miller's most elaborate fantasy concerns the apparition of an Aztec Indian, named Chi-wan-to-pel. She imagines him in various situations – on a horse, in battle, in a wood – and in particular being threatened by another Indian, dressed in buckskin, who makes ready to shoot him with an arrow but who eventually slinks away and disappears into the forest. Thereupon Chi-wan-to-pel delivers an extensive soliloquy (in English), in which he tells of all the women he has known, none of whom has apparently been able to understand him. Eventually Chi-wan-to-pel is bitten by a green viper and dies during an earthquake. Again, Miss Miller records this small 'melodrama in one act' in almost perfect detail, and concludes that, given its strangeness and complexity, 'this hypnagogic fantasy is well worth a little attention.'[14]

For Jung the Miller case is a classic example of the unconscious manifestations that invariably precede a severe psychic disorder and, in over four hundred densely packed pages, Jung sets about unravelling them. The method he employs in this, and indeed in all his subsequent cases, he calls the *method of amplification*. This method requires the analyst to collect as much information as possible about the dream or image being employed by the patient. This information, according to Jung, can be derived from an enormous variety of sources: not merely, of course, from the personal history of the person being analysed, but from historical and anthropological references, from archeological findings or literary sources, from myths and fairy-stories – from anything, in fact, that can illuminate the nature and character of the image being displayed. Jung's diagnosis begins, however, with an important preamble. It is a commonplace of psychology to suppose that the dreams and fantasies of people like Miss Miller are to be taken as libidinal signs: in other words, that they contain a hidden meaning emanating from an unknown part of the psyche, and further, following Freud, that these images invariably express some kind of erotic conflict. In this sense, a dream or fantasy is a pathological product from which we may discover the complexes of the patient: it does not, as it were, possess a life of its own but is rather explicable retrospectively, that is, by reference to some definite past experience or trauma. Jung does not deny the validity of this approach but he does deny its exclusivity. This he does by defining the act of dreaming as a particular *mode of thought*. In the first instance, dreaming (or 'fantasy-thinking') is to be distinguished from 'directed thinking,' that is, from that process which is entirely verbal, communicative and almost solely concerned with matching our language to the outside world. Directed thinking is therefore 'reality-thinking,' and it is this form of thought which we find pre-eminently expressed in the modern preoccupation with science.[15] Fantasy-thinking, on the other hand, begins when reality-thinking comes to an end, and to this extent represents not just a shift away from the materialist demands of the present-day, but even more significantly, a dramatic backwards move to an earlier, more ancient mode of thought; indeed to a form of thinking, familiar to the classical mind, in which the dream or fantasy or myth is the only means of expressing an experience which completely eludes rational formulation.

> What happens when we do not think directly? Well, our thinking then lacks all leading ideas and the sense of direction emanating from them. We no longer compel our thoughts along a definite track, but let them float, sink or rise according to their specific gravity.... [This] sort of thinking ... leads away from reality into fantasies of the past or future. At this point thinking in verbal form ceases, image piles on

image, feeling on feeling, and there is an ever-increasing tendency to shuffle things about and arrange them not as they are in reality but as one would like them to be. Naturally enough, the stuff of this thinking which shies away from reality can only be the past with its thousand-and-one memory images. Common speech calls this kind of thinking 'dreaming.'[16]

In dealing, then, with Miss Miller's fantasies and dreams Jung adopts a significantly different approach from Freud. Freud's method is causal and reductive: the dream encapsulates the pathological effects of a regression back to certain infantile and libidinal desires, and can therefore be reduced down to a composite of camouflaged neurotic motives. For Jung, on the other hand, far from being a symptom of pathological complexes, the dream is an entirely normal and constructive psychic function, in which the repetition of infantile reminiscences parallels and reflects an altogether more archaic mode of thinking. The basis of a dream or fantasy is therefore only apparently infantile: its true source lies further back, even beyond the individual experiences of childhood, but nevertheless made more accessible in infancy by virtue of the child's inherent gift for fantasy and less rational and objective view of things. What we are in fact dealing with here is an altogether more ancient layer of the human mind, buried deep within the psyche, and from which emerges the instinctive and unconscious repetition of certain primitive fantasy-processes. Freud, it will be remembered, was quite ready to accept in both *Totem and Taboo* and *Moses and Monotheism* that the unconscious contains residues of an archaic heritage – 'memory-traces of the experience of earlier generations'[17] – and indeed was equally ready to acknowledge his debt to Jung in this respect; but whereas Freud concentrates exclusively on the ontogenetic repetition of a specific phylogenetic inheritance – the re-enactment in every individual life of the Oedipal drama of the primal horde – Jung now extends the range of this legacy to encompass a whole host of primordial images, which are the most ancient and most universal 'fantasy-thoughts' of humanity. In this sense, then, the dream does not rest exclusively on personal memories, infantile or otherwise, but rather on a still deeper level of the unconscious, in which we meet once again the images and perceptions of a vanished world. Jung writes:

> The psychologist should accept this view without qualification. The Dionysian phallagogies, the chthonic mysteries of classical Athens, have vanished from our civilization, and the theriomorphic representations of the gods have dwindled to mere vestiges, like the Dove, the Lamb, and the Cock adorning our church towers. Yet all this does not alter the fact that in childhood we go through a phase when archaic thinking and feeling once more rise up in us, and that all through our lives we possess, side by side with our newly acquired directed and adapted thinking, a fantasy-thinking which corresponds to the antique state of

Archei 2
Mind

mind. Just as our bodies still retain vestiges of obsolete functions and conditions in many of their organs, so our minds, which have apparently outgrown those archaic impulses, still bear the marks of the evolutionary stages we have traversed, and re-echo the dim bygone in dreams and fantasies.[18]

This conclusion governs Jung's analysis of Miss Miller. We see now that her apparently chaotic and random dreams are less masks of her own neurotic and libidinal past but more spontaneous reversions to primitive and archaic motifs and ideas, and thus manifestations of a level of the unconscious independent of her own experience but nevertheless typical of fantasy-thinking throughout the ages, be it in myths, fairy-tales, dreams, visions or, as in this case, the delusional systems of a schizophrenic. Each of Miss Miller's fantasies are treated in this manner, but as an example let us take her second poem, 'The Song of the Moth.' Here Miss Miller equates the moth's desire for the sun with her own desire for God; and, as Jung then proceeds to show, this identification of God with the intensity and power of the sun finds countless parallels not just among the religions of the ancient Near East – in Mithraic liturgy, in Egyptian symbolism, in the visions of the Johannine Apocalypse – but in literature generally, as can be seen in the poetry of Goethe and Nietzsche. For Jung these correspondences are too obvious to be ignored; and since we cannot suppose any direct connection between these sources, we must assume that we have 'dug deep down into the historical layers of the psyche.'[19] In Miss Miller's hymn we have consequently uncovered symbols and images that belong to no single place, time or individual but are rather inherited and collective.

During the course of his analysis of Miss Miller's 'Song of the Moth,' Jung refers to another, even more extraordinary example of this phenomenon; and, since he frequently recalls this case, it is worth mentioning here. At the Burghölzli in 1906 Jung came across a young male paranoid schizophrenic suffering from a curious delusion. One day he told Jung that he wanted to show him something very interesting: 'he told me he could see an erect phallus on the sun. When he moved his head from side to side, he said, the sun's phallus moved with it, and *that was where the wind came from*.'[20] As Jung makes clear, he himself knew nothing of mythology at the time, and it was not until four years later, and after his mythological studies had begun, that he came across a book by the well-known philologist, Albrecht Dieterich, concerning a certain Greek papyrus. The text consisted of a series of instructions, invocations and visions; and in these Dieterich believed he had discovered elements of a Mithraic liturgy. One of the visions reads as follows: 'The path of the visible gods will appear through the disc of the sun, who is God my father. Likewise the so-called tube, the origin of the ministering wind. For you will see hanging down from the disc of the sun something that looks like a tube.'[21] This, then, was further evidence of an unconscious content generated outside the realm of the individual's experiences. For not only could Jung's patient have had no knowledge of this Greek papyrus, but, as Jung was to discover later, the idea of a wind-tube connected with God or the sun occurs at other times and in other places – as, for example, in the ancient idea of the procreative pneuma and in certain medieval representations of the Conception, where the fructification of Mary is depicted as a hose-pipe coming down from heaven and passing under her robes. For Jung, accordingly, these parallels could not be the purely chance coincidences of two isolated cases. They were rather empirical evidence of a common psychic and *collective* substrate, present in all of us but of a suprapersonal nature, the contents of which is expressed in universal images that have existed from the remotest times. It is true that, for a while, Jung thought that these contents might be explained by racial inheritance, and this led him to undertake various researches on the dreams of mentally deranged blacks in the USA. These, however, only confirmed his hypothesis of a collective unconscious, particularly when, in the dreams of an uneducated male, he found the ancient mythological motif of crucifixion on the sun-wheel, which can be traced as far back as the Mesolithic and Paleolithic ages. As he remarks:

> These and other experiences like them were sufficient to give me a clue: it is not a question of a specifically racial heredity, but of a universally human characteristic. Nor is it a question of *inherited ideas*, but of a functional disposition to produce the same, or very similar, ideas. This disposition I later called the *archetype*.[22]

In the next chapter I shall have much more to say about the notion of the collective unconscious and its archetypal contents. For the moment, however, it is worth pausing here to clarify two points.

1   The first has to do with Jung's definition of the psyche. From what has been said thus far, we can see that the psyche is composed of three diversified but interacting levels. These are *consciousness*, the *personal unconscious*, and the *collective unconscious*. Consciousness is that part of the mind directly accessible to the individual and contains those attitudes through which he or she adjusts to the outside world.[23] Beneath this is the personal unconscious. This, as its name suggests, is unique to the individual concerned and acquired by him during his own lifetime. Here we find not just those infantile drives and desires that Freud enumerates in his theory of repression, but more generally all psychic material that has yet to reach the threshold of consciousness but has the capacity to do so – in other words, material that Freud previously assigned to the so-called 'pre-conscious.' It contains 'lost memories, painful ideas that are repressed (i.e., forgotten on purpose), subliminal perceptions, by which are meant sense-perceptions that were not strong enough to reach consciousness, and finally, contents that are not yet ripe for consciousness.'[24] The collective unconscious, on the other hand, can be

distinguished from the personal unconscious by the fact that it does not depend on personal experience and accordingly cannot be personally acquired. In this, the deepest and most extensive stratum of the psyche, we meet a reservoir of unconscious contents that have never been in consciousness but which are rather, as the Miller case clearly indicated, *primordial images common to all humanity*. Accordingly the collective unconscious represents the impersonal and transpersonal foundation of the psyche, undergirding both consciousness and the personal unconscious. We may say, then, that the history of individuals, either in their conscious encounter with the external world or in their unconscious encounter with their own unique past, is not left unaffected by their own ancestry but rather bears witness to it in the deepest level of their psyche and by their constant repetition of the most ancient and most universal images of humanity.

2   It is also worth mentioning at this point a criticism often levelled at Jung's account of the origin of the collective unconscious. Jung was always particularly sensitive to the charge that, by describing the contents of the collective unconscious in terms of inherited primordial images, he, like Freud before him, was subscribing to the discredited Lamarckian theory of the inheritance of acquired characteristics. Certainly there are passages in which this seems to be the case, particularly when Jung talks of archetypal experiences being 'engraved' upon our psychic constitution through 'endless repetition.'[25] Elsewhere and more generally, however, Jung was adamant that his theory did not require Lamarckianism. So the term 'archetype' is not meant to denote an inherited idea, but rather an inherited mode of psychic functioning, corresponding to the inborn way in which the chick emerges from the egg, the bird builds its nest, a certain kind of wasp stings the motor ganglion of the caterpillar, and eels find their way to the Bermudas. In other words, it is a '"pattern of behaviour." This aspect of the archetype, the purely biological one, is the proper concern of scientific psychology.'[26]

What Jung has in mind, therefore, is much more akin to a theory of instincts – indeed at one point he goes so far as to suggest that the contents of the collective unconscious (the archetypes) are in fact the 'unconscious images of the instincts themselves. . . .'[27] No one denies the existence of certain instincts common to man and animals, like the reproductive instinct; and no one denies that these instincts have an hereditary and impersonal character, which set up patterns of response. Why, then, should one deny much the same of the collective unconscious? For here too we find certain dispositions of the mind, similarly developing through generations, and configuring themselves into patterns of imagination, perception and thinking. The primordial images of the collective unconscious are not, therefore, inherited in the sense that people consciously remember or have transmitted to them the images of their forebears, but are rather the predispositions or potentialities for experiencing and responding to the world in the same way that their ancestors did. Jung makes this point even clearer when, much later, he distinguishes between the 'form' and 'content' of these primordial images. What is inherited is the form alone, the capacity to create the image; but what is created, the contents, is not inherited but filled out with the material of conscious experience.[28] In this respect, the theory of the collective unconscious is, as Anthony Stevens remarks, 'biologically unimpeachable' and fully consistent with the approach adopted by ethologists studying animal behaviour.

> In this manner, our archetypal propensities have become adapted to the typical situations encountered in human life. The repeated selection of fortuitous mutations, occurring through thousands of generations and over hundreds of thousands of years, has resulted in the present genotype or archetypal structure of the human species. And this expresses itself as surely in the structure of the psyche as it does in the anatomy of the human physique.[29]

THE ENERGIC CONCEPT OF THE LIBIDO

Symbols of Transformation, in proposing a three-tiered structure of the psyche, makes quite clear Jung's dissatisfaction with the Freudian method of analysis. Freudian psychoanalysis is mainly concerned with the history of a symptom, and accordingly ascribes particular value to the repressed experiences of childhood and to the therapeutic value of bringing these experiences back into consciousness. For Jung, however, a true analysis of the individual can only begin when the contents of the personal unconscious have been exhausted and when the focus of attention can therefore shift to the collective unconscious – to those irreducible and primordial psychic images that exist in their own right. Unconscious contents are not therefore identical with repressed contents but embrace a still deeper level.

It was not, however, the novel hypothesis of the collective unconscious that caused the break with Freud. As we have seen already, Freud indeed comes very close to a similar idea himself. For example, in *The Ego and the Id* (1923), Freud is willing to allow that the experiences of the ego, if repeated often enough through successive generations, can transform themselves into 'experiences of the id, the impressions of which are preserved by inheritance.' Thus in the id 'are harboured residues of the existences of countless egos,' and these can be inherited.[30] It was not this, then, that caused the break. That came when Jung, in the second section of *Symbols of Transformation*, proceeded to attack the pivotal concept of Freudian psychology – the libido – specifically reducing its sexual component and replacing it with a more generalized notion of the libido as 'psychic energy.' As Jung makes clear, this fundamental correction came about in the first instance because an exclusively sexual interpretation could not adequately explain the phenomenon of schizophrenia. For while the repression of the sexual libido undoubtedly plays a great part in the development of neurosis, this alone could not account for a condition like schizophrenia, where far more is lacking than sexuality, where indeed the individual's whole relation to reality, including his erotic interest, disappears entirely.[31] In neurosis there is never an actual loss of reality but rather a falsification of it; but in schizophrenia, as we found with Miss Miller, the real world is replaced by a world of archaic images, the lack of adaptation to reality being compensated by a progressive increase in the creation of fantasies. But this was not all. Even more contentiously, Jung also challenges Freud's notion of infantile sexuality. For in considering how far the first traces of sexuality go back into childhood, Jung concludes that though sexuality exists implicity *ab ovo*, it only manifests itself between the first and fourth years of age and consequently after a long period of extra-uterine life. We are thus left with the conclusion that there exists a 'presexual' stage of human development, in which the central preoccupation is with the biological functions of nutrition and growth. Thus, where Freud is inclined to see in the infant's sucking at its mother's breast an essentially sexual act, Jung sees it as a nutritive function and thus initially devoid of any sexual connotations, if only because the sexual instinct is at this stage hardly developed and clearly subservient to the instinct of self-preservation. This being the case, it was impossible to explain the neuroses of children in terms of a sexual trauma occurring in a period generally characterized by an absence of any sexual function. Clinical experience of other disturbances, most notably schizophrenia and epilepsy, seemed only to confirm the existence of this presexual stage. Jung mentions two cases. In one a young girl developed a catatonic state during her engagement and, on seeing Jung for the first time, kissed him, saying, 'Papa, give me something to eat!' In another a young servant-girl complained that people were pursuing her with electricity and that this caused a queer feeling in her genitals, 'as if it ate and drank down there.'[32]

It was because Freud's notion of an exclusively sexual libido could not explain these and other functional disturbances that Jung proposes his *energic concept of the libido*, and to this we must now turn. Jung's discussion is a good example of his unfortunate style – by turns elusive, ambiguous and poetic, and which Raymond Hostie has fittingly characterized as 'more like a lyrical flight than a description of empiric fact.'[33] What follows, however, is an essential prologue to his redefinition of neurotic illness and thus, by implication, of his rejection of Freud's claim that religion is a neurosis.

As we have seen, the human psyche is composed of two complementary but antithetical dimensions – consciousness and the unconscious – the second of these being further divided into two spheres, the personal unconscious and the collective unconscious. Taken together, these three constitute what Jung calls a 'relatively closed system,' by which he means that the psyche functions as a phenomenon in its own right and generates an energy unique to itself.[34] It cannot therefore be regarded as an epiphenomenon – as a by-product of physical processes – but as a unitary, self-contained and self-regulating system. This system is characterized by constant and dynamic movement. What stimulation it does receive from outside through the senses is consumed by the psyche and converted into further psychic energy. Jung calls this psychic energy *libido*. Just as with physical energy, psychic energy or libido can only be known through its manifestations and effects, actual and potential. When actual, libido appears in the specific, dynamic phenomena of the psyche – in such things as instinct, wishing, willing, remembering, feeling and capacity for work; and when it is only potential, it manifests itself in various states, in possibilities, aptitudes and attitudes. Despite all these manifestations of libido however, the thing itself remains unknowable: we can say *that* it is but not *what* it is. In other words, libido is a *conceptual necessity* for the explanation of certain psychic phenomena, abstracted, like all scientific explanatory concepts, from experience. As Jung remarks in his Fordham lectures of 1913, 'the libido with which we operate is not only not concrete or known, but is a complete X, a pure hypothesis, a model or counter, and is no more concretely conceivable than the energy known to the world of physics.'[35]

This analysis of libido in terms of energy leads on to Jung's account of the form and direction of the movement taken within the psyche – as we shall discover, it is this which not only governs the relations between the various elements of the conscious and unconscious mind, but which, when disrupted, accounts for pathological illness. The first thing to note is that, while the libido does not move according to any set pattern, it does operate according to certain observable principles. The first of these is the *principle of opposites*. This principle, taken from Heraclitus' notion of *enantiodromia* – that sooner or later everything runs into its opposite[36] – establishes that the movement of the libido involves a constant dynamic oscillation between contrasting poles, somewhat akin to the diastole and systole of the heart, in which the amount of energy generated is in direct proportion to the presence of conflicting opposites. Various examples can be given. Love becomes hate, virtue turns into wickedness, organization degenerates into disorganization, old age longs for youth and youth for maturity. Another way of looking at this, since we are here talking about various expenditures of energy, is to describe the various directions taken by the libido in terms of the *psychic value* attributed by the individual in any given case. That is to say, 'values are quantitative estimates of energy'[37] – an observation which frequently functions as an important explanatory principle in the analysis of human conduct. When, for example, we come across a person of extreme prejudices, we can translate the values there expressed as an excess of libido. Conversely, an individual with a low estimate of himself and his opinions can be said to be suffering from a lack of libido. In both cases, the value ascribed is an indicator of libidinal energy.

In explaining the distribution of energy throughout the psyche, Jung mentions two further principles, both of which he derives from physics. These are the *principle of equivalence* and the *principle of entropy*. The principle of equivalence states that 'for a given quantity of energy expended or consumed in bringing about a certain condition, an equal quantity of the same or another form of energy will appear elsewhere.'[38] In other words, following the first law of thermodynamics (the conservation of energy), the sum total of energy within the psyche remains constant, and is susceptible neither of increase nor of decrease. Thus no energy is lost from the psyche; rather, the disappearance of a given quantum of libido is followed by the appearance of an equivalent value (or amount) in another form. What this means is this. Because we are dealing with a relatively closed system in which there is only a given quantity of energy expendable, it follows that any decrease in energy in one area of the psyche will require a corresponding increase in another, and vice versa. So, for example, as a child's attachment to the parents decreases, an equivalent value appears elsewhere and the libidinal energy may now be transferred to other substitute parents, such as a teacher or older friend; and this transference will in the long run also prove untenable as the maturing personality achieves authority, responsibility and independence. In the lifetime of the individual such transformations are the normal evidence of libidinal movement, inevitable and of almost limitless modulation, but in the treatment of neurotic illness they are of great explanatory importance. In a neurotic symptom, such as a phobia or obsession, we find the generation of an unconscious substitute, over-invested with libido, at the expense of consciousness – this disparity manifesting itself in a variety of disturbances from slight neurosis to the total dissociations found in schizophrenia. For energy lost by consciousness must, by the principle of equivalence, be transferred with equal energic force into the unconscious, that is, into either the personal unconscious or the collective unconscious. Once there, the libido transforms and activates the content of the unconscious; and thus energized, this content embarks on a life of its own and irrupts into consciousness, thereby accounting for the full range of neurotic disturbance.

While the principle of equivalence accounts for the transformations of energy within the psychic system, it does not explain the directions taken by them. For this we must turn to another and complementary principle, to the second law of thermodynamics (the principle of entropy). This law states that when two bodies of different temperatures come into contact, the flow of energy will always be from the hotter to the colder, a process which accordingly entails the heating of the colder body and the cooling of the hotter. Thus, when left to itself, what Jung calls a 'levelling process' takes place within the system and a thermal equivalence is reached,[39] with the two bodies eventually reaching the same temperature. Now, Jung continues, this same principle of entropy operates within the psychic system. Here, too, energy will always flow from a stronger to a weaker body until an equilibrium is achieved. Here, too, the libido seeks a balance of opposites. The psyche, in other words, can be viewed as a system 'in which transformations of energy lead to an equalization of differences.'[40] As we have seen, the greater the tension between the pairs of opposites, the greater the energy generated between them; but where these opposites are of unequal strength, energy will tend to pass from the stronger into the weaker until a balance is reached. Thus we speak of the 'storms of youth' yielding to the 'tranquillity of age,' the resolution of doubts into a 'confirmed belief,' and so on. In these cases, the personality is seeking a complete balance between contending forces. Since, however, the psychic system is a 'relatively closed system,' this ambition can never be fully realized and is constantly being frustrated by the energies which impinge from outside. It is this introjection of added external stimulation which creates imbalances, and replaces the feelings of quiescence with feelings of tension and conflict. Under normal conditions this new energy can be assimilated within the psyche without causing serious disruption. Alternatively, others may develop different strategies to protect themselves: they may shut their minds to anything other than their own prejudices, remove themselves from fresh experiences and thus come close to an entropic state. More drastically, in situations where the psyche has already lost its equilibrium through an uneven distribution of energy, and where outside influences cannot adequately be dealt with, the individual may protect him or herself by withdrawing from reality altogether. This condition may explain the so-called 'dulling of affect' in schizophrenia, where all connection with the environment is severed. Equally, and at the other end of the scale, the flow of psychic energy from one structure to another can, like the flow of water, be dammed up and so reversed. Thus what was already strong becomes stronger still and the personality becomes one-sided in its functions. But such individuals are always inherently unstable. For whatever stability may be achieved, the danger always remains that the stronger impulse will finally succumb through the operation of the entropy principle. This explains why someone of dominant personality can suddenly change in character and become subservient and submissive. The libidinal energy that has been amassed in such large quantities on one side of the psyche has suddenly shifted and been deposited in its opposite.

Jung clarifies the directions here taken by the libido with the help of two additional concepts. If, by analogy, we take the transfer of energy to be somewhat akin to the movement of water, then the natural movement of the libido is forwards and backwards. Jung calls this forward movement, which satisfies the needs of the conscious, *progression*, and the backward movement, which satisfies the needs of the unconscious, *regression*. Progression, to be more precise, takes place when the psyche adjusts to the ever-changing demands of the environment, when the individual's mental habits adapt to the needs of external reality. We can see this happening, for example, when new information requires an alteration in a firmly held attitude, when a difficult decision is required through force of circumstance. But what happens when this process becomes impossible – when, for whatever reason, the flow of libidinal energy is halted in its progressive movement? Then, says Jung, the flow is reversed, regression occurs, and the energy previously directed outwards is now directed inwards, down into the levels of the unconscious. Thus it is that the unconscious becomes over-charged with energy, the decrease in value of the psyche's conscious activity being in proportion to an increase in its unconscious processes. Gradually consciousness becomes inundated by the contents of the unconscious and there appear from below all those elements – what Jung calls 'slime from the depths'[41] – which Freud has classically defined as the main causes of neurosis: primarily those of an infantile-sexual character, together with those incompatible and rejected remnants of everyday life that are the focus of repression.

This, however, is far from being the whole story, and here Jung makes a crucial amendment to this Freudian schema. While it is true that the autonomous forces of the unconscious, if not held in check, may in extreme cases swamp the conscious to the point where a psychosis develops, this is not to say that the psyche is to be forever safeguarded from the unconscious contents that are dredged up by the process of regression. Quite the reverse, in fact. *For the regression of psychic energy reactivates the contents of the unconscious and thus reveals the possibilities of renewal and regeneration that lie within them.* This makes quite clear that regression, far from being a retrograde step in the sense of a backwards degeneration, is a *necessary step* in the development of the human personality.

To understand the important point that Jung is making here, we should remember that in all the examples of neurotic illness given thus far, neurosis is characterized by a lack of balance within the structure of the psyche. Sometimes, it is true, the origin of the illness can be traced to infantile traumas of a sexual nature – as Jung remarks, 'no experienced psychotherapist can deny having met with dozens of cases whose psychology answers in all essentials to that of Freud'[42] – but to suggest for that reason that sexuality is the sole origin of neurosis is an unjustified and fantastic generalization, tantamount to discussing 'Cologne Cathedral in a text-book of mineralogy, on the ground that it consisted very largely of stones.'[43] More accurately, then, we should categorize neurosis as a *disturbance within the distribution of libidinal energy*, as a failure to achieve a balance of opposites, as a failure in reciprocity, if you will, between the progressive demands of the conscious mind and the regressive demands of the unconscious.

If, then, neurosis is inherently *a dissociation of the psyche*, an inner cleavage between the conscious and the unconscious in which the patient remains at war with himself, it follows that the therapeutic ambition is to resolve this disharmony, which is the real basis of neurosis, by confronting the contents of consciousness with those of the unconscious, to provoke thereby an interaction between them in order to achieve a proper equilibrium. Jung cites innumerable examples of this process. Take, for example, the case of the man whose neurosis lay in an imbalance between the opposites of thinking and feeling. So intellectual was he that he could understand quite clearly Jung's explanation of why he should fantasize about his fiancée's suicide, but understanding produced no alleviation of his depression. Why? The reason, explains Jung, was because the man could not yield to his unconscious, had become so caught in a conflict of opposites that the 'feeling' side of his psyche had to assert itself in the fantasies that assailed him. Following the law of energy, displacement of libido had taken place, and value had accumulated in his unconscious and held him fast in its fantasy-images.

too rational

> The conscious attitude of my patient is so one-sidedly intellectual and rational that nature herself rises up against him and annihilates his whole world of conscious values. But he cannot de-intellectualize himself and make himself dependent on another function, e.g., feeling, for the very reason that he has not got it. The unconscious has it. Therefore we have no alternative but to hand over the leadership to the unconscious and give it the opportunity of becoming a conscious content in the form of fantasies. If, formerly, my patient clung to his intellectual world and defended himself with rationalizations against what he regarded as his illness, he must now yield himself up to it entirely, and when a fit of depression comes upon him, he must no longer force himself to some kind of work in order to forget, but must accept his depression and give it a hearing.[44]

What the patient, in other words, is enjoined to do is follow the path of his neurosis, to let himself be led into the world of his unconscious by the very thing that torments him. Considered from this viewpoint, a regression represents an attempt to activate in the unconscious that which has been excluded from the conscious attitude, to redress the balance of the psyche. Thus, if thinking fails in its adaptation to the outside world because it is dealing with a situation to which one can adapt only by feeling, then the unconscious material activated by regression will contain the missing feeling function. Conversely, regression will activate a thinking function in order to compensate an inadequate feeling function. This process operates along the whole range of functions and attitudes, and is to be seen not just in the functions of thinking and feeling but also in those of sensation and intuition and in the basic attitudes of extraversion and introversion.[45] These functions and attitudes combine to form a whole range of personality types, and each type has a tendency to develop a particular form of neurosis. The extraverted-feeling type is predisposed to hysteria, the introverted-feeling type to neurasthenia, the sensation types to phobias, compulsions and obsessions. But however diverse these pathologies, they all have a common cause and a common cure: they result from a disturbance of psychic balance, from a disruption within the flow of libidinal energy, and this can only be restored

different types different illness

107

by integrating both parts of the psyche, consciousness and the unconscious, into a dynamic and reciprocal unity. In this sense, then, whatever form the neurosis takes it points to its own therapy: it unlocks the inner world of the psyche and brings to the surface those elements which will establish a new equilibrium within the personality. Jung calls this therapeutic procedure the 'process of individuation,' and I shall return to it in Chapter 9.

SOME DIFFERENCES BETWEEN FREUD AND JUNG ON RELIGION

We have now traversed some of the most complex aspects of Jung's analytical psychology; and it may be helpful at this point to summarize our findings so far, and to begin, if only in a rudimentary way, to relate them to the matter of religion. Once again the most instructive comparison is between Jung and Freud. As will be remembered, *Totem and Taboo* contains Freud's first speculations on the correspondences between certain neurotic-obsessional rituals and the totemic observances of primitive tribes. Following these comparisons, Freud goes on to argue, in both *The Future of an Illusion* and *Moses and Monotheism*, that religious phenomena are similarly symptoms of neurosis, and, to be more specific, of a neurosis related to the unconscious sexual anxieties of children in relation to their parents (the Oedipus complex). These neuroses may be understood in two ways: either as proceeding from the individual and ontogenetic experiences of each one of us, or as common inheritances descending from the phylogenetic reactions of former generations – these forming the 'archaic heritage of mankind' and proceeding from the experiences of the primal horde.

What does Jung make of this? There are, I think, five points to be borne in mind.

1   The first thing to say is that *Jung rejects Freud's definition of religion as a sexual neurosis*. For even if we were to accept, for the purposes of argument, that religion is a neurosis, this does not mean that we have to accept that it is a neurosis of a particular type. As far as Jung is concerned, this equation is not merely a mistake on Freud's part but a logical blunder, an example of *petitio principii*, the fallacy of begging the question.[46] For the issue to settle first, the logically prior question, is not whether religion as a neurosis is sexual, but whether neurosis is sexual – whether Freud's general classification of this whole *class* of mental disturbance of which, it is alleged, religious neurosis is an instance, is correct. As we have seen, Jung's disavowal of Freud at this point proceeds from his own presentation of an energic concept of libido, which strips Freud's use of the concept of its exclusively sexual connotation, and thus allows for its application to a much wider range of mental illnesses, many of which, according to Jung, cannot otherwise be explained in Freudian

terms (e.g., schizophrenia). Freud, therefore, was not wrong to see sexuality as a cause of a neurosis but he was wrong to see it as the origin of all neuroses.

2   A second point follows on from this, namely, that *Jung rejects Freud's account of the mechanism of religious neurosis*. For Freud the primary mechanism of neurosis is the *repression* of infantile sexual impulses. Here certain emotionally charged events, ideas or fantasies are excluded from consciousness because of their sexually painful, immoral, anti-social or repugnant character and, thus disowned and unable to find direct expression and discharge, they give rise to neurotic symptoms. In the case of religion, the sexual character of the neurosis is best seen in the obsessional form of religious ritual, in which the believer seeks to assuage his sense of Oedipal guilt in relation to the father. For Jung, however, this account, as a general description of religious practice, cannot be correct. Again, this is not because religion can never be neurotic in Freudian terms – there are clearly cases of religious behaviour in which repression best fits the facts – but because it is not the sexual instinct alone, but rather an imbalance within the distribution of psychic energy, that is responsible for the formation of neuroses. In other words, the sexual impulse is but one instance of the energic transformation of libido, and cannot therefore stand as the sole dynamic of neurosis. This being the case, it follows that religion, like any other human disposition, will be neurotic when it upsets the psychic equilibrium, when it disrupts the flow of libidinal energy and fails to integrate the conscious and unconscious dimensions of the personality. It also follows, however, that religion will not be neurotic if no such disruption takes place, if it displays a harmonious conjunction of the disparate sides of the psyche, the conscious and the unconscious. Should this occur, the study of religious experience cannot be regarded as the analysis of sexual sublimation and repression but as the study of a fundamental, natural and therapeutic psychic process, in which the individual seeks self-knowledge, self-regulation and self-fulfilment.

3   A third point to note is that *Jung denies Freud's exclusively negative account of religion as a neurosis*. For Freud, as we have seen so often, the neurosis of religion is generated on the basis of a conflict between the conscious and unconscious mind, in which individuals in the act of repression refuse to admit the infantile and Oedipal impulses that fuel their obsessions. To acknowledge these impulses and their past associations thus becomes the first step in the defeat of this particular illness. For Jung, however, this assessment of religion is fundamentally misconceived. For it assumes that a neurosis, whether its form is religious or not, *has no positive attributes*, and that the unconscious is no more than a lumber-room of uncomfortable material drawn from the patient's infantile past – of thoughts and impulses so feared that repression becomes necessary. But this is not the case. Far from being negative, neurosis can also be a positive step in psychic development

by unlocking, in the process of *regression*, the deepest and most creative level of the unconscious mind, namely the collective unconscious. Thus Freud's denunciation of religion, far from fostering individual maturity, aggressively blocks it. For so concerned is he to find the biological root of this neurosis, and to locate it within the Oedipal experiences of the personal unconscious, that he has entirely overlooked religion's more positive, profound and therapeutically necessary focus, which is upon the collective, primordial and archetypal images of humanity.

4   A fourth, and perhaps less obvious, implication of Jung's shift away from sexual repression as the determinative factor in mental illness, is that *he denies Freud's exclusively retrospective account of religion as a neurosis*. Freud locates the cause of neurosis back to the sexual impulses of childhood, and it is these impulses, once constellated within the obsessions of religion, that demarcate religion as infantile. For Jung, by contrast, this classification could only work if the past-historical movement of the libido is exclusively sexual and determinative for all its subsequent formations – a conclusion which would in fact render Jung's energic concept of the libido entirely static. The system of the psyche, we remember, is only a *relatively* closed system, and in part draws its energy from being open to new and external experiences – from the demand to adapt the unconscious to changing environmental conditions. This being the case, the cause of neurosis cannot be exclusively sexual – indeed, in its earliest manifestations, the psyche will be more concerned with channelling itself into the biological functions of nutrition and growth – but is much more likely to depend on a lack of equilibrium engendered by a much wider range of influences and by the patient's attitude to them in both their present and future situation; not, then, on their perception of what has happened but of what is happening or may happen. To dismiss religion because it is infantile is thus to ignore its *present and prospective character*, and to fail to see that it may also be expressive of an attempt to integrate the conscious and unconscious aspects of the psyche under the changing conditions of the life, to nurture the psychic balance of the individual not just for the present but through all the vicissitudes of later experience. That said, religion, far from being neurotic, is revealed as a constant and evolving process in the development of the psychic personality.

5   Each of the four points I have mentioned so far meet together in a final and more general point. This is that *Jung rejects Freud's account of the symbolic character of religious phenomena*. For Freud the symbol, no matter how it may appear in language or ritual, is a static representative of a symptom causally connected with a repressed impulse, that is, it can be decoded on the assumption that its primary function is the concealment of something within the unconscious. Thus Freud interprets the symbols of religion *semiotically*, as signs of something else that can be rationally explained, and explained

110

within the context of our infantile and Oedipal desires. This, after all, was the method employed in *Totem and Taboo*, where the forms and practices of totemic religion can be unmasked as organized sexual repressions, as neurotic because they involve the renunciation of things desired. For Jung, however, this procedure is almost entirely inappropriate, and in its preoccupation with scientific and causal explanation, is a good example of 'reality-thinking' – Jung's only concession being, as before, that sexual repression can, in certain quite specific cases, be the cause of religious obsession and can therefore generate overtly sexual imagery. And yet, even when religion does employ such imagery, the question still remains: is this imagery *symptomatic or symbolic?* Is it, in other words, no more than a disguise for an impulse or is it a symbol of something else – of something operating on a level beyond that of personal desire? Jung's answer is that it is invariably symbolic, and for the reasons already given. Religion does not primarily signify the repression of a sexual and infantile impulse but rather the energic movement of the libido towards the deepest layer of the psyche, in which reside the universal and primordial images of the collective unconscious. Thus religious symbols are revealed as expressions of a *form of regressive experience* or, to put the matter differently, as *manifestations of collective contents*. And, to that extent, they open up a psychic level that completely eludes rational definition, that is primordial and independent of personal experience but which is nevertheless *of supreme value for the present and future development of the human psyche.* The symbol, we may say, is the pre-eminent creation of 'fantasy-thinking,' and by it Jung can demonstrate a fundamental identity between, say, the schizoid dreams of a Miss Miller, the rituals of a religion, and the myths of the most ancient and primitive cultures. For however differentiated, the symbol is a revelation of our inner psychic life, not of our creation but autonomous – a spontaneous and unreflective formulation of certain irreducible, universal and timeless images.

All the points that I have listed here are contained, admittedly in various guises, in *Symbols of Transformation*, and they make clear the completeness of Jung's break with Freud that was occasioned by its publication in 1912. For whatever Jung's concessions to Freudian orthodoxy, he could not conceal, and indeed had no wish to conceal, his very real doubts about the notion of an exclusively sexual libido, particularly when applied to religion. Indeed, as Jung saw it, the caricature of religion that results is further evidence of the erroneous nature of the concept.

I have said earlier that Freud *sexualizes* religion: religion is a neurotic expression of sexual repression.[47] For Jung, this conclusion is symptomatic of Freud's inability to see beyond his own sexual theory and to realize that the human libido is motivated by more than this biological drive: that, indeed, it is also governed by the necessity to experience a more universal, timeless and collective aspect of the unconscious mind. Religion, in this sense, is expressive of this experience. In repudiating religion, therefore, Freud has not merely misunderstood its function but, more seriously, denied the existence of a whole dimension of the unconscious – the collective unconscious – which is the one dimension, indeed, that allows human beings some intuition of the ultimate meaning of life.

8

GOD AS ARCHETYPE OF THE COLLECTIVE UNCONSCIOUS

Jung's earliest discussions on the existence of God are distinctly Freudian. Freud, of course, was delighted. One of his letters to Jung (of 1 September 1911) concludes with an exultant 'Bravo!' on receiving further evidence that his young colleague had become 'aware that the Oedipus complex is at the root of religious feeling.'[1] And there was ample evidence for Freud's satisfaction. Between 1909 and 1911 Jung wrote a series of five articles very much in the Freudian mode and in one of these – 'The Significance of the Father in the Destiny of the Individual' (1909) – he not only endorses Freud's claim that 'all "divine" figures have their roots in the father-imago,' but goes on to sketch a brief history of religion based on this premiss.

> The religion of the Old Testament exalted the paterfamilias into the Jehovah of the Jews, whom the people had to obey in fear and dread. The patriarchs were a stepping-stone to the Deity. The neurotic fear in Judaism, an imperfect or at any rate unsuccessful attempt at sublimation by a still too barbarous people, gave rise to the excessive severity of Mosaic law, the compulsive ceremonial of the neurotic.[2]

We have seen, however, that by the end of 1912 matters stood very differently. The friendship with Freud had only a few weeks to run, and passages like the one I have just quoted were deleted from later editions. What precipitated this change was the publication of the second part of *Symbols of Transformation*. For here Jung had not only 'desexualized' Freud's concept of the libido to the point where the Oedipus complex could no longer operate as the exclusive generative force in the formation of a religious neurosis – or indeed of any neurosis – but, equally dramatically, he had replaced Freud's idea of a sexual libido with his own much more inclusive concept of an 'energic libido.' This allowed for an altogether different perception of religion. Religion need no longer be perceived as a conglomerate of guilt-ridden repressions and ritualized obsessions, but as a natural and legitimate dimension of psychic activity. This does not mean, of course, that religious experience can never be neurotic. Neurosis, as a symptom of libidinal

113

imbalance, can occur in this area of life as in any other. But it does mean that where specific examples of religious neurosis do exist, these examples can no longer be used to characterize all religious phenomena. Religious activity, as a distinct class of activity, may contain instances of obsessive conduct but these instances do not themselves decide the nature of the class as a whole.

In many ways Jung's own analysis of religion begins at this point. For once we jettison Freud, once we realize that the worship of God can no longer be explained in terms of a fantasy substitute for the earthly father, then we must look elsewhere for an explanation of the nature and content of religious belief. The question becomes not so much whether religion has father-images, but rather what other explanation can be given for their occurrence and for their continuing hold upon the human imagination. Jung's answer to these questions is, as we shall now discover, quite specific and to the point: God's reality is that of the archetypal father of the collective unconscious. God, so conceived, is an irreducible and inescapable psychic reality, experienced by the individual in the deepest level of his being. Quite how Jung arrives at this conclusion is, however, a matter of considerable complexity.

THE ARCHETYPES OF THE COLLECTIVE UNCONSCIOUS

The first thing to do is to remind ourselves of Jung's most important and radical claim so far. This is that there exists, in addition to the personal unconscious, a still deeper level of the unconscious mind, the collective unconscious, which is of an impersonal and universal character and which is thus identical in all of us. The collective unconscious, we should stress again, is not therefore dependent on the personal history of the individual: it is not something acquired by us during our lifetime but is rather something 'suprapersonal,' preceding us in time and containing the 'primordial images' of our ancestral life. It is, accordingly, 'a great mistake to suppose that the psyche of a new-born child is a *tabula rasa* in the sense that there is nothing in it.'[3] Rather, every infant, like every adult, is determined by influences emanating from the collective unconscious; and these influences, operating independently of the personal unconscious, guarantee in every single individual a similarity and even a sameness of experience and representation. We should stress again that in making this claim, Jung is not attempting to *prove* the existence of the collective unconscious: he rather assumes its existence as part of his working hypothesis to explain the almost *universal parallelism* of imagery in, for example, the dreams of children, the fantasies of neurotics, the schizoid visions of a Miss Miller and, at the ethnological level, the mythologies of primitive cultures.

Jung takes his next important step when he turns to consider more exactly the contents of the collective unconscious. *The contents of the collective unconscious are called archetypes.* As we have seen, Jung first introduces the concept of the archetype, if not the term, in *Symbols of Transformation* (1912) where he speaks of 'primordial images' to designate the myths, legends and fairy-tale motifs that characterize universal modes of human perception and behaviour;[4] and it appears again in *Two Essays on Analytical Psychology* (1916) as 'dominants' of the collective unconscious.[5] But it is not until 1919, in his essay 'Instinct and the Unconscious,' that Jung makes specific use of the term.[6] Plato is credited with the discovery of the concept – the word 'archetype' being taken as an 'explanatory paraphrase' of the platonic 'idea' (*eidos*), of which all existent things are imitations. Other uses occur as early as Philo Judaeus with reference to the *Imago Dei* (God-image) of man, and can also be found in Irenaeus and Dionysius the Areopagite. Saint Augustine also employs the concept when he speaks of *ideae principales* – ideas which are themselves not formed but are contained in the divine understanding. A more recent variant is to be found in the work of the French anthropologist, Lucien Lévy-Bruhl (1857–1939), who coined the term 'représentations collectives' to indicate those socio-cultural forms which are imposed upon the primitive mind while yet pre-existing and surviving the individual members of the tribe.[7] From these and other references it becomes clear that for Jung his concept of the archetype does not stand alone but is something that is recognized and named in other fields of knowledge. But whatever the varieties of usage, the idea underlying them is essentially the same. The archetypes are those pre-existent forms or primordial types that have existed since the remotest times of humanity. This does not, however, mean that they are forms or types consigned merely to the past. For the archetypal images, precisely because there are images emanating from the depths of the collective unconscious, are manifestations *of the structural nature of the psyche itself*, and thus expressive of a universal and common substratum which is present in all human beings and constantly and dynamically operative. This has the further implication that the archetypes are not, as Freud might claim, *exclusively symptoms of neurotic states*. As Jung remarks: 'it must constantly be borne in mind that the constellation of archetypal images and fantasies is not in itself pathological.'[8] While conditions like schizophrenia may therefore provide the occasion for the appearance of archetypes in an acute and dramatic form, this is not to say that these conditions alone bring archetypes into being. Indeed, to suppose as much is to adopt once again the mistaken Freudian doctrine of causation, which claims that any unconscious fantasy must be the product of repression. Archetypes, to repeat, are constituent elements of the unconscious mind; and the fact that they are essentially archaic in character, while yet constantly manifesting themselves under present conditions, does not indicate a neurotic reversion to an out-moded form of thought, but rather – and much more interestingly – that 'every civilized human being, however high his conscious development, is still an archaic man at the deeper levels of his psyche.'[9]

As many commentators have pointed out,[10] Jung's discussion at this point remains highly ambiguous, and this becomes particularly evident when we come on to the innumerable examples he gives of archetypes. We have, for instance, the archetype of the Mother, observed not just in the goddesses of religion but, amongst others, in the recurring symbols of fertility and fruitfulness (the cornucopia, a ploughed field, a garden).[11] We have the widespread archetype of the Child God, evident in the miraculous birth-stories of Jesus and Moses, in the visions of Meister Eckhart and the poetry of William Blake, and also in the fairy-stories of the king's son or witch's child possessed of daemonic powers.[12] We have the archetype of the Hero embodied in the various hero-cycles prevalent in almost every culture, in which the brave individual is not devoured by the monster but subdues it and thus obtains the prize (David and Goliath, Hercules and the Lion, Theseus and the Minotaur). These are just three examples, but Jung lists many others, often given in personified form. In addition to the archetypal figures just mentioned, there are archetypal events (e.g., birth, creation, death, marriage, betrayal) and archetypal objects (e.g., the dragon, snake, sphinx, helpful animals).[13] The question is: When Jung defines the 'contents' of the collective unconscious as archetypal, does he mean that archetypes like the Mother or Child God are 'inherited ideas' – images passed on and duplicated through the generations without substantial variation – or does he mean that the archetype determines only the 'form' of these images, acting therefore as a kind of template for all subsequent representations? Are we talking here of the transmission of replicas or of something less specific, of the transmission of a disposition? Jung was well aware of this confusion and replies in detail:

> Again and again I encounter the mistaken notion that an archetype is determined in regard to its content, in other words that it is a kind of unconscious idea (if such an expression be admissible). It is necessary to point out once more that archetypes are not determined as regards their content, but only as regards their form and then only to a very limited degree. A primordial image is determined as to its contents only when it has become conscious and is therefore filled out with the material of conscious experience. Its form, however, as I have explained elsewhere, might perhaps be compared to the axial system of a crystal, which, as it were, preforms the crystalline structure in the mother liquid, although it has no material existence of its own. This first appears according to the specific way in which the ions and molecules aggregate. The archetype in itself is empty and purely formal, nothing but a *facultas praeformandi*, a possibility of representation which is given *a priori*. The representations themselves are not inherited, only the forms, and in that respect they correspond in every way to the instincts, which are also determined in form only. The existence of the instincts can no more be proved than the existence of the archetypes, so long as they do not manifest themselves concretely. . . . The same is true of the arche-

type. In principle, it can be named and has an invariable nucleus of meaning – but always only in principle, never as regards its concrete manifestations. In the same way, the specific appearance of the mother-image at any given time cannot be deduced from the mother archetype alone, but depends on innumerable other factors.[14]

In one respect, this goes some way towards clarifying what an archetype is. An archetype arises from the *a priori* structure of the psyche, its 'form' being an inborn predisposition or tendency of the psyche to create an image of a universal and uniform character. This is not to say, however, that the image thus created – the 'content' of the archetype – is similarly of a universal and uniform character. For while the 'form' may be innate to the psyche, the manner in which this is expressed, its concrete manifestation, will be diverse and will depend much more on individual and social experience. Indeed, if this were not the case, we could not account for the great variety of ways in which the same archetypal image is presented in all periods of history, in symbol, myth and ritual. But an ambiguity still remains, and this has to do with the origin of archetypes. If the archetypal 'form' is part of the *a priori* structure of the psyche, what are we then to make of Jung's other remarks to the effect that archetypes are 'the precipitate of the psychic functioning of the whole ancestral line; the accumulated experiences of organic life in general, a million times repeated, and condensed into types'?[15] Granted that the particular 'content' of the archetype is a product of experience, can this not be said also of its 'form,' that this too has been acquired through the accumulated experience of centuries? Although aware of this difficulty, Jung's response is still equivocal. 'The images,' he writes, 'are "primordial" images in so far as they are peculiar to whole species, and if they ever "originated" their origin must have coincided at least with the beginning of the species.'[16] This is tantamount to saying that archetypes are not the creation of recurring experiences, and gives credence to Joland Jacobi's statement that they 'exist *a priori* . . . are inherent in the collective unconscious, and hence unaffected by individual growth and decay.'[17] In another passage, however, Jung sidesteps the problem altogether: 'Whether this psychic structure and its elements, the archetypes, ever "originated" at all is a metaphysical question and therefore unanswerable.'[18] This does not prevent Jung from concluding that the archetype is metaphysical because it is an 'eternal presence' and because it 'transcends consciousness.'[19]

This answer, Jung adds, recalls Kant's famous discussion of the *a priori*, in his *Critique of Pure Reason* (1781).[20] For Kant the objects of experience ('phenomena') are unknowable without the imposition by the mind of such categories as space, time and causality: these are the *a priori* forms to which all our experience must conform, and it is accordingly impossible to perceive any object as a thing-in-itself ('noumenon'), that is, apart from the categories. Thus it is that the organizing mind participates in the construction of the phenomenal world; and here too we must distinguish between the form of a judgment and its content, between the pattern that is permanent and the individual experiences which constantly change. Jung adopts much the same argument:

> It should on no account be imagined that there are such things as *inherited ideas*. Of that there can be no question. There are, however, innate possibilities of ideas, *a priori* conditions for fantasy-production which are somewhat similar to the Kantian categories. Though these innate conditions do not produce any contents themselves, they give definite form to the contents that have already been acquired.[21]

Archetypes are therefore the 'unconscious organizers of our ideas,'[22] representing only the 'possibility of a certain type of perception and action,'[23] the 'uniform and regularly recurring modes of apprehension';[24] but the archetypes themselves can only be observed in their manifestations not independently of them. 'What we mean by "archetype" is in itself irrepresentable, but has effects which make visualizations of it possible, namely, the archetypal images and ideas.'[25] The contents of the archetypes therefore belong to the phenomenal world; but of the archetype itself – of the form without content – nothing can be known because 'of what lies beyond the phenomenal world we can have absolutely no idea.'[26] The claim, therefore, that archetypes exist as *a priori* categories of the psyche depends on an inductive inference drawn from the constant appearance of certain motifs and patterns in human experience. Their existence, as Jung never tires of saying, is in this respect like the existence of the collective unconscious and the libido, namely, a *conceptual necessity* required to explain the patterns and repetitions of psychic phenomena.

While theoretically there is no limit to the number of archetypes, practically speaking some are more important than others, and Jung gives systematic treatment to five in particular. These are the Persona, the Shadow, the Anima and Animus, and the Self. I shall deal with these in some detail because they provide the clearest illustration of what Jung means by an archetype. We will then be in a better position to see how Jung then applies this concept, without any great modification, to the concept of God.[27]

The Persona

The term 'persona' originally referred to the mask worn by actors to indicate their role in a play; and the archetype indicates much the same psychological tendency, that is, an individual's concern to conceal what he really is for the sake of what society thinks he ought to be. The Persona, accordingly, is an example of 'feigned individuality' in which the controlling influence is social expectation: for example, 'a man who is a parson must not only carry out his functions objectively, but must at all times and in all circumstances play the role of parson in a flawless manner.'[28] These pretences can bring great advantages – for example, the individual is not thought unpredictable or unreliable and his career flourishes – but also great disadvantages. For the Persona is equally a 'very fruitful source of neuroses,'[29] particularly when the artificial personality dominates to the point where all other and more typical characteristics are suppressed. This generates the imbalance that is the nucleus of neurosis: the individual becomes persona-ridden, literally 'inflated' with his own public image of himself, either inflexible or too malleable, either suffering delusions of grandeur or of insignificance, but in all cases becoming incapable of relating to the other and complementary sides of his personality. All these examples indicate adequate or inadequate relationships to the Persona archetype; and here we see the Persona, as an archetype, operating as a structural component of the psyche, thus guaranteeing that each one of us, irrespective of time or place, will meet the same conflict between personal need and public expectation. And for the same reason, the Persona guarantees the constant repetition of the same images to represent itself. So, as examples of social submission, Whitmont quotes the recurring dreams of being unable to take off one's clothes or of being stuck in heavy armour; and as examples of a refusal to adapt, the dreams of being at a party stark naked, of being in filthy rags at a reception, and so on.[30]

The Shadow

In contrast to the Persona, the archetype of the Shadow designates that side of an individual that he or she prefers not to reveal. It consists of the dark, unadapted or repressed parts of oneself, or, in Jung's words, of 'everything that the subject refuses to acknowledge about himself and yet is always thrusting itself upon him directly or indirectly – for instance, inferior traits of character and other incompatible tendencies.'[31] As the personification of, amongst other things, the human capacity for evil, the Shadow is suppressed because it is considered alien to one's own Persona, either because it embodies qualities that are contrary to one's conscious moral principles, or to what society disapproves of, or because it calls up impulses born of the instinctual and animal side of human nature. This suppression, however, can lead to psychic imbalance and so to the creation of an artifical, neurotic and one-sided personality. The Shadow has therefore to be assimilated, no matter how unwilling the individual may be to expose the darker side of his character, because indeed to deny the Shadow is to deny a structural element of the psyche and thus a part of one's total self. As with the Persona, the Shadow, as an archetypal form, manifests itself in a great variety of ways. For example, it can appear individually in the shape of a person said to embody evil (e.g., a mother-in-law, an estranged wife, an unruly neighbour), but it is equally apparent in a more general form, for instance in the ancient mythologies of the fiend, the tempter, the evil power, the Titans or Satan. Fiction has conjured many images of the Shadow: Shakespeare's Caliban, Mrs Shelley's Franken-stein, Oscar Wilde's Dorian Grey, Stevenson's Mr Hyde.[32]

Anima and Animus

The Anima and Animus archetypes stand for the contrasexual side of the psyche – the Anima is the feminine side of the male, the Animus the masculine side of the female – and just as we usually experience our Shadow through someone else, so we experience our own attributes of the opposite sex through another person. In the male, for example, the Anima is first encountered in the mother, just as in the female the Animus is first met in the father, and subsequently his Anima will be projected on to those females who awaken positive or negative feelings within him. So if he feels strongly attracted to someone, the object of his desire will invariably be a female who possesses the same characteristics as his own Anima-image. Conversely, if he experiences antipathy or aversion, this is because the woman possesses qualities that conflict with his Anima-image. Seen in this light, therefore, the Animus and Anima become indispensable for the selection of a mate and thus for the survival of the species, although, as with all psychic structures, the possibility of imbalance remains, the male accentuating his female character-istics, thereby becoming more possessive and submissive, or the female her male characteristics, thereby becoming more competitive and aggressive. As archetypes, Anima and Animus appear in a great variety of images. The Anima, for example, can take the form of a pure virgin, a goddess or a seductress, or appear in mythological figures like Eve, Kundry and Androm-eda, or in fictional heroines like Helen of Troy or Dulcinea. Typical Animus representations are the Hero or Wise Man, Dionysus or the Flying Dutch-man, ranging down to a friend or seducer. Both may also appear as animals or objects: the Anima perhaps as a cow, cat, ship or cave, the Animus as an eagle, bull, lance or tower. All these, we should remind ourselves, are the *contents* of the archetypes, not the archetypes themselves. They are the phenomenal *effects* of the mind's *a priori* disposition to express itself in terms of Anima and Animus.[33]

The Self

The Self is the most important, and yet most elusive, structural component of the psyche. To understand what Jung means by it, it is worth repeating that, for Jung, the system of the psyche is not a fixed or static system but a dynamic one, a system subject to a constant process of interaction and change. In the previous chapter, we saw this in Jung's claim that psychic energy operates according to the principle of opposites (*enantiodromia*), and further, that neurosis arises from a failure to achieve a proper equilibrium be-tween the disparate sides of the psyche – between the conscious and the unconscious.[34] Psychic balance, however, is not only therapeutically in-dispensable. We also saw that the integration of conscious and unconscious contents, quite apart from its beneficial effect, constitutes a task or goal to which all human beings, with greater or lesser degrees of success, devote themselves; that, in other words, the very disjunction between the conscious and unconscious sets up a demand within each of us to overcome it, to synthesize these disparate elements. The goal of psychic balance is thus intrinsic to the psyche itself, its irreducible prospective component, its life's purpose, as it were. And this is best indicated by the fact that this direction of the psyche towards its goal of wholeness is itself archetypal, that is, it is an aim that is an *a priori* human disposition, and that *the archetype of wholeness is the archetype of the Self*. The Self is accordingly 'our life's goal, for it is the completest expression of that fateful combination we call individuality. . . .'[35] The beginnings of 'our whole psychic life seem to be inextricably rooted in this point, and all our highest and ultimate purposes seem to be striving towards it.'[36] What we have here then is an archetype of psychic integration which confronts the individual as an inner guiding factor, as an innate teleological and psychic component, but which, like the other archetypes, presents itself not in its 'form' but only in its phenomenal 'contents.' The Self therefore manifests itself in dreams, images and visions of many and varied types. Archetypes of the Self can be seen, for example, in human or animal figures of power and prestige (kings or queens, the lion, the bear), in suprapersonal entities (gods and goddesses, the sun, nature, the universe), in outstanding religious personalities (Christ, Buddha), in plant symbols (the lotus and rose), in inanimate objects (a jewel, a ball, a chalice), and so on. Symbols of the Self also appear as geometric figures (the circle, the sphere, the square, the quaternity, the clock) and as mandalas.[37] The last-named was of particular importance for Jung, and he wrote about them extensively. Derived from the Sanskrit word for 'magic circle,' the mandala is a design based on a perfectly balanced square or circle, in which the mid-point is given particular prominence. Although found in the art of the Western Middle Ages and Renaissance – the depiction, for instance, of Christ surrounded by the four evangelists is one example[38] – the most impressive mandalas are to be found in Tibetan Buddhism. Although Jung gives many illustrations of mandalas, and drew many himself, their central motif remains an archetype of the Self. They involve, as he makes clear, a 'premonition of a centre of personality, a kind of central point within the psyche. . . . This centre . . . is the *self*.'[39]

If the mandala is the archetype of the Self most frequently invoked by Jung, it is by no means the most extraordinary. That distinction undoubtedly belongs to medieval Hermetic philosophy or *alchemy*. Jung's interest in alchemy began in 1927, when the distinguished Frankfurt sinologist, Richard Wilhelm, sent him the manuscript of a Taoist alchemical text entitled *The Secret of the Golden Flower*. From then on Jung enthusiastically devoted himself to a study of alchemy, amassing a huge collection of alchemical texts, and producing in 1944 his remarkable *Psychology and Alchemy*.[40] Space forbids a detailed account of Jung's research in this area but it is sufficient for our purposes to note that it was not the alchemical attempt to transmute base substances into gold that fascinated Jung, but rather that alongside this chemical aspect lay a psychological one, in which the union of opposites was sought through the agency of the 'philosopher's stone.' The quest for the *lapis philosophorum* may thus be read as another archetype of the Self, and so as another attempt to express in concrete form the desire for psychic integration. The secret of alchemy lies therefore, says Jung, 'in the transformation of personality through the blending and fusion of the noble with the base components, of the differentiated with the inferior functions, of the conscious with the unconscious.'[41]

Let us now take stock. As I said at the outset, Jung's discussion of these five archetypes – the archetypes of the Persona, the Shadow, Animus and Anima, and the Self – gives us a clearer picture of what exactly Jung means by an archetype; but it will, I think, be helpful at this point to be more precise and to attempt some more general classification. We shall then be in a better position to pass on to the next phase of Jung's argument and see how, from his theory of archetypes, Jung goes on to develop his own highly distinctive notion of God as an archetype.

Jung's notion of an archetype contains the following components:

1   An archetype is a manifestation of the deepest level of the unconscious mind, the collective unconscious.

2   A distinction must be drawn between the *form* of an archetype and its *contents*. The form of an archetype is a structural component of the psyche or, more precisely, an *a priori* disposition of the unconscious mind to construct uniform images. The content of an archetype is the manner in which the form is realized – its concrete representation.

3   As an *a priori* disposition, the form of an archetype is unknowable, independent of experience and unacquired, eternal and transcendent. Its existence can therefore only be postulated as a conceptual requirement, necessary for the explanation of the uniform imagery apparent in the archetypal contents.

4   The contents of an archetype, by contrast, are known and compounded of elements drawn from the acquired personal and social experiences of each individual. While the form of an archetype may therefore be deduced from its manifold contents, the contents of an archetype cannot be deduced from its form.

5   From this it follows that the archetypal form, being unknown, can only be expressed indirectly, namely, in the images, metaphors and symbols of the

archetypal contents. In the archetypal contents we find therefore the indirect expression of that which cannot be expressed directly.

6   While the form of an archetype is unknowable, it nevertheless has certain effects which make the symbolic representation of it possible, namely, the contents of an archetype. These effects are virtually inexhaustible. So, for example, the archetypal form of the Shadow, which is a structural component of the psyche, manifests itself only in the distinct but infinitely various responses of each one of us to his or her capacity for wrongdoing. By the same token, how the archetypes of Anima and Animus are revealed will depend very largely on the sexual history of each individual, and so on. This is true of all archetypes: the form is the mode of perception, not its concrete realization.

7   An archetype is dynamic and dualistic, which means that it operates, like all psychic phenomena, according to the law of opposites. Every archetype therefore contains the possibility of psychic imbalance, of an unequal distribution of libidinal energy. So an individual can become too obsessed with his public Persona and suppress his own distinct individuality, he can repress the necessary Shadow-side of his personality or orientate himself too far towards his own contra-sexual nature, and so on. No matter what the archetype, it will possess this potential for neurotic disturbance and, where it occurs, will reflect it in the symbols and images of its archetypal contents.

8   Just as an archetype possesses, as an innate characteristic, a capacity for psychic imbalance, so it also possesses a teleological and prospective dimension, which is the goal of psychic balance between its disparate elements. This goal is itself archetypal and expressed in the archetype of the Self.

GOD AS ARCHETYPAL FORM

The central proposition of Jung's concept of God is that *God is an archetype*. This proposition immediately ascribes to God a particular property, one which is, as we have just observed, a defining property of all archetypes. This is that, as an archetype, *God is a manifestation of the deepest level of the unconscious mind, the collective unconscious*. From the claim, however, that 'God is an archetype,' we may further adduce another important distinction, again in common with other archetypes. This is between God as archetypal *form* and God as archetypal *contents*. Jung's discussion of God is thus essentially bipartite. On the one hand, we have an analysis of God *an sich*, or in itself, the God that is unknowable, timeless and eternal; on the other, an analysis of God as represented to us in the infinitely various images and symbols of religion. In this section I shall deal with the first of these – God as archetypal form.

The claim that God is an archetypal form carries with it the immediate implication that God is an *a priori structural component of the psyche*, evident as a '"disposition" which starts functioning at a given moment in the development of the human mind and arranges the material of consciousness into definite patterns.'[42] This means that all conceptions of God, no matter how sophisticated or primitive, no matter whether dealing with the subtleties of Trinitarian thought or with the animal deities of polytheism, proceed from an inherent and prior mode of perception, that is, from the archetypal form of God. Nor is this all. This archetypal form of God must be further considered, like all archetypal forms, as a *psychic reality*, as something not extrinsic but intrinsic to the individual, as an active dimension within his or her own psychic life. Given Jung's earlier correlation of archetypes with the instincts, we may even speak here of an 'instinct for God,' not as something individually acquired but as something universally operative, as an elemental force within each of us but perceptible only in its effects, namely, in the indirect archetypal contents of metaphor and symbol. Another way of expressing the same point would be to say that the religious attitude, however it may be personally or socially realized and irrespective of time or place, proceeds from the fact that within the deepest level of our being there exists an archetypal form of God deeply and indelibly engraved upon our psyche. This religious disposition functions, if you will, as an internal activity of the psyche, generates an energy unique to itself, issues forth from the collective unconscious, and manifests itself in the visible and multifarious phenomena of religion.

Needless to say, Jung's argument at this point raises a number of important questions. The first is this: Does Jung's claim that the archetypal form of God exists within the human psyche constitute a proof for the objective existence of God? Does the fact that God is experienced in this fashion constitute a demonstration of the fact that there is a God to be experienced? Jung answers as follows:

> ... when I say as a psychologist that God is an archetype, I mean by that the 'type' in the psyche. The word 'type' is, as we know, derived from *typos*, 'blow' or 'imprint'; thus an archetype pre-supposes an imprinter.... We simply do not know the ultimate derivation of the archetype any more than we know the origin of the psyche. The competence of psychology as as empirical science only goes so far as to establish, on the basis of comparative research, whether for instance the imprint found in the psyche can or cannot reasonably be termed a 'God-image'. Nothing positive or negative has thus been asserted about the possible existence of God, any more than the archetype of the 'hero' proves the actual existence of a hero.[43]

And again:

> We know that the God-images play a great rôle in psychology, but we cannot prove the physical existence of God. As a responsible scientist

I am not going to preach my personal and subjective convictions which I cannot prove. . . . To me however, personally speaking, the question whether God exists at all or not is futile. I am sufficiently convinced of the effects man has always attributed to a divine being. If I should express a belief beyond that or should assert the existence of God, it would not only be superfluous and inefficient, but it would show that I am not basing my opinion on facts. When people say that they believe in the existence of God, it has never impressed me in the least. Either I know a thing and then I don't need to believe it; or I believe it because I am not sure that I know it. I am well satisfied with the fact that I know experiences which I cannot avoid calling numinous or divine.[44]

I have quoted Jung at some length here because, these and other remarks notwithstanding, it remains a vexed question whether Jung did or did not believe in the existence of God. One way of resolving this problem is to note here yet another similarity between Jung's argument and that deployed by Kant in his *Critique of Pure Reason*. We have already seen how indebted Jung is to Kant in his distinction between the form and content of an archetype; but Kant's influence is equally apparent in Jung's repudiation of the theistic proofs. Indeed, Macquarrie is not far wrong when he describes Jung as *a Kantian agnostic*.[45]

We need only note here that Kant's famous rejection of the cosmological and design arguments – the two arguments which attempt to establish the existence of God from empirical observations – proceeds on the basis that no argument from experience can prove (or indeed disprove) the existence of anything that lies beyond the boundaries of human experience, and so cannot establish the reality of any transcendent and supersensible entity, such as God. This does not imply, however, that God does not exist, nor does it expose the futility of religious belief – indeed, as Kant makes clear in his Preface to the second edition of the *Critique*, these limitations on human knowledge 'make room for faith.' In his *Critique of Practical Reason* (1788), Kant underscores this point when he argues that the human capacity for moral thought requires the existence of something outside the individual which impels him to think and act in a moral way, and that this is God. Although the purely rational proofs of God are rejected, the experience of moral obligation makes it necessary nevertheless for us to *postulate* God's existence.

Now it seems to me that Jung is employing an argument very similar to Kant's. He has made it quite clear that the existence of God cannot be proved. Thus the question whether God actually exists or not can never be logically demonstrated. What we can say, however, is that human beings possess a certain characteristic – the property of formulating God-images – and that this characteristic is as certain and self-evident as the property Kant ascribes to them, namely, a moral capacity. In other words, just as Kant infers that man is moral from the plain evidence of moral experience – from our immediate and certain consciousness of moral freedom and from the clear and perceptible instances in which that freedom is exercised – so Jung, in very similar vein, infers from the innumerable and incontestable evidence of God-images that man possesses as an *a priori* component of his psychic nature a particular disposition, namely, the archetypal God-form. But this is all that can be inferred. Again, we may *postulate* from the 'imprint' of the archetype the existence of an 'imprinter,' and so from the existence of the archetypal God-form the existence of a God; but when we do this we are doing no more than classifying these archetypes as *specific psychic experiences*, which we understand to be and formulate as God. These experiences say nothing, therefore, about whether there is a God, or whether the images they generate correspond to the existence of a Deity. 'The psyche,' as Jung remarks, 'cannot leap beyond itself. It cannot set up any absolute truths.'[46] This does not imply that nothing exists apart from the psyche, and so does not imply that no God exists; but it does imply that psychic experience is the only experience we have, that 'we are hopelessly cooped up in an exclusively psychic world,'[47] and that accordingly there can be no demonstration of whether these are (or are not) experiences of a being that has an objective existence, that exists apart from these experiences. All that individuals can mean, therefore, in affirming the existence of God is that for them God is a *psychic phenomenon*; that he is an immediate, direct and self-evident fact of psychic experience en-countered by them within the depths of their own beings; that he is a psychic reality attested to and known by each individual's response to the archetypal images of God.

> I make no transcendental statements. I am essentially empirical, as I have stated more than once. I am dealing with psychic phenomena and not with metaphysical assertions. Within the frame of psychic events I find the fact of the belief in God. It *says*: 'God is.' This is the fact I am concerned with. I am not concerned with the truth or untruth of God's existence. *I am concerned with the statement only*, and I am interested in its structure and behaviour.... It is obvious that if man does not exist, no such statement can exist either, nor can anybody prove that the statement 'God' exists in a non-human sphere.[48]

This goes some way towards explaining Jung's much-publicized remark in his BBC interview with John Freeman in 1959. When asked if he believed in God, Jung replied: 'Difficult to answer. I know. I don't need to believe. I know.'[49] Now, as I see it, this is not a confession of belief – because belief, as Jung has just noted, implies that 'I am not sure that I know it.' Jung's statement is rather a statement of fact: that a particular individual, in this case Jung himself, has undergone a particular psychic experience, and that this experience is of the 'God within' – certain, immediate and indisputable. It is this experience which certifies the existence of God as a psychic reality, and which therefore makes the statement that 'God exists' psychologically true.

To 'know God' is therefore to admit to the psychological truth of this experience.

> I beg leave to point out that it is not a question of belief but of experience. Religious experience is absolute; it cannot be disputed. You can only say that you have never had such an experience, whereupon your opponent will reply: 'Sorry, I have.' And there your discussion will come to an end.[50]

God exists, therefore, as a psychic reality, as a fundamental and psychologically demonstrable factor in human experience; and all that Jung is concerned with is the fact of this phenomenon, with the undeniable reality of this psychological condition. The next question is: Does this mean that God is the product of such experience? Has Jung, in other words, by his repudiation of the theistic proofs, reverted, unwittingly perhaps, to a thoroughgoing subjectivism – to a position in which 'God' becomes a synonym for the act of believing rather than what is believed? This Jung strenuously denies. We remember that God as archetypal-form is not individually acquired but is, *a priori*, an inborn mode of apprehension which belongs to the collective unconscious as 'unknowable' and 'eternal' but which is yet manifested in the symbols of religion. Jung requires, in other words, that we draw an absolute distinction between the archetypal God-form as *imperceptible cause* and the archetypal God-contents as *perceptible effects*. The result of this is that, while individual experiences will inform and flesh out the archetypal God-contents, they are yet totally incapable of generating the God-form. So, while one part of the archetypal image may be characterized in terms of particular and social experiences, another part will be utterly distinct from them because it belongs to that stratum of the psyche which is primordial and not individual. When therefore Jung refers to God as an immediate and undeniable experience, as a psychic reality, he is not assuming that this experience covers the totality of that reality, that the reality is equivalent to that experience, but rather that this experience also involves something that is not and cannot be known. For the experience of God issues from a dimension of the psyche that is greater than and prior to the personal part of the unconscious; it springs rather from that which is unacquired, pre-existent, timeless, impersonal and universal: in a word, from the collective unconscious.

This feature of the psychic knowledge of God – that it includes the archetypal God-form as an impersonal, timeless element, that it is autonomous and not a mental product – also explains other notable characteristics of religious experience. It explains, for example, why religious people so invariably conceive of their faith as something originating outside themselves, as something happening upon them, as something spontaneous and of eternal and authoritative value. It also explains the enormous frequency of independent and autonomous personalities within religious imagery, of figures endowed with consciousness, intellect, free-will and purpose. Angels and archangels, St Paul's 'principalities and powers,' the archons of the Gnostics, the heavenly hierarchy of Dionysius the Areopagite – all are personifications of the autonomy of the God-archetype.[51] Most significantly of all, of course, we have the traditional representations of God himself as omnipotent and omniscient, as the dispenser of justice and love, as the all-merciful Father and Creator of the world. It is interesting to note, therefore, that for Jung the attribution to God of such qualities as power and fatherliness is not, as Freud would have it, a sign of the infantile and neurotic character of religious belief, but rather a reflection of its psychic origin in the autonomous form of the God-archetype.

This allows us to answer the question with which this chapter began. Why is it that believers conceive of God as a father? If the reason is not Oedipal, what is it? The answer is, according to Jung, that the concept of God as father is archetypal: it proceeds, that is, from the activity of an unconscious and innate disposition. To conceive of God in these terms is thus evidence of the operation of the archetypal God-form, which determines that the father-image is one of the universal and inescapable images employed by belief in its worship of a god. In the words of Victor White: 'The way is now open to us ... no longer to conceive of God as a substitute for the physical father, but rather the physical father as the infant's first substitute for God, the genetically prior bearer of the image of the All-Father.'[52]

GOD AS ARCHETYPAL CONTENTS

In turning now to God as archetypal contents, we come to the most extensive and elaborate part of Jung's theory of religion. This is so because, in effect, we are now dealing with every image of God in the entire history of religion, East and West; with every belief, myth, rite and doctrine that has ever been concerned with representing the God-form. Jung's researches in this area are remarkable and justly famous, and it is quite impossible in such a short space to give an accurate idea of the extent and depth of his interests. Two books are, however, worth special mention: *Aion* (1951) and *Answer to Job* (1952). *Aion*, as its name suggests, deals with a specific period of history – the 'Christian aeon' – and explores the symbolism of the Christ-figure and of the devil, provides a lengthy study of fish-symbolism in both Christian and alchemical texts, and concludes with an account of the symbolism found in the ancient belief of Gnosticism. *Answer to Job*, although very much a continuation of *Aion*, is an altogether more contentious work. Here Jung uses the conflict between Job and Yahweh as a paradigm for the way in which God may be perceived, and concludes, much to the outrage of some contemporary theologians, that God contains his own 'shadow-side' and that he is thus implicated in the existence of evil. But in addition to these two books, and to give a short selection, there are studies on the Incarnation, the

Trinity, the Mass, the doctrine of Mary's Assumption, discussions on the differences between Protestantism and Catholicism, and extended studies of the visions of the fifteenth-century Swiss mystic, Brother Klaus, and the theology of Meister Eckhart in the thirteenth century. The list is extraordinary and exhaustive and it is a fitting tribute to Jung's scholarship that commentators rarely tackle him on matters of historical or textual detail.[53]

However, of more importance for us is the fact that, irrespective of this range of discussion, Jung's distinction between archetypal God-form and archetypal God-contents remains intact. When speaking of demons, angels, spirits or God himself, or when considering any of the myths, rites or dogmas of religion in which these so-called 'metaphysical' beings appear, we are, he says, making no claims whatsoever about what may or may not lie behind these images, and thus no assessment of whether they do or do not conform to any kind of objective reality. For what we are concerned with here is the archetypal God-contents – with, if you like, the empirical phenomena of religion – and not with unanswerable questions about whether the innate human disposition to think about God implies that there is a God to think about. All that is of importance now is the indisputable and observable fact that such phenomena exist and that they are manifestations of inner psychic processes. The archetypal God-contents, in other words, can demonstrate nothing other than the psychic experience of God which generated them, and to that extent they are the only subject-matter of psychological enquiry.

The second thing of importance to notice is that the archetypal God-contents, as the concrete manifestations of an *a priori* human disposition (the God-form) which is itself unknowable, can only adopt *one mode of expression*. For no matter what individual or social experiences may contribute to the formation of the images of God, they are all necessarily expressions of that which cannot be expressed directly, and for that reason alone the archetypal God-contents *can only be expressed symbolically*. The symbol is, in other words, the particular form of expression required of the God-contents for its representation of the God-form. Symbolic language thus becomes *the language of religion*, the only language appropriate for the expression of the individual's immediate and absolutely certain psychic experience of God within him.

In order to understand, therefore, what Jung means by the archetypal God-contents, we must first be clear what Jung means by 'symbol.' A handy definition of the term is provided in *Psychological Types* (1921).[54] Here Jung makes three important points:

1 A symbol must be distinguished from a *sign*, the latter having a *semiotic* meaning. That is to say, a sign designates something that is known. A symbol, on the other hand, 'is the best possible formulation of a relatively *unknown* thing.' Jung gives an interesting example of this distinction. If the Christian

cross is conceived as a direct designation of divine love, then this interpretation is semiotic; it becomes symbolic 'when it puts the cross beyond all conceivable explanations, regarding it as expressing an as yet unknown and incomprehensible fact of a mystical or transcendent, i.e., psychological, nature, which simply finds itself most appropriately represented in the cross.'[55]

2 A symbol is 'a living thing:' it is alive 'only so long as it is pregnant with meaning,' but it will die if replaced by another, more appropriate symbol. The way in which St Paul and the earlier speculative mystics speak of the cross indicates that for them it was still 'a living symbol which expressed the inexpressible in unsurpassable form.' But this viewpoint is not exclusive, and it is not difficult to see how the once-potent symbol of the cross can be viewed by others as 'merely a conventional sign for associations that are more completely and better known elsewhere.'[56]

3 It follows from this that whether something becomes a symbol or not will depend chiefly upon the attitude of those considering it; upon whether or not the individual concerned will regard 'the given fact not merely as such but also as an expression for something unknown.' This is the same as saying that nothing will be considered symbolic unless it is apprehended in a *symbolical attitude*, namely, in a 'definite view of life' which endows events with a deeper level of meaning beyond their phenomenal reality. The only attitude, therefore, which cannot think symbolically is that which 'lays the accent upon pure actuality, and subordinates meaning to facts.'[57]

Let us now apply these three points to Jung's concept of the archetypal God-contents. The first thing to say is that Jung's rejection of any attempt to interpret the God-contents in terms of signs rather than symbols is another barely concealed attack upon Freud's semiotic view of religion, in which religious phenomena are ascribed with a quite definite and fixed nucleus, namely the Oedipus complex, in which, accordingly, any religious belief will be analysed retrospectively, as pointing back to something which, if not known to the patient, is at least capable of being disclosed to him. Jung has of course taken Freud to task on this point already,[58] but it is still worth repeating his criticism. Freud interprets the God-contents 'symptomatically,' and thereby indulges in a form of 'reality-thinking' totally inappropriate for the subject at hand. For while it is certainly true that the God-contents come clothed in images drawn from personal experience, the archetypal core to which these images refer – the archetypal God-form – remains inaccessible and unknowable. To suppose, therefore, that religious belief is no more than the encoding of certain emotional attitudes – and neurotic attitudes at that – is to assume an illegitimate identity between the non-perceptible 'archetype as such' and its perceptible manifestation, between its irrepresentable form and its representational contents. It is, in a word, to adopt a 'non-symbolical attitude' which assumes that the language of religion can be reduced to the point where it encapsulates no more than certain psychological states.

In his *Two Essays on Analytical Psychology* (1917) Jung gives an interesting example of the point he is making here – of how Freudian analysis can misread the nature of a neurosis when reducing it to no more than the repression of infantile tendencies. He cites the example of a woman patient who came to him suffering from a 'father complex,' to use the familiar Freudian terminology. Since her relationship with her late father had been highly emotional, she had sought to extricate herself by accentuating the intellectual, thinking side of her personality and had thus become a student of philosophy. This, however, had little effect and only resulted in a further, more aggravated form of psychic imbalance, leading to physical discomfort. Nor was treatment with Jung immediately successful. All that happened was that the woman transferred to Jung the self-same feelings that she had had for her father, making him her substitute father and thus another object of conflict. Both Jung and his patient were at a complete loss what to do next. As a possible step forward, Jung suggested that they analyse her dreams. Most of these dealt with Jung himself as her doctor, and generally included a remarkable distortion: he appeared of enormous size and extremely old. At other times he resembled her father. One dream was particularly significant:

> Her father (who in reality was of small stature) was standing with her on a hill that was covered with wheat-fields. She was quite tiny beside him, and he seemed to her like a giant. He lifted her up from the ground and held her in his arms like a little child. The wind swept over the wheat-fields, and as the wheat swayed in the wind, he rocked her in his arms.[59]

Jung's breakthrough came when he realized that this elevation of himself to a gigantic and protective father of superhuman proportions was nothing other than a symbolic presentation of a 'vision of God,' reactivating the ancient symbolism in which the wind, both in Greek (*pneuma*), Hebrew (*ruah*) and Arabic (*ruh*), stands for God and spirit. Since the patient herself was totally unaware of this connection, Jung concludes that what was emerging here was not, as Freud might have supposed, the repressions of early childhood, but an archaic, primordial image of God, admittedly encased within her own personal experience of Jung himself, but nevertheless shaped and directed by a collective, impersonal fantasy-pattern (i.e., the archetypal God-form). Therefore, despite her own agnostic tendencies, this woman was expressing from the depths of her own unconscious not a desire for a father-lover but a still deeper *passion for God himself*. At first this explanation was unacceptable to the patient but Jung records that, following this diagnosis, the woman gradually lost her fixation with him and began to assimilate what she had learned into a 'guiding function' of life, with the result that her own personal relationships with others deepened immeasurably.

Jung's theory of symbolism indicates another characteristic of the archetypal God-contents. Now conceived as a constellation of symbolic images, the God-contents can, like all symbols, degenerate into signs and so die. Whether this occurs or not will depend in part on whether the particular image of God being employed does or does not 'express the inexpressible,' namely, on whether it has the *symbolic structure necessary for the expression of the archetypal God-form*. To repeat, the God-form is an archaic, primordial and collective psychic disposition, utterly distinct from the countless images of God that it generates – the one in principle unknowable, the other immediately perceptible among the phenomena of religion. So, in the case just cited, what was evident were the images of God fashioned by Jung's female patient; but what predisposed her to fantasies of this kind was not susceptible to scrutiny but something *a priori* and collective, indefinable and imageless, something generated from within the deepest level of her unconscious mind. It follows, therefore, that what is manifested through these images cannot be identified with them – that the God-contents is the vehicle of revelation, not what is revealed – and that accordingly the God-form is not being revealed if such an identification takes place. To suppose otherwise is to convert the symbol into a sign, to indulge in a form of literalism, and to imply that what is being expressed does not emanate from the depths of the collective unconscious and that it can be rationally understood. This robs the symbol of its meaning and psychic power. Without being symbolic, therefore, the archetypal God-contents cannot disclose the collective and non-personal psychic dimension *that only symbols can reveal*.

This conclusion explains Jung's unremitting attack upon any image of God that is considered definitive. Whether found in a book or picture, creed or dogma, ritual or myth, or in the life of an historical personality or institution, any such assessment implies an ignorance of what is being revealed in these situations and of the form appropriate for its revelation. *For the archetypal God-contents is always symbolic and never literal*. The importance of these symbols depends, in other words, on their expression of the God-form as something unknown and unknowable; but this requirement is not met if the object, dream, person or event, which here serves as the vehicle of revelation, is elevated to the dignity of the God-form itself: in a word, if it ceases to be symbolic. Jung's female patient had an image of God as Dr Jung; but Dr Jung was not God. Indeed, on the basis of this image, no property can be ascribed to God whatsoever, not even that he exists. All that can be said is that these images point to the psychological fact of a particular experience had by this woman and that, once stripped of their personal associations, what emerges is a form of imagery not unique to her but collective and archetypal, 'an historical image of world-wide distribution that has come into existence again through a natural psychic function.'[60] This image was the primordial one of a powerful and protecting father, of a creative deity breathing life into her. In her dreams about Jung, this woman had thus reactivated these ancient symbolisms, and thereby indicated the *a priori* psychic disposition of human beings to conceive of God in these terms. Indeed, it is precisely this innate disposition to employ universal imagery that makes this stratum of the unconscious *collective*; and it is precisely for that reason that the archetypal God-form must transcend the symbolism through which it is revealed. It is, accordingly, the first step in the deterioration of any God-contents as archetypal that it is perceived as the source, and not the agent, of this revelation.

By a slight alteration of this argument, we can also see why certain archetypal God-contents do not die but continue to operate as living symbols, pregnant with meaning. Jung has made clear that this largely depends 'on the attitude of the observing consciousness,'[61] on whether these images of God are received as symbols and not as a signs; on whether, that is, the person concerned accepts that the meaning of these symbols does not derive from what can be known and is conscious but from what cannot be known and is unconscious. When Jung says, however, that a symbol exists as a symbol because it has been observed as a symbol, we should be careful to note what he is *not* saying. Jung is not concluding by this that the symbol is created solely by the percipient. A symbol is not a construct of the imagination alone. True, a certain meaning is being ascribed to something when it is called a 'symbol,' but we should not forget what this designation also implies. When a person acknowledges that something is a symbol he is not, admittedly, assuming that the particular picture or ritual that he considers symbolic is symbolic for everyone – as Jung remarks, what is considered a living symbol for one person may be dead for another, and one cannot accordingly manufacture symbols either for oneself or for the benefit of others; but he is acknowledging that through the medium of these images something has been conveyed to him that is *unconscious, a priori and collective*, something, in other words, which is *archetypal* and which thus stands over and above the specific and individualized images through which it is expressed.

A particular image of God, therefore, does not live because it has retained an historical or philosophical significance or because it has continued to arouse intellectual or aesthetic interest. No potent image of God can be created consciously because to do so would be to deny its origin, which is unconscious. It is not, after all, the archetypal God-contents that activate the archetypal God-form, but the form the contents – the one being logically prior, as a unconscious disposition to act, to the act itself. The archetypal God-contents, however it may be presented, lives only because it is symbolic, because it possesses the capacity to reveal through its imagery the deepest and most potent level of the psyche, because through it is activated the archetypal and collective dimension of the unconscious mind, which is the archetypal God-form. Through the medium of the God-contents, individuals thus feel that they have experienced an aspect of themselves, of their inner life, which transcends their own situation and which is timeless and universal. The image is alive because through it people touch that part of themselves which is eternal and which thus transcends their own particularity. It is thus the archetypal God-form which elevates the symbolic archetypal God-contents beyond the world of signs and which gives to every image of God its universal meaning and psychic potency.

Again, an example will clarify Jung's argument. The Christian doctrine of the Trinity is, for him, 'the most sacred of all dogmatic symbols,'[62] but one which can easily be reduced to the status of a sign, to the level of a mathematical configuration which is nevertheless taken, despite all its contradictions and controversial interpretations, as a demonstration of the nature of the Deity. When this occurs, the dogma, indeed any dogma, 'no longer formulates anything, no longer expresses anything; it has become a tenet to be accepted in and for itself, with no basis in any experience that would demonstrate its truth.'[63] To rescue the symbol of the Trinity from this fate, it is accordingly necessary to show that the symbol gives expression to an unconscious and collective experience. True to his method, Jung applies the technique of *amplification* in order to uncover the archetypal roots of the dogma. So we are told of its pre-Christian parallels in Babylonian thought (the triad of Anu, Bel and Ea), in Egyptian theology (the triunity of God, king and Ka-mutef), and in the mathematical speculations of the Greek philosophers (the number symbolism of Pythagoras, Plato's triadic God-image in his *Timaeus*). From this evidence Jung concludes that the trinitarian idea is archetypal, and that what, for instance, the Church Fathers were doing when they devised the *homoousios* formula was in fact to reactivate this archetype and thus to reproduce in new forms 'the timeless truths that are innate in man's nature.'[64] The dogma of the Trinity is not therefore to be assessed in terms of its logical formulae but in terms of the 'psychological reality' it expresses, that is, in terms of its symbolic presentation of an unconscious and primordial image. Despite all the controversies surrounding it, the dogma thus becomes a psychological phenomenon, the immediate and undeniable evidence of a particular psychic experience; and it is this, and this alone, which rescues it from redundancy. The doctrine of the Trinity can now be perceived not as an empty fantasy irrelevant to the concerns of modern people but as the symbolic activation of a universal human disposition. In other words, the image that it presents becomes part of the archetypal God-contents, through which is revealed the archetypal God-form – which in this case is a disposition to conceive of God not as a unitary and static being but as a dynamic and triadic force.[65]

Jung employs the same argument not only to cover other religious phenomena – the Mass, for example, is accorded very similar treatment[66] – but also to assess the significance of certain religious personalities. How, then, does he view the figure of Jesus of Nazareth? Here too the requirement is made that any archetypal image must be presented symbolically. Since this also involves a distinction been the archetype itself and the medium of its revelation, it is not difficult to see how this allows Jung to give a new twist to the old theological distinction between the historical Jesus and the biblical Christ; between, that is, the outward details of Jesus' life, which Jung considers unreliable and of scarcely any importance, and faith's belief in him as presented in the New Testament, which Jung now translates as the perception that Jesus is the *exemplification of an archetype*. Thus we are once more on the familiar territory of assessing an image – in this case, a biblical image – not on grounds of historical reliability or rational consistency, but in terms of its expression of a particular psychic and primordial experience. This explains, says Jung, the 'unhistorical character of the gospels, whose only concern was to represent the miraculous figure of Christ as graphically and impressively as possible.'[67] Even the earliest literary witness, Paul, overlays the figure of Jesus with metaphysical conceptions: he is the ruler of all daemonic forces, the cosmic saviour, the mediating God-man. Indeed, if it had not been for this downgrading of the earthly man, Jesus could not have emerged as 'the collective figure whom the unconscious of his contemporaries expected to appear.' The gospels, accordingly, do not provide historical evidence that Jesus was the Christ, but only bear witness to a particular psychic experience evidently had by their authors: 'Here is the living and perceptible archetype which has been projected upon the man Jesus and has historically manifested itself in him.'[68]

What then is the archetype being displayed by the Christ-figure? It is, Jung continues, the archetype familiar to us in individual dreams and fantasy-projections: the idea of an overpowering, all-embracing, complete or perfect being, which is invariably represented by a man of heroic proportions. In the case of Jesus, this being is depicted as possessing heroic attributes: 'improbable origin, divine father, hazardous birth, rescue in the nick of time, precocious development, conquest of the mother and of death, miraculous deeds, a tragic, early end, symbolically significant manner of death, post-mortem effects (reappearances, signs and marvels, etc.).'[69] In Christian iconography the same image of perfection is depicted in the mandala of Christ surrounded by the four evangelists or in the presentation of saints, angels and elders grouped around his central figure. All these symbolisms, to repeat, adumbrate an archetype; and we can now see why they remain significant despite their often fantastical presentation. For the image of completeness being presented by these images is the expression of an archetype which encapsulates a fundamental and *a priori* requirement of human nature, namely, *the demand to unify the disparate elements of the psyche*. This demand, we remember, Jung has already categorized as the archetype of the Self.[70] What the individual identifies in Christ, therefore, is the archetype expressing his own inner psychic need for wholeness and unity: Christ, that is, 'exemplifies the archetype of the self.'[71] Jesus, accordingly, is called the Christ not because the historical details of his life confirm him as the Christ – this would be to treat the biblical narrative literally, as a composite of signs –

but because the observing consciousness experiences the archetype of the Self through the symbolic medium of that life. The symbol of the Christ, just like the doctrine of the Trinity, is thus saved from oblivion and reanimated by the immediate and certain experience of its universal, collective and archetypal validity.

Jung's discussion of the Self-archetype figures prominently in the last stages of his argument, and I shall return to it in the next chapter. What needs to be emphasized at this point is the extent to which Jung, in making these references to the various images of God incorporated within the creeds, dogmas and rituals of religion, repeatedly discounts any consideration of their so-called 'metaphysical' truth. So the doctrine of the Trinity provides no demonstration of the nature of the deity, and the gospels provide no evidence that the historical Jesus was actually the God-man. By the same token, neither does this mean that no God exists or that Jesus was not the Christ. This follows, as we have seen, both from the absolute restriction Jung places upon the human capacity either to verify or to falsify such transcendental ideas and from the necessity to present such ideas non-literally. These, then, are questions impossible to resolve, and every attempt to do so is, for him, an exercise in sustained futility – a presumption of the human mind unconscious of its limitations. Importantly, however, silence on these matters does not imply that such metaphysical speculations are meaningless. For however remote they may appear at first from everyday experience, their meaning can be restored once they are perceived to be rooted in universal psychic processes. Read aright, in other words, *the metaphysical concepts of religion may also stand as archetypal God-contents*, and as such may also be regarded as the phenomenal effects of an innate psychic disposition to deploy the collective and primordial images of the archetypal God-form – in the cases just mentioned, the images of God as a trinity or perfect man.

Therefore, despite Jung's reservations about metaphysics in general, specific metaphysical speculations – in theology, for example, about whether the death of Christ brought us redemption or whether there is life after death – can be rescued from oblivion if they are seen to derive from the transpersonal and universal experiences emanating from the collective unconscious; if they are taken, that is, as the 'abbreviated descriptions' of certain psychic facts, issuing from the immediate psychic experience of the God-archetype. As Jung makes clear, it is not 'the concept that matters; the concept is only a word, a counter, and it has meaning and use only because it stands for a certain sum of experience.'[72] While, therefore, it is invariably the fate of metaphysical ideas or outmoded theological concepts to lose their relevance and die, this is not inevitable if they continue to evoke and recall the original archetypal experiences upon which they are based. In that sense, too, they become an historical witness to the fact that such experiences have occurred: they become, like all the symbols of religion, the perceptible effects of an imperceptible cause. It is, therefore, the archetypal core of the doctrine, dogma, ritual or personality which elevates them to the level of archetypal God-contents, through whose symbolic formulations and imagery is mediated the archetypal God-form. Thus it is that the often alien and unintelligible speculations of religion have universal and collective meaning conferred upon them.

THE NATURE OF RELIGIOUS EXPERIENCE

Jung's distinction between the archetypal God-form and the archetypal God-contents has allowed him to distance himself from any suggestion that the images of God are, as Freud would have it, figments of the neurotic imagination. The God-contents, while certainly utilizing imagery drawn from individual experience, are at the same time actualizations of an *a priori* psychic disposition, of an unconscious substratum which is universal and collective and thus independent of any personal history. This is the archetypal God-form, the God-archetype *an sich*, the matrix or precondition to which every symbolic representation of God conforms. If religion constantly employs images of the father, this is not then evidence of its Oedipal origin but of its deployment of a suprapersonal and archetypal motif. Accordingly, it is not infantile need that makes the father-image potent, but the experience that is obtained through that image of a particular and primordial level of psychic being.

As we have seen already, in this argument religious experience plays a quite decisive role. The archetypal God-contents are symbolic because it is only through the medium of a symbol that an illimitable reality, the archetypal God-form, can be experienced; and at the same time the fact that an individual has had this experience certifies that this symbol is indeed a symbol and thus a medium of this revelation. In this sense, religious experience has a two-fold character: it is the reception of something that is given; it is, as we have noted before, the perceptible effect of an imperceptible cause. Thus, on the one hand, this experience is independent of the subject, something that is manifested to him within the depths of his own being but which is uncreated, 'eternal,' collective and impersonal; but, on the other, it is having this experience in relation to, say, a particular image or dogma that confirms that these phenomena are living symbols, still active in their presentation of an archetype.

But this is not all that Jung has to say about religious experience.[73] To begin, let us turn to Jung's most famous definition of religion, given in the Terry lectures at Yale University in 1937. As we might expect, here he defines religion not by its creeds and rituals but by the original religious experiences upon which they depend. That is to say, religion is a 'peculiar attitude of the human mind' in which 'certain dynamic factors' are observed and considered 'beautiful and meaningful enough to be devoutly adored and loved.' This attitude is further characterized as possessing 'the highest or strongest value' and an 'important, even overwhelming, psychical intensity.'[74]

> Religion, as the Latin word denotes, is a careful and scrupulous observation of what Rudolf Otto[75] aptly termed the *numinosum*, that is, a dynamic agency or effect, not caused by an arbitrary act of will. On the contrary, it seizes and controls the human subject, who is always rather its victim than its creator. The *numinosum* – whatever its cause may be – is an experience of the subject independent of his will. At all events, religious teaching as well as the *consensus gentium* always and everywhere explain this experience as being due to a cause external to the individual. The *numinosum* is either a quality belonging to a visible object or the influence of an invisible presence that causes a peculiar alteration of consciousness. This is, at any rate, the general rule.[76]

Ten years later, in 1947, Jung is still more explicit about what he means by the 'numinosum' that religion so carefully observes and to which it attaches such significance. Religion, he says, does not rest upon tradition and faith but originates with the archetypes, 'the "careful consideration" of which – *religere*! – constitutes the essence of religion.'[77] Again, this is not unexpected. For to define religion in terms of the archetypes is to do no more than reassert that the religious attitude is an *essential component of the psyche*. This is a by now familiar argument. Every individual possesses an *a priori* 'religious instinct' – an impulse for religion that is a psychic function – and it is this instinct which provides the occasion and the pattern for all his subsequent religious imagery and activities. Put otherwise, this definition of religion *requires that the religious attitude is the collective attitude* . Any expression of the religious attitude will therefore require the recreation of these unconscious and psychic impulses in symbolic, universal and archetypal form.

The second point to note is Jung's description of religious experience as a 'dynamic' activity, in which the 'value' being attributed to the *numinosum* involves a psychological condition of great 'psychic intensity.' Furthermore, there appear to be two reasons for the special character of this activity: it proceeds, in the first instance, from a peculiar quality of the experiencing subject, and in the second, from a peculiar quality of the experienced object. Let us take each of these in turn.

When Jung speaks of the act of ascribing meaning to something as a dynamic and psychically intense act, he is recalling his earlier theory of psychic energy.[78] The relatively closed system of the psyche is, we remember, characterized by the constant and dynamic movement of the libido. Although the libido itself is not observable, its course can be charted in terms of the 'value' being attributed in any given case. Values are 'quantitative estimates of energy,' so that for a person to place a high value on, say, a work of art is the same as saying that this art-object has been invested by him or her with a large amount of psychic energy. What has happened here is that psychical energy has been 'transformed' or 'canalized' into a particular cultural phenomenon – the value being attributed to it being directly calculable in terms of the intensity of its libidinal effect.

Jung transposes this argument directly into his account of religious experience. Through the medium of the symbolic God-contents a person experiences the revelation of the archetypal God-form; and because of this experience he or she attributes the 'highest or strongest value' to these contents and so calls them 'archetypal.' This can now be translated as follows: the symbolic God-contents are images into which a specific quantity of psychic energy has been canalized. These symbolic images, whatever form they take, are thus the manifestation and expression of the libido, and the intensity of their effect derives directly from the energic movement of the psyche, of the infusion of these images with libidinal power. The believer, in according these images the highest value, in confessing that they are the vehicles of revelation, is thus attesting to the fact that they are transformers of energy in the psychic process. They become 'numinous,' in other words, because of a particular quality they possess, namely, that they carry with them a dynamic of concentrated libidinal power, which is simultaneously an expression of life-energy within the psyche.

This, then, is the first strand of Jung's analysis of religious experience: a religious experience is identified as a numinous experience, and a numinous experience is in turn connected to the psychic processes of the experiencing subject. In the second strand, however, Jung turns to consider religious experience as an effect produced by the experienced object, by the numen or archetype itself which impacts upon individuals through the medium of symbols. This is the 'invisible presence' which seizes and controls the human subject as its 'victim' and not its 'creator.' In a striking passage, again very reminiscent of Rudolf Otto, Jung describes this experience as an encounter with 'holiness'.

> 'Holiness' means that an idea or thing possesses the highest value, and that in the presence of this value men are, so to speak, struck dumb. Holiness is also revelatory: it is the illuminative power emanating from an archetypal figure. Nobody ever feels himself as the subject of such a process, but always as its object. *He* does not perceive holiness, *it* takes him captive and overwhelms him; nor does *he* behold it in a revelation, *it* reveals itself to him, and he cannot even boast that he has understood it properly. Everything happens apparently outside the sphere of his will, and these happenings are contents of the unconscious.[79]

Once again, Jung is here concerned only with *phenomenal religion*, with the immediate and undeniable fact that certain people have a particular type of experience which they consider overwhelming and revelatory and which may therefore be called 'numinous.' Lest it be supposed, however, that this experience is self-generating, Jung now repeats his earlier argument but with a significant addition. Not only may we postulate, if not demonstrate, that this experience has a real origin – that it is the mediated effect of an archetypal cause – but we may further postulate, if not demonstrate, *that the characteristics of the effect require certain characteristics in the cause.* In other words, because the religious experience is 'numinous,' we may presume not only that it is activated by an archetype but further that this archetype is a 'numen' – that it has the qualities necessary to generate this experience, that it possesses 'highest value,' that it is a 'revelation,' that it 'captures and overwhelms' its recipient, and so on. All these, then, are qualities that may be inferred from the nature of the experience obtained through the medium of God-images. But this inference, as Jung is quick to point out, does not demonstrate the existence of God. All that can be empirically established are certain phenomenal effects in the numinous experience – that, for example, one feels the 'victim' and not the 'creator' – but these psychic effects are sufficient for us to conclude that in a numinous experience the numen is disclosed as an autonomous and creative agent, as a reality standing apart from the receiving subject.

> The difficulty which gives rise to misunderstandings is that archetypes are 'real.' That is to say, effects can be empirically established whose cause is described hypothetically as *archetype,* just as in physics effects can be established whose cause is assumed to be the *atom* (which is merely a model). Nobody has ever seen an archetype, and nobody has ever seen an atom either. But the former is known to produce numinous effects and the latter explosions. When I say 'atom' I am talking of the model made of it; when I say 'archetype' I am talking of ideas corresponding to it, but never of the thing-in-itself, which in both cases is a transcendental mystery.
>
> ... Only it is news to me that such knowledge is accounted 'metaphysical.' You see, for me the psyche is something real *because it works,* as can be established empirically. One must therefore assume that the effective archetypal ideas, including our model of the archetype, rest on something actual even though unknowable, just as the model of the atom rests on certain unknowable qualities of matter. But science cannot possibly establish that, or to what extent, this unknowable substrate is in both cases God. This can be decided only by dogmatics or faith. . . .[80]

In summary, then, a religious experience is a numinous experience, and a numinous experience carries with it certain necessary psychic processes. These processes distinguish what is given and received in a numinous situation. On the one hand, we have a process generic to the human psyche which issues forth from the collective unconscious. This process is conceived as archetypal, primordial, universal and eternal, as being utterly different from the individualized products of the personal unconscious, as possessing a unique power of its own, sufficient to determine in every single individual a similarity of experience and representation. This is the archetypal God-form. On the other hand, the experience of the archetypal God-form is a mediated experience: the God-form cannot be known directly but only through its effects, namely, through the medium of the archetypal God-contents. Thus, through the symbolic images of religion, the individual receives and expresses a revelation of the immanent-transcendent, of the suprapersonal centre of his own existence, the numen, 'God within us.' This is an immediate experience of an absolutely convincing character, guaranteed by its own dynamic intensity and by the absolute value that is attributed to it.

The fact of this experience is all that the psychologist is concerned with: it is only this that can be empirically established. Strictly speaking, then, all that we can say is that religious experience establishes God as a psychic reality, and that there exists an archetypal image of God indelibly engraved upon our psyche. Psychology cannot demonstrate the existence of God; but in establishing the existence of this archetypal image it can confirm religion as a fundamental activity of the human psyche, as a necessary expression of the deepest level of our unconscious being, the collective unconscious.

9

GOD AND INDIVIDUATION

We come now to the final stage of Jung's account of religion, in which, as we shall see, he argues that religion is necessary for human psychic development. This argument turns on Jung's important concept of *individuation*. Jung himself regarded this idea as 'the central concept of my psychology',[1] and for many commentators it remains his most enduring achievement. It also provides us with yet another illuminating contrast with Freud. Freud, we recall, is particularly dismissive when he considers the advantages of being religious. Religion, it is true, has performed the valuable service of providing rules and regulations for the taming of our asocial instincts, but it has done little else. It has not made us happy, it has not allowed us to come to terms with our sexual impulses, and, above all, it has not fostered any process of individual growth. Religion is an obsessional neurosis, and to be religious is thus to be locked into a childish and illusory form of life. But Freud is not downhearted. Such infantilism, he predicts, is bound to be discarded as people mature. Men and women cannot remain children for ever, and 'a turning-away from religion is bound to occur with the fatal inevitablity of a process of growth....'[2] This claim is denied by Jung. Once the religious attitude is revealed as a *collective attitude* – once, in other terms, it is recognized as expressing an archetypal dimension that is intrinsic to human nature – it cannot any longer be regarded as something that should be, or even could be, discarded. Indeed, Jung goes further. Precisely because religion is a psychic function, as inseparable from the individual as any other instinct, any attempt to deny its significance will result in a loss of psychic equilibrium and thus a descent into neurosis.

As I have pointed out before,[3] both Freud and Jung are here taking as their common starting-point the *vis medicatrix naturae* – the healing power of nature – and thus the view that every individual has the inherent capacity to regain health. Thereafter, however, the difference between them is quite stark. For Freud, this therapeutic process requires unravelling the repressions of our Oedipal past, and thus must involve the unmasking of religion as part of that inheritance. For Jung, therapy requires uniting the disparate parts of the psyche – consciousness and the unconscious – into a living relation, and thus must involve the recognition of religion as a vital component in that process. The religious experience is a numinous experience of the archetypal and eternal foundations of humanity itself, and to that extent it enables the individual to lift himself above his personal problems and to relate instead to the indestructible and primordial dimension of his own psychic being. It is not therefore the acceptance of religion that is psychologically damaging but its rejection. Jung makes this clear in a famous passage:

> I should like to call attention to the following facts. During the past thirty years, people from all the civilized countries of the earth have consulted me. Many hundreds of patients have passed through my hands, the greater number being Protestants, a lesser number Jews, and not more than five or six believing Catholics. Among all my patients in the second half of life – that is to say, over thirty-five – there has not been one whose problem in the last resort was not that of finding a religious outlook on life. It is safe to say that every one of them fell ill because he had lost that which the living religions of every age have given their followers, and none of them has been really healed who did not regain his religious outlook. This of course has nothing whatever to do with a particular creed or membership of a church.[4]

THE PROCESS OF INDIVIDUATION

Jung calls the process by which the individual integrates the conscious and unconscious parts of the personality the *process of individuation*. The concept of individuation first appears in *Psychological Types* (1921) – although traces of the idea are to be found in Jung's doctoral thesis of 1902 – and it receives its fullest treatment in his last major work, *Mysterium Coniunctionis* (1956). The term 'individuation' denotes not a state but a living and dynamic 'process by which a person becomes a psychological "individual", that is, a separate, indivisible unity or "whole."'[5]

> Individuation means becoming an 'in-dividual,' and, in so far as 'individuality' embraces our innermost, last, and incomparable uniqueness, it also implies becoming one's own self. We could therefore translate individuation as 'coming to self-hood' or 'self-realization.'[6]

The process of individuation, Jung continues, is a totally spontaneous and natural process within the psyche, on a par with the physical processes of growth and ageing; it does not therefore exist as something that can be externally stimulated, but as something that is potentially present in all human beings, although most of us are unaware of it. The personality is thus destined to individuate just as surely as the body is biologically destined to decay. This process should occur naturally but can easily be thwarted by any number of factors – by heredity, the adverse influences of parents, education and

environment. It is therefore one of the principal tasks of practical psychotherapy to identify these obstructing elements and so assist the personality
along his or her particular path of individuation.

Another way of indicating that individuation is a process inherent to the
psyche is to define it in terms of its goal. For Jung individuation is a 'coming
to selfhood,' and thus the goal of individuation is the realization of the Self:

> ... the self has somewhat the character of a result, of a goal attained,
> something that has come to pass very gradually and is experienced with
> much travail. So too the self is our life's goal, for it is the completest
> expression of that fateful combination we call individuality, the full
> flowering not only of the single individual, but of the group, in which
> each adds his portion of the whole.[7]

I have already said something about Jung's concept of the Self in the
previous chapter.[8] The Self, we recall, is *the archetype of wholeness*, and so
testifies to the fact that seeking a proper equilibrium between the disparate
sides of the psyche, between the conscious and the unconscious, is an *a priori*
human disposition. This immediately tells us more about the individuation
process. If the goal of individuation is the realization of the Self, then this
process becomes one which is not only therapeutically necessary but one
which is also *archetypally directed*. The Self, in other words, must be
conceived not just as the goal of individuation but also as its originating
impulse: it is both *result* and *agent*. This means that the desire to integrate
conscious and unconscious elements is itself primordial and collective in
origin, that it is an actualization of the archetype of the Self. Individuation is
thus innate to individuals, a natural law of the psyche, the psyche's irreducible
'prospective' and 'teleological' component. The task of self-realization is,
accordingly, one to which all human beings must devote themselves, albeit
with differing degrees of success.

Jung's identification of the goal of individuation as the realization of the
Self allows him to be fairly precise about what is entailed in the programme
of individuation. Individuation is concerned with achieving psychic balance,
that is, it seeks the union of opposites. This means assimilating or integrating
into consciousness the various unconscious parts of the psyche: it requires
becoming sensitive and receptive to those aspects of oneself that one has
neglected and so left undeveloped. What these are will depend very much on
the person concerned; but in all cases the demand is to bring forth into
experience what has been devalued and repressed – whether this be personal
characteristics that one prefers to hide (the Shadow), values that one considers
at odds with one's public Persona, unconscious male or female patterns of
emotion and behaviour (Anima/Animus), a particular non-dominant or
inferior attitude (extraversion or introversion), or a particular non-dominant
and inferior function (sensation, intuition, thinking or feeling). It is scarcely
surprising that individuation is a difficult, painful and sometimes dangerous

process.[9] Psychic harmony and the realization of the Self, as Jung makes clear, can only be achieved by first exposing the most intimate parts of an individual's inner life, and for this the individual requires considerable courage – after all, the issue at this point is not so much how to deal with certain desires or tendencies but rather to admit that one has them. But that difficulty overcome, the psychic harmony that results invariably produces an improved capacity for relationships with others, with, for instance, members of one's own family or with the community in general. Individuation, therefore, is not merely the resolution of inner conflict, but impels us towards a more harmonious relation with society as a whole. To give one example: acceptance of our Shadow-side, of our own hostile and aggressive impulses, may in turn unlock other capacities for spontaneous affection, and so enable us to treat those who are hostile to us with greater tolerance and warmth.

Jung cites many case-studies revealing the process of individuation.[10] We have come across one already in the example of the man whose fantasies about his fiancée's suicide revealed an imbalance between his dominant thinking and inferior feeling functions – this disharmony pointing to the therapeutic need for him to reactivate in his unconscious what he had excluded from consciousness.[11] However, Jung's most detailed and intriguing case concerns an unmarried American woman of fifty-five – Miss X – who began treatment with Jung in 1928. She was highly educated, had studied psychology for nine years, and was suffering from an imbalance between her Animus and Anima. This was the result of what Jung calls her 'positive father complex': she was very much 'her father's daughter' and consequently did not have good relations with her Danish mother. Realizing that these relations left much to be desired, 'the feeling had gradually grown up in her that this side of her nature might have developed differently if only the relation to her mother had given it a chance.'[12] So Miss X turned to Jung. Jung's analysis is based on the paintings she produced over ten years, and which he describes as 'a kind of ideogram of unconscious contents.'[13] He gives twenty-five illustrations of her work, beginning with an image of Miss X surrounded by egg-like rocks, with half her body stuck in Mother Earth – the implication being that she is waiting to be released from her imprisonment by a sorcerer (i.e., by Jung himself). In the next picture, the rocks are no longer eggs but complete circles, one of which has been blasted by a golden flash of lightning – this last feature indicating that she will now be released not by a magician but by a natural process. The fourth picture is the most important. Not only is the total image now circular but at its centre we find the female organ, stylized to look like a plant with silver petals, being fertilized by a black snake with a pale yellow halo. The sexual significance of this was not lost on Jung's patient, and gradually her pictures depict the assimilation of the snake into the nucleus, its blackness being compensated by a golden light radiating out from the centre. This was the beginning of the integration of her Animus and Anima, and by picture nineteen the process was almost complete. This series of pictures, Jung concludes, 'illustrates the initial stages of the way of individuation,'[14] but unfortunately we do not know whether they provided Miss X with any therapeutic benefit. Jung seems to have lost track of her, although her paintings were left to him after her death.

Jung's analysis of Miss X is extraordinarily complicated, so complicated in fact that it is difficult to imagine many patients making anything of it at all. That said, it does give us an excellent practical demonstration of Jung's amplification technique. The circles drawn by her are, of course, mandalas, and so indicate the unconscious duplication of perhaps the greatest of all archetypal images of the Self's totality.[15] But Jung is quick to point out other resemblances. When Miss X paints a rightward-moving swastika (picture six) this is connected with a Buddhist emblem, indicating a spin out of unconscious chaos; if she paints an equal-armed cross or an eye (pictures seven and eight), reference is made to similar images in the work of the sixteenth-century mystic Jacob Böhme; if she draws six sets of sunbeams (picture nine), then this recalls the Buddha's Discourse on the Robe, although in the same picture the three white birds signify the Christian Trinity. However, these connections, although fascinating, are as nothing compared to the parallels Jung draws between Miss X and alchemy – indeed he freely admits that it was one picture in particular (picture three) which gave him the 'definitive incentive to make a thorough study of the works of the old adepts.'[16] This picture depicts a free-floating sphere, across which which runs a vibrating silver band, stamped in the middle with the number twelve. Jung points out that all these are alchemical symbols. The silver is quicksilver, the vibrations are the wings of Mercury, and the number twelve has to do with the alchemical process known as *tetrameria*. But other alchemical symbols abound. The egg-like boulders refer to the Orphic egg (the *rotundum*) – the vessel from which, at the end of the alchemical process, the homunculus emerges, namely the Anthropos, the spritual and complete man. The liberating lightning-flash is a symbol often used by Paracelsus and the alchemists to indicate Mercurius as both god and the element of quicksilver; and in Miss X's picture of the snake and the flower we find another powerful alchemical idea: the two silver petals representing the receptive vessel, the moon-bowl in which the seed (gold) is destined to rest.

Jung makes clear that Miss X knew nothing of alchemy, and that his own lack of knowledge ruled out any suggestion of 'my having unintentionally infected her with alchemical ideas.'[17] This possibility ruled out, all that was left was to suppose that both Miss X and the alchemists were here *under the unconscious influence of an archetype*, that they were in their very different ways employing similar images to express an intense inner experience – the experience of an archetype – and that this experience, being archetypal, was not something unique to them but age-old and collective. Miss X's pictures are, then, like the symbolical ideas of alchemy, genuine creations of the unconscious: they are not the products of conscious reflection but are instead the spontaneous revelation in symbolical form of the actual state of Miss X's collective unconscious. More exactly, what is being transmitted here is an archetypal demand for Self-hood and what Miss X is now being enjoined to do is, as it were, to listen to the messages being transmitted through her paintings, and so to begin the process of individuation that they call for: in other words, to release those dormant and inferior aspects of her personality which her own psyche has identified as essential for psychic balance and for the attainment of Self-hood. Here, then, it is not just that the desire for individuation is archetypal, but that the archetypes themselves provide specific psychological information about how individuation is to be obtained.

THE TWO STAGES OF INDIVIDUATION

The goal of the individuation process is, then, to unite the disparate aspects of the psyche and so realize the archetypal unity of the Self; and to this end, as the case of Miss X makes clear, the unconscious operates in a compensatory role to consciousness: that is, it provides symbolic material in which are expressed those features of the individual, hitherto undervalued or repressed, which must be taken up if any kind of psychic equilibrium is to be achieved. The archetypal content of Miss X's pictures were not therefore random and due to chance, but their appearance was relative to certain existing imbalances within her personality: the images she employed are indicative of her own unconscious demand to rectify this situation, and in that respect they provide a commentary on her own progress towards individuation. Her need to achieve psychic balance remains archetypal, an *a priori* human disposition, but the form in which this is expressed remains individual to her and dependent on her own personal and cultural situation. In this sense her paintings become commentaries on both a universal and particular condition.

That said, whether achieved naturally or through psychotherapy, the individuation process follows a fairly regular pattern. Broadly speaking, it falls into two major phases, one in the first half of life (from infancy to young adulthood) and the other in the second half of life (from middle age to old age).

The first half of life

This phase begins at birth, includes the onset of puberty or sexual maturity, and ends around the ages of thirty-five or forty. Initially the young infant has no problems: its perceptions are sporadic, it has almost no continuous memory, little sense of personal identity, and is almost completely dependent on its parents. The child's behaviour is 'anarchic or chaotic' and governed almost entirely by impulse.[18] Gradually, however, the ego begins to develop, memory lengthens, and a sense of personal identity – an 'I-ness' – arises. This first stage of consciousness comes to an end, however, with the eruption of sexual life at puberty. This 'physiological change is attended by a psychic revolution.' The young ego, now consciously distinguished from its parents, is for the first time burdened with 'the demands of life which harshly put an end to the dream of childhood.'[19] There are problems of sex, feelings of inferiority which spring from an almost unbearable sensitivity, the need to adapt to social life, and the necessity of finding a vocation. If the individual is sufficiently well prepared and adjusted, this transition from childhood to youth can occur quite smoothly; but if he or she clings to illusions that contradict reality, underestimates difficulties or is unjustifiably optimistic, then problems will arise and psychic disturbances result. This first phase is more generally characterized by the adaptation of the psyche to the demands of the environment and by the expansion of experience, by the establishment of personal relationships and the development of a suitable Persona.

The second half of life

Just as the first half of life is distinguished by initiation into external reality, so the second half is distinguished by initiation into inner reality. Here the former concern for material and attainable goals – money-making, social existence, family – gives way to a different set of priorities. Philosophical and spiritual questions are now asked about the meaning of life and the purpose of existence. Often this dramatic change of attitude is precipitated by the so-called 'midlife crisis.' Around middle-age physical energies decrease, there are fewer opportunities for success, youthful ambitions have either been met or relinquished, and old convictions or moral principles are no longer felt to be adequate to present needs. The individual thus experiences a sense of emptiness and inadequacy. This loss of value – or displacement of psychic energy – provides, however, the impetus for a fundamental psychological transformation. In the quest for significance, the person now turns inward, and begins a self-exploration of those aspects of his or her nature which have, in the struggle for survival, been ruthlessly repressed. In other words, a new meaning and purpose in living is to be found by forging a link between the conscious and unconscious aspects of the psyche, by realizing, on the one hand, what is personal to the individual, and, on the other, what binds the individual to the collective form of humanity. Individuation is therefore almost exclusively an activity of maturity – Miss X, we recall, was over fifty-five at the time of her analysis. But this task continues into old age. Even here, as death approaches, the search for meaning and the movement towards wholeness are indispensable. As Jung remarks: 'For a young person it is almost a sin, or at least a danger, to be too preoccupied with himself; but for the ageing person it is a duty and a necessity to give serious attention to himself. After having lavished its light upon the world, the sun withdraws its rays in order to illuminate itself.'[20] Gradually, as we get older, the outside world recedes and the demands of the inner world become more urgent. The individual, having as an infant struggled to assert his own identity, now towards the end of life again becomes child-like, unworried by his state of consciousness. The cycle of individuation thus closes meaningfully and harmoniously, with a coincidence of beginning and end, with the assimilation of the unconscious and conscious dimensions. Accordingly the natural end of life, as Jung was fond of saying, 'is not senility but wisdom.'[21]

Edinger has helpfully characterized the difference between the first and second phases of the individuation process in terms of the dialectical relation between ego and Self:

1 ego identified with Self;
2 ego alienated from Self; and
3 ego reunited with Self.[22]

According to this scheme, the first half of life sees the gradual separation of ego from Self, and the second half the gradual reunion of the two. At birth no ego exists and there is a complete identification with the Self, that is, with a state of unconscious wholeness and perfection. At this point we cannot differentiate between ourselves and the world of the collective unconscious from which we originate: we are, as it were, immersed in the images of the archetypes and thus, not unnaturally, we see ourselves quite literally as the centre of the universe – a condition which, incidentally, can continue past childhood and lead to serious psychoses. This condition cannot, however, persist for long. As reality impinges, the ego and the Self become alienated from one another, and we find the first appreciable indications of an ego-personality now emancipated from the collective psyche, a separation best illustrated by the aggression and self-assertiveness of adolescence. But this too is only a stage to be superseded, and the experience of alienation is a necessary prelude to a rediscovery of the Self. For more and more the ego-Self produces a state of meaninglessness, a state that can only be terminated by re-establishing the connecting link between the ego and its suprapersonal and collective origins. This becomes the major task in the second phase of life, and to which the remainder of our lives must be dedicated. Maturity thus brings with it the realization that the true goal of existence lies in the attainment of Self, that is, in becoming a 'whole,' someone who has discovered that their ego has an *a priori* and transpersonal origin. Meaning can thus be restored to individuals once they see themselves as participating agents in a universal and collective experience.

As with any archetypal process, the way of individuation can be charted through the symbols spontaneously generated from the unconscious – hence the explanatory character of Miss X's paintings. However, an archetype can also be further clarified through amplification, that is, through the use of analogous images drawn from the collective repository of mankind. So in order to explain Miss X's condition, Jung found innumerable parallels between her images and those in mythology, folklore and alchemy. But at this point Edinger's comparisons are even more breathtaking in their scope. To quote just a few: the original ego-self identity is found in all those myths which depict the original state of man as one of roundness, wholeness, perfection or paradise (e.g., the Platonic myth of original man, the Garden of Eden); the beginnings of ego-consciousness are indicated in the story of Adam's expulsion, in the myths of Prometheus, Icarus, Phaeton and Ixion, and in Herodotus' story of the tyrant Polycrates; we find the eventual estrangement between ego and Self presented in the biblical stories of Cain and Ishmael – the latter developed by Melville in *Moby Dick*. We find it also in the autobiography of Tolstoy and in the opening lines of both Dante's *Divine Comedy* and Goethe's *Faust*. The movement towards the third stage of the process – that in which ego and Self are reunited – is often symbolized as a 'moment of breakthrough': Moses' encounter with Yahweh in the burning bush, Jacob's dreams of the heavenly ladder, Jonah's experience of God within the belly of the whale, the dramatic conversion of the apostle Paul.[23] All these stories and myths illuminate, as Edinger makes clear, the journey to be undertaken by the individuating personality. They are all archetypal symbols of the evolution of the Self, and as such indicate that the wish for completeness or wholeness is not just a wish of the few but a collective and inherent desire found in all human beings. This perhaps explains why neo-Jungians have not been slow to provide other examples of individuation in the fictional and non-fictional lives of others. So Esther Harding sees Bunyan's *Pilgrim's Progress* in these terms; Barbara Hannah the lives of the Brontës; Daryl Sharp the life of Kafka; Liliane Frey-Rohn the tragedy of Nietzsche; John Sanford the drama of King Saul, and Timothy O'Neill, in *The Individuated Hobbit*, the adventures of Frodo.[24]

INDIVIDUATION: GOD AND THE SELF

Many of Edinger's examples, and for that matter Jung's, are religious in content. The question therefore arises: Is the process of individuation a religious process? Or, to put it otherwise: Is the goal of the individuation process – that is, the realization of the Self – identifiable as a religious goal?

As is often the case with Jung, his answer appears, initially at least, to be unequivocal. Individuation may be defined as religious because it is an *archetypal* process, and because any such orientation towards archetypes is religious. This conclusion follows directly from Jung's previous account of religious experience.[25] A religious experience is the 'numinous' experience by the individual of that aspect of his own psyche that is primordial, archetypal and collective. It is the experience of his own suprapersonal form, of the immanent-transcendent, 'God within us.' Because therefore individuation is similarly motivated by an archetype – in this case the archetypal desire for wholeness – it may also be construed as a religious and numinous process. Admittedly this process does not depend on a particular metaphysical system, creed or rite, but derives its religious quality solely from being a *collective experience*: it requires, in other words, a 'religious outlook on life' by demanding of the individuating self insight into his own psychic nature; that he perceives that his conscious ego is grounded on something that is deeper than, prior to, and more fundamental than his own distinct personality, and that his desire to become an integrated human being is at the same time an experience of the eternal and archetypal foundation of his own psychic being.

By the same token, we can also identify the goal of individuation as a religious objective. To realize the Self is, as we have noted, a collective and archetypal ambition: to that extent alone it may be considered of religious concern. But this is not the only reason why Jung considers the goal of individuation to be religious. Individuation is also religious because Jung maintains that *the God-archetype and the archetype of the Self cannot be empirically distinguished from one another.* So, in *Mysterium Coniunctionis*, he writes:

> The extraordinary difficulty in this experience [of the self] is that the self can be distinguished only conceptually from what has always been referred to as 'God', but not practically. Both concepts apparently rest on an identical numinous factor which is a condition of reality.[26]

Jung's view that the concepts of God and the Self 'rest on an identical numinous factor' derives from what he takes to be a universally attested and empirical fact, namely, that 'the symbols of divinity coincide with those of the self: what, on the one side, appears as a psychological experience signifying psychic wholeness, expresses on the other side the idea of God.'[27] This hypothesis, as Jung makes clear, does not establish a metaphysical identity between God and the Self 'but merely the empirical identity of the images representing them.'[28] The Self, as he says elsewhere,

> stands for the psychic totality. So formulated, it is a psychological concept. Empirically, however, the self appears spontaneously in the shape of specific symbols, and its totality is discernible above all in the mandala and its countless variants. Historically, these symbols are authenticated as God-images.[29]

It has to be admitted that this identity between God and the Self is extremely confusing, and commentators have laboured valiantly to make sense of it. The most important available evidence on the subject is to be found in the series of letters written by Jung to the Catholic theologian Gebhard Frei. Frei was concerned that Jung had substituted the Self for God, a conclusion which prompted a vehement response for Jung. Writing in September 1944, Jung replied:

> I was astonished to find that even you, too, did not understand the concept of the 'self.' How on earth did you get the idea that I could replace God – and with a concept at that? I can establish the existence

of psychological wholeness to which our consciousness is subordinate and which is, in itself, beyond precise description. But this 'self' can never take the place of God, although it may, perhaps, be a receptacle for divine grace. Such regrettable misunderstandings are due to the assumption that I am an irreligious man who does not believe in God, and should be shown the road to faith.[30]

Jung's position, however, is by no means clear-cut. Following another letter, written in 1948, Frei's criticisms become much more understandable:

I could say that the 'self' is somehow equivalent to God. To a theological mind, such an assertion must undoubtedly be disturbing, for it sounds as if some substitute for God has been made. But to a psychologist this interpretation seems equally absurd, and he can hardly believe anyone capable of such stupidity. This is how he understands these things: When (as a psychologist) I speak of 'God' I am speaking of a psychological image. Similarly, the 'self' is a psychological image of human wholeness, and it also is of something transcendental – because it is indescribable and incomprehensible. We observe that both are expressed by identical symbols, or by symbols so alike as to be indistinguishable. Psychology deals with these images only in so far as they come under our experience, and their formation and behaviour in the context of life can be studied by comparative methods. This has nothing to do with God as such. How could any sane man suppose he could displace God, or do anything whatever to him? I am not so mad that I could be suspected of intending to create a substitute for God. How could any man replace God?[31]

The confusion at this point derives from the fact that Jung is speaking on two different levels: he is talking on the one hand about archetypes as such, which remain imperceptible and unknowable, and on the other about the perceptible and known manifestations of these archetypes in their symbolic images. Given this, we may say that just as the archetypal God-form is known only through the images it generates (the archetypal God-contents), so too the archetype of the Self is known only through its symbolic representations. Although Jung does not speak in these terms, it would be quite legitimate at this point to distinguish between the archetypal Self-form and the archetypal Self-contents, this distinction between form and contents *being appropriate to all archetypes*. But beyond this nothing more can be said about the archetypal God-form or the archetypal Self-form. The link between the two is, then, that both are, in the words just quoted, 'transcendental,' 'in-describable' and 'incomprehensible.' Aniela Jaffé is right to remark here that the 'unfathomability of God and the unfathomability of the self account for the synonymity, not the identity, of the two concepts.'[32] This explains why no pronouncements can be made on either the existence or nature of God or the existence or nature of the Self. Indeed, to speculate about a possible identity between the two, on whether one has replaced the other, is to indulge in the kind of metaphysical thinking that Jung consistently abhors.

The archetypes of God and the Self are not therefore identical in Jung's thought. However, when it comes to the images of these archetypes, the matter is quite otherwise. Here the psychologist can directly observe, in the archetypal contents, the phenomenal results of the activity of the otherwise imperceptible archetypal forms – these contents being, to repeat, the in-disputable empirical evidence of a particular psychological effect. What conclusions are we to draw, then, from a comparison between the images of God and the images of the Self? It is that these images cannot in practice be distinguished from one another. Why? Because both the symbols of God and the symbols of the Self are *symbols of unity*. All representations of God and the Self must therefore be regarded as symbols of *psychic wholeness*. Accord-ingly, God and the Self coincide in that each is expressive of the goal of the individuation process. This is, to repeat, the only conclusion that can be reached on the basis of the available empirical evidence.

> It is not possible to distinguish between symbols of God and symbols of the 'self'; i.e., it is not possible to *observe* the distinction empirically. I cannot help this being so; I mean that the manifestation of the 'self' should have this Godlike character. *I* did not make it so.[33]

Jung gives many examples of how comparative research has confirmed this coincidence between images of the Self and images of God. Three areas are of particular interest: early Christianity, medieval and late alchemy, and mysticism. Early Christianity was clearly well aware of the Self as a God-image, or at least that it could not be distinguished from one. 'Otherwise,' says Jung, 'Clement of Alexandria could never have said that he who knows himself knows God.'[34] Likewise the alchemists, in their complicated fish symbolism (which also extends back to the very beginnings of Christianity), fuse together notions of God and the Self. As Jung reports: '. . . the alchemical fish symbolism leads directly to the *lapis*, the *salvator*, *servator*, and *deus terrenus*: that is, psychologically to the self. We now have a new symbol in place of the fish: a psychological concept of human wholeness. In as much or in as little as the fish is Christ does the self mean God.'[35] Later alchemists, like Dorn, went still further and were quite specific in equating, 'the transcendent centre in man with the God-image. This identification makes it clear why the alchemical symbols for wholeness apply as much to the arcanum in man as to the Deity.'[36] As for mysticism, 'the symbols of the self coincide with the God-images, as for instance, the *complexio oppositorum* of Cusanus with the dyad . . .';[37] and in some later forms of it, like the *Cherubinic Wanderer* of Angelus Silesius, 'God and the self coincide absolutely. The times have undergone a profound change: the procreative power no longer proceeds from God, rather is God born from the soul.'[38]

For Jung, then, the wealth of symbols, myths, rituals and dogmas which constitutes the history of religions consistently indicates that, if the archetypes of God and the Self are not identical, the images generated by these archetypes cannot practically be separated from each another. 'Unity and totality,' he remarks, 'stand at the highest point on the scale of objective values because their symbols can no longer be distinguished from the *imago dei*. Hence all statements about the God-image apply also to the empirical symbols of totality.'[39] In other words, the archetypal God-contents may be of an almost infinite variety; but, this fact notwithstanding, these contents will always in some sense express the unconscious quest for wholeness. Put otherwise, because the demand for psychic unity, being archetypal, is an *a priori* and essential characteristic of every personality, this demand is an intrinsic part of any image of God created by the individual. Individuation is thus an integral part of the religious attitude: the God that is presented to the individual as an archetype within the depths of his or her own psychic being – the 'God within' – is apprehended by the religious mind as the God of wholeness or totality. The immediate and phenomenal experience that, for the believer, guarantees the existence of God as an unquestionable 'psychic fact' is thus indistinguishable from the believer's experience of his own archetypal Self. For this reason it becomes inappropriate to conceive of God as a 'wholly Other,' as being '"cut off" from man and existing outside and beyond all human conditions.'[40] Rather, following Meister Eckhart, we should now speak of the 'relativity of God,' of a God united with the human soul, with the soul now being considered the 'birthplace of God.' This view, Jung explains, 'is purely psychological': Eckhart is here conceiving God as *a psycho-dynamic state* or as *a psychological function of man*. God is no longer to be thought of as an object exerting an overpowering influence over a slavish subject, but rather as the personification of a supreme psychological value found within, and not outside, the human psyche.

> Henceforth the determining factor is no longer the overvalued object, but the unconscious. The determining influences are now felt as coming from within oneself, and this feeling produces a oneness of being, a relation between conscious and unconscious, in which of course the unconscious predominates.[41]

Not surprisingly, the fact that images of God are considered by Jung to be empirically identical with images of the Self has important implications for the final stages of his discussion. I want now to deal with two in particular.

THE PROBLEM OF EVIL

The first of these I shall mention only briefly. This has to do with Jung's examination of the problem of evil, of how to reconcile the existence of suffering in the world with the belief in an omnipotent and benevolent God.

Jung's discussion, as I have already pointed out,[42] is contained for the most part in his *Answer to Job*, a book that created a storm of theological protest on its appearance in 1951. Nor is it difficult to see why. According to Jung the Persona that Yahweh presents to Job – the mask of supreme goodness, justice and mercy – disguises the inner reality of his personality: that he is unjust and violent, jealous and unreliable. The encounter between Job and Yahweh thus becomes as psychologically traumatic for Yahweh as it is for Job: Job has made Yahweh aware of his own Shadow-side. In this respect, indeed, Job is morally superior to Yahweh in the sense that Job, by appealing to the compassionate side of God, is more aware of God's goodness and justice than God is himself. This conclusion also allows Jung to reverse the traditional doctrine of the Incarnation. However reluctantly, Yahweh has to admit Job's moral superiority and that consequently he has 'to catch up and become human himself.' Thus God becomes man not because of what man has done to God but because God must atone for his own crime against Job. 'Yahweh must become man precisely because he has done man a wrong. . . . Because his creature has surpassed him he must regenerate himself.'[43]

In this argument, as Don Browning has rightly observed, Jung is not employing some Manichaean dualism between good gods and evil gods or some gnostic distinction between good gods and evil demiurges, but rather speaking 'of both good and evil right at the heart of a single god.'[44] Good and evil, as Jung would have it, when 'reduced to their ontological roots . . . are aspects of God, names for God.'[45] This leads him to reject the Augustinian notion that evil is a negative absence of good. For the argument that evil is a *privatio boni* not only nullifies the reality of evil, but is built upon the doctrine that since God is good, what he creates must be good. Evil is thus taken to be not a thing in itself but a malfunction of the good – in the same way that deafness is a malfunction of hearing or war a malfunction of peace. But for Jung the image of God presented in the Book of Job is not of a *summum bonum*, but of an ambivalent and contradictory being, of a being with a dual nature, in which good and evil sit side by side.

Now however extraordinary Jung's argument may be – and setting aside the question of whether it completely misunderstands the doctrine of *privatio boni*[46] – the point to bear in mind is that Jung himself saw it as no more than a natural extension of his claim that images of God and images of the Self functionally coincide by both being symbols of wholeness and totality. The structure of the archetypal God-contents is, to repeat, empirically identical with the structure of the archetypal Self-contents: both are the visible effects of the innate human and archetypal disposition to construct images *of a particular type*, that is, images that have a *teleological or prospective character*, expressing the individual and collective desire to attain the goal of individuation, *Self-hood*. And this coincidence has an important consequence for God-images. For just as the Self is a dynamic and unifying concept, co-ordinating the two disparate elements of consciousness and the unconscious, so too God-images, as symbols of unity, must embrace the same disparity and so reflect *the nature of the opposites which is characteristic of all psychic phenomena*. Thus, as a totality, the archetypal God-contents are by definition a *coincidentia oppositorum*, integrating into a dynamic union the self-same archetypal impulses that the individual seeks to integrate in the process of individuation (i.e., the Persona, the Shadow, the Animus and the Anima). It follows from this that an image of God that does not include God's 'dark side' could not stand as a unifying symbol, and that without the presentation of God's 'shadow' the archetypal God-contents could not be formulated as images of the Self. As the personification of evil, the Devil must therefore assume his rightful place in the Godhead, a conclusion which adds a fourth figure to the Trinity, converting it into a quaternity.[47]

INDIVIDUATION AND IMAGES OF GOD

The coincidence between God-images and images of the Self has a second implication. It is that these images of God, because necessarily incorporating symbols of individuation, *can always be employed by the psychologist to reveal the stage attained by the individuating personality*. In other words, the archetypal God-contents, like the pictures of Miss X, can always be utilized for amplificatory and therapeutic purposes, giving to the patient some indication of his or her relative position along the path of individuation. This conclusion further suggests that the archetypal God-contents will, broadly speaking, change as the individual moves from the first into the second half of life, and that, following Edinger's classification, these images will be divisible into three categories, each category corresponding to the dialectical relation between the ego and the Self.

Now there is little doubt that, for Jung, because God-images are inseparable from Self-images in being expressive of the universal and collective disposition towards wholeness, they may be categorized in terms of the three stages of the individuation process. Jung makes this clear in several places, but his most important discussion is found in his 'A Psychological Approach to the Dogma of the Trinity' (1942).[48] From a psychological viewpoint, the Trinity denotes a 'process of unconscious maturation taking place within the individual.'[49] Here the three stages are enumerated in terms of the Trinity-symbol: that is, a Father-stage, a Son-stage, and a spirit- or Holy Ghost-stage. Let us look at each in turn.[50]

The Father-stage

This stage corresponds to the first stage of the individuation process, the period of infancy in the first half of life.

> Generally speaking, the father denotes the earlier state of consciousness when one was still a child, still dependent on a definite, ready-made

pattern of existence which is habitual and has the character of law. It is a passive, unreflecting condition, a mere awareness of what is given, without intellectual or moral judgment. This is true both individually and collectively.[51]

If we now ask what kind of God-images this stage generates, the answer is that it produces those of *primitive religion* – the consciousness of primitive man being identified as 'that of a child.' Here, then, we find the childhood identification with parental figures. At this level, the most immature and uncritical of human consciousness, 'man, world, and God form a whole, a unity unclouded by criticism. It is the world of the Father, and of man in his childhood state.'[52] The Father is, by definition, the prime cause, the creator of everything good and beautiful, there being no capacity to criticize God's handiwork. There is accordingly no problem of evil and the Oneness of God is unchallenged by any Other. 'A feeling of oneness, far removed from critical judgment and moral conflict, leaves the Father's authority unimpaired.'[53]

The Son-stage

The transition from the Father-stage to the Son-stage occurs when the state of unreflecting and uncritical semiconsciousness changes into a reflective and rational state of total consciousness, and so corresponds to that midpoint in the individuation process when the maturing ego begins to assert and emancipate itself.

> This state is not only in opposition to the still-existing earlier state, but, by virtue of its conscious and rational nature, it also contains many latent possibilities of dissociation.... The stage of the 'Son' is therefore a conflict situation *par excellence*: the choice of possible ways is menaced by just as many possibilities of error. 'Freedom from the law' brings a sharpening of opposites, in particular of the moral opposites.[54]

What kind of God-images does this stage generate? Just as adolescents distinguish themselves from their parents and begin to develop their own personalities, so here the images of God likewise become more differentiated. We have already seen this process at work in the *Book of Job*, where Satan is regarded as the shadow-side of Yahweh; but we find it also in the appearance of masculine and feminine attributes of the deity, mythologically presented in images of the 'syzygy' or divine pair, such as Adonis and Aphrodite, Osiris and Isis, and reflected again in the Judaeo-Christian tradition, with the appearance of Yahweh's feminine counterpart, the divine Sophia as the Old Testament embodiment of Wisdom. Pre-eminently, however, and as the *Book of Job* has already indicated, the most significant symptom of this 'irreversible increase in man's consciousness' is to split the original unity of the Godhead and to activate the notion of a Father incarnating in the God-man. 'Hence the One has to be supplemented by the Other, with the result that the world of the Father is fundamentally altered and is superseded by the world of the Son.'[55] The Son is the revealed God 'who voluntarily or involuntarily offers himself for sacrifice as a man, in order to create the world or redeem it from evil . . .; '[56] This idea is of course central to Christian teaching, but many other parallels are to be found, for example, in the Purusha of Indian philosophy, in the Persian conception of the Original Man (Gayomart, son of the god of light), in the gnostic redeemer-figure of Anthropos, and in the Egyptian belief that Pharaoh was both an incarnation and son of God.

The Holy Ghost-stage

The stage of the Son is, however, only 'a transition stage, an intermediate state, part child, part adult.'[57] It is therefore only in the third stage that genuine adulthood is achieved. Accordingly, the stage of the Holy Ghost corresponds to the final phase of the individuation process. Here, we recall, during the second half of life, the individual is gradually initiated into the inner world of the unconscious, and the ego begins to rediscover its collective and suprapersonal root.

> Accordingly, the advance to the third stage means something like a recognition of the unconscious, if not actual subordination to it. . . . Just as the transition from the first stage to the second demands the sacrifice of childish dependence, so, at the transition to the third stage, an exclusive independence has to be relinquished. . . . This third stage . . . means articulating one's ego-consciousness with a supraordinate total-ity, of which one cannot say that it is 'I,' but which is best visualized as a more comprehensive being, though one should of course keep oneself conscious all the time of the anthropomorphism of such a conception. Hard as it is to define, this unknown quantity can be experienced by the psyche and is known in Christian parlance as the 'Holy Ghost,' the breath that heals and makes whole.[58]

It is worth underscoring the last lines of this quotation. What in Christianity is called the 'Holy Ghost' is something unknown but yet experienced. In other words, 'Holy Ghost' *is a name for the archetypal God-form as experienced by the human psyche in the final stage of individuation and as perceived through the medium of the archetypal God-contents.* We can be equally specific about the imagery to be employed at this level. For since Jung has already claimed that empirically there is no difference between images of God and images of the Self, we can extend this equation and say that all images of the Holy Ghost are likewise images of union and wholeness, of a *complexio oppositorum* between the personal world of the ego and the suprapersonal world of the collective unconscious. Symbols of the Holy Ghost thus act like all other symbols of the Self: they represent to human beings the fulfilment of their own psychic development.

It is in this sense, then, that the stage of the Holy Ghost should be properly understood: not, as its title may suggest, as a stage exclusive to Christianity, but as a paradigm of the final stage of the individuation process, paralleled in the various symbolisms of other religions and cultures. Or to put the matter differently, each stage of the Trinitarian dogma represents a particular phase in the development of the God-archetype, with the Holy Ghost standing as the 'final, complete stage in the evolution of the God and the divine drama.'[59] First, as we have seen, there is the 'Father-stage,' in which the God-archetype is first distinguished as an autonomous Creator, one and indivisible. Then there is the 'Son-stage,' in which the God-archetype becomes differentiated through the appearance of the God-man. And finally there is the 'Holy Ghost-stage' in which the original unity is re-established, but in a higher and more elevated condition. This is because the preceding duality is not denied but rather reconciled in a new synthesis of opposites. Here the identity (or *homoousia*) asserted between Father and Son is, through the 'deifying effect of the Holy Ghost,'[60] asserted of all men, so implying a 'broadening process of incarnation':

> Since the Holy Ghost is the Third Person in the Trinity and God is present entire in each of the three Persons at any time, the indwelling of the Holy Ghost means nothing less than an approximation of the believer to the status of God's son. One can therefore understand what is meant by the remark 'you are gods.' ... God, in the shape of the Holy Ghost, puts up his tent in man, for he is obviously minded to realize himself continually not only in Adam's descendents, but in an indefinite number of believers, and possibly in mankind as a whole.[61]

Language like this might suggest that, for Jung, the doctrine of the Trinity is not just the representation of a three-fold human development but also the description of a particular life-process within a transcendental reality. This is not the case. Jung remains true to his earlier position by having 'no intention of involving myself in the metaphysics of the Trinity.'[62] Whether God exists, or whether he exists as a trinity, is not a question for the psychologist but for the theologian. Indeed, here it is not even a question of God at all but of *human images of God*, that is, of the archetypal God-contents, here presented in ternary symbolism. All that the psychologist can do, therefore, is uncover the psychological validity of the dogma by revealing its collective foundation: by showing, as Jung has done, how the movement from Father to Son to Holy Ghost corresponds to the three-fold archetypal cycle of individuation. To speak, then, of the 'indwelling of the Holy Ghost,' or of the believer becoming 'God's son,' is to utilize a particular set of images which are valid because, being archetypal, they are *personifications of unconscious contents*. These images, in other words, have an immediate and absolutely certain phenomenal validity: they reveal certain psychological facts about those individuals who employ them – in this case, the realization of their own innate human wholeness and the discovery of their *a priori* relation to a supra-individual centre. All such images of the Holy Ghost stand, then, as images of the Self, and incorporate the unconscious perception that the process of individuation is the proper focus of human aspiration.[63]

We are now in a better position to see why a person's adherence to a particular image of God is so instructive for the psychologist. Any God-image, like 'Father,' 'Son' or 'Holy Ghost,' is the spontaneous expression of a certain predominant psychic condition: it thus indicates the stage to which that person has progressed along the path of individuation. Nor is the psychologist deceived by the image. The image chosen, because it proceeds from the unconscious, cannot be the product of deliberate choice, nor can it be foisted on others, and for the same reason: the validity of any image of the Self, including therefore any God-image, depends on the extent to which it expresses the archetypal experience of the particular individual involved. All images of God, in other words, are *psychic products of an essentially unconscious origin*, and so manifest themselves only in the effect they have on the observer. Whether or not they have this effect will not depend on any allegiance to a particular church or creed, but only on whether these images do or do not open up or manifest the *a priori* and collective dimension. As Jung remarks, 'Belief is no adequate substitute for inner experience, and where this is absent even a strong faith which came miraculously as a gift of grace may depart equally miraculously.'[64]

There is an important point to notice here. If the validity of a God-image depends on the inner experience it evokes in the percipient, then any image, even the most primitive, will be valid provided it fulfils this function. Individuation certainly sets up a model of progressive development, of how the individual should psychically evolve; but it provides, it should be stressed, no chronological account of how a particular individual will evolve. Indeed, given what Jung has already said about the difficulties of the process, it is more than likely that many of the images of God we encounter will reflect immaturity rather than maturity. As Jung says, even today 'in a civilized community the people who form, psychologically speaking, the lowest stratum live in a state of unconsciousness little different from that of primitives.'[65] For them, God is still conceived in archaic terms, as a power ruling us from the external world, beneficent and father-like.

Equally, and at the other end of the scale, there is no reason why the mature individual, progressing towards Self-hood, should employ images of an overtly religious character. For the rule here is a simple one. As an archetypal process, individuation will express itself in the archetypal images of Self, and, on the empirical level, these images are indistinguishable from the archetypal God-contents. But should these God-images lose their vitality or numinosity, new images of Self will replace them. Thus even comparatively sophisticated images, like the Trinitarian symbolism, will become redundant if they do not correspond to any archetypal experience, and will vanish like the ancient gods of Greece and Rome. The fact, therefore, that God-images have dominated in one age is no guarantee that they will dominate in another, or even that the notion of God will be employed at all. Even today 'we can see in individuals the spontaneous genesis of genuine and valid religious symbols, springing from the unconscious like flowers of a strange species, while consciousness stands aside perplexed, not knowing what to make of such creations.'[66]

> The psychological interest of the present time is an indication that modern man expects something from the psyche which the outer world has not given him: doubtless something which our religion ought to contain, but no longer does contain, at least for the modern man. For him the various forms of religion no longer appear to come from within, from the psyche; they seem more like items from the inventory of the outside world. No spirit not of this world vouchsafes him inner revelation; instead he tries on a variety of religions and beliefs as if they were Sunday attire, only to lay them aside again like worn-out clothes.[67]

This explains various contemporary phenomena. It accounts, for example, for the extraordinary interest in spiritualism, astrology, theosophy and, much more extensively, Eastern religions. It also explains the resurgence of 'abstract symbolism' like quaternity symbols and mandalas – these being symbols of, not substitutes for, the deity, 'typical of people who cannot project the divine image any longer.'[68] Even the belief in 'flying saucers' or 'Unidentified Flying Objects' can be construed as a 'modern myth,' replacing a God-symbol with an extra-terrestrial 'heavenly power,' whose 'simple, round form portrays the archetype of the self. . . .'[69] All these, then, are examples of what happens when human beings move away from concepts of God that they consider outmoded and irrelevant. To use an earlier analogy, these concepts have been drained of libidinal energy and have thus become valueless. Like a dammed-up water-course, the lidido is accordingly channelled in different directions, infusing fresh symbols with power and significance.

But here we should ask: What happens when no new symbols are created? What occurs when, after the disintegration of the old images of God and in the absence of any 'religious outlook on life,' no new images are forthcoming to replace them? Jung's answer is that we become ill. But what is the nature of the illness?

The immediate answer, as we have noted many times before, is that the individual becomes neurotic. Without the experience of his own archetypal centre, as it is mediated to him through the enormous variety of archetypal symbols, he will become unbalanced, unable to integrate the conscious and unconscious elements into a psychic totality. And the causes of this neurosis may have nothing to do with past associations but be entirely located within the present situation. In the first stage of life, an undeveloped ego-consciousness is quite normal – as normal indeed as is its development when the individual moves through adolescence into adulthood. But if these forms persist into the second stage of life they can produce neuroses. What was supposed to be a transitory phase has now become ossified into a permanent condition, with the ego estranged from its collective base. All this, however, is reflected in the archetypal contents generated by the unconscious, and to that extent the unconscious itself advocates the therapy. Any archetypal image, whether a God-image or not, must therefore be taken as something positive and therapeutic. Properly understood, it will reveal the nature of the disturbance and so indicate to the individual or psychologist the nature of the task ahead.

But is there an illness which is peculiar to the loss of God? On the face of it, this is impossible to answer. The fact that images of God and images of the Self are, for all practical purposes, identical makes it true to say that the loss of God is the loss of Self – that is, of a transpersonal centre. The difference between them does not lie, then, at the point of reference – both are individuation symbols and so both can illustrate the same psychic imbalance – but lies rather in the way this imbalance is presented in the image. And here it may be the case that one image is more potent than another. Consider, for example, the following passage:

> It is a psychological rule that when an archetype has lost its metaphysical hypostasis, it becomes identified with the conscious mind of the individual, which it influences and refashions in its own form. And since an archetype always possesses a certain numinosity, the integration of the numen generally produces an inflation of the subject.[70]

The particular state of 'psychic inflation' which Jung is describing occurs when, following the breakdown of the archetype, the ego personality, in an extraordinary act of self-assertion, deifies itself and attributes to itself the contents of the collective unconscious. We can see this happening, for example, when an individual identifies himself with his particular Persona, with his business or his titles. 'L'état c'est moi is the motto of such people.'[71] But when the lost archetype is a God-archetype the result can be still more dramatic, leading to the colossal pretension that one is something extraordinary, 'godlike' or 'superhuman.'[72] At its most virulent, this can develop into megalomania, as in the case of the locksmith's apprentice, who believed that the world was his picture-book.[73] But more generally it leads to an elation based upon illusion: the illusion, namely, that 'we are the culmination of the whole history of mankind, the fulfilment and the end-product of countless generations.'[74] In this sense, the death of God has, as its corollary, the birth of man as a god. All the libidinal energy which once suffused the belief in God is now redirected into a belief in human beings. God has become a mere 'sign' or 'name,' divested of any numinous power, and accordingly men and women construct other belief-systems, with themselves at their centre: beliefs, for example, in their own rational and scientific capacities, or beliefs in some secular or political movement that deifies mass-man (e.g., communism). Such inflations of an egocentric consciousness inevitably lead, however, to an alienated and 'despiritualized' world, empty and meaningless. For the fact is

> that an inflated consciousness is always egocentric and conscious of nothing but its own presence. It is incapable of learning from the past, incapable of understanding contemporary events, and incapable of drawing right conclusions about the future. It is hypnotized by itself and therefore cannot be argued with.[75]

It is Jung's conviction, however, that the egoism of individualism is only a stage along the path of individuation; that although assertive ego-consciousness may be the prevailing mood of today, it is nevertheless an inevitable prelude to the reintegration of ego with Self. In this sense, alienation is a necessary step towards restitution, and the fact that it appears that this transition is taking place today, however fitfully, constitutes for Jung the great spiritual change overtaking the modern world.

> The gods whom we are called upon to dethrone are the idolized values of our conscious world. Nothing, as we know, discredited the ancient gods so much as their love-scandals; and now history is repeating itself. People are laying bare the dubious foundations of our belauded virtues and incomparable ideals, and are calling out to us in triumph: 'There are your man-made gods, mere snares and delusions tainted with human baseness – whited sepulchres full of dead men's bones and of all uncleanness'. We recognize a familiar strain, and the Gospel words, which we failed to digest at Confirmation, come to life again.[76]

The contemporary reappearance of God or Self imagery is therefore symptomatic of an unconscious awareness of what happens when human beings become the centre of their world, of the psychic disruptions that result. This elevation of ego-consciousness, although an essential concomitant of the individuation process, leads to an arbitrary and dangerous restriction of the psyche, removing individuals from those *a priori* and collective aspects of their personality which are necessary for psychic health. All these images, whether overtly religious or not, thus correspond to a profound and very definite psychological need, not just of those who employ them but of all human beings. For it is only by turning to these great archetypal images that we can relocate the meaning of our lives. What we find in these images is the expression of our own archetypal nature: that we are not merely personal and subjective beings, but beings also possessing an impersonal and objective dimension, and that in this dimension lies a meaning that is neither transitory nor partial but which is rather infinite and universal. Accordingly, individuals no longer feel isolated but discover, through the medium of these images, their own supra-individual and eternal foundation. For Jung the whole process of life may be construed as adapting to this truth – communicated to us from the depths of the unconscious through archetypal symbols. Admittedly, this is less apparent to us in the first half of life; but in the second half of life, as we turn from the external world to the inner world, the images of God and Self reassert themselves, and the quest for individuality takes on a new seriousness. For these images, we recall, not only express life's task, the attainment of Self, but also indicate the means of achieving it, of what it is within the psyche that needs to be adjusted. To that extent they impose upon all individuating personalities a unique duty and responsibility: to experience these images as expressing their own inner need for wholeness, and to construct their lives according to that need.

CONCLUSION

We are now as far away from Freud as it is possible to be. For Freud the images of religion contain nothing more than repressed contents, these contents being constellated around the figure of the father. Thus both the belief which created them and the belief which even now venerates them remain locked into a particular Oedipal neurosis about a dominant male. To maintain the image is therefore to maintain the obsession, and religious worship becomes no more than the unconscious desire to remain infantile, submissive and dependent. Maturity, accordingly, lies in a movement away from the protective and consoling embrace of these images, but quite how the particular individual will develop thereafter it is impossible to say. For Freud all that can be said is that life is bounded by the certainties of birth and death, by the struggle against external forces and by the continuous conflict between the powers of the ego and id. But to suppose that it contains a universal and progressive instinct towards higher development is another of those 'benevolent illusions' that should be abandoned.[77]

For Jung, it is one of the great ironies of modern psychology that Freud, who did so much to awaken interest in the unconscious, and who therefore stands as one of the great heroes of the modern world, should ultimately have misunderstood the precise nature of his own discoveries. Freud indeed presents an instructive reminder of what can happen when an assertive ego-consciousness forgets its own collective base: the unconscious itself becomes one-dimensional, no more than a repository of repressions, and so devoid of precisely that eternal and impersonal element which is its most distinctive and precious characteristic. Correcting Freud's error thus produces a completely different picture of humanity and a completely different interpretation of religion. There exists within the human psyche an *a priori* potentiality of wholeness, an instinct of dynamic intensity, which seeks to integrate conscious and unconscious contents into a coherent psychic totality. Jung calls this 'the Self,' and the process by which it is realized 'Individuation'. This process follows a fairly regular pattern, distinguishable primarily in the second stage of life, and this pattern may be discerned in the Self-images that spontaneously emerge from the unconscious. God-images, however, are also symbols of the Self, and for that reason they too are symbols of individuation, archetypal in origin, and may be employed to reveal the process by which Self-hood is achieved. Freud's advice – that these fabricated images must be discarded to achieve maturity – only serves, then, to hinder, if not actually prevent, the very process he is seeking to advance. For these images are not substitutes or 'signs' for something else (e.g., an Oedipus complex), but natural manifestations of the psyche, genuine psychic phenomena, which provide access to the contents of the unconscious, and so crucial insight into the current state and progress of the individuating personality. Through them human beings discover both what they are and what they are capable of becoming.

10

A CRITICAL APPRAISAL

Although invariably sympathetic towards attempts to systematize his thought, Jung was generally less happy with the results. For him, the elusive character of his thinking reflected the elusive character of the psyche itself, to the point indeed where ambiguity became a necessary component of his arguments. This in itself presents us with yet another contrast with Freud. For whatever one may think of Freud's theories, he remains one of the great literary figures of his time, presenting his ideas in a style that is always clear and invariably persuasive: it is small wonder, indeed, that Thomas Mann considered *Totem and Taboo* 'a literary masterpiece allied to, and comparable with, the greatest examples of literary essays.'[1] But the same can hardly be said of Jung. Indeed, as Anthony Storr has remarked, 'it is easy to lose patience with Jung.'[2] Jung's habit, for example, of personifying unconscious contents can be highly confusing to all but the uninitiated, and it is not always easy to see how a disquisition on the alchemical *lapis philosophorum* or the visions of Brother Klaus will have any therapeutic value except to the highly educated. This is not an entirely trivial point. If Jung's amplificatory technique involves this degree of erudition, then it lays him open to the charge of 'élitism.' It is not merely that the analyst must be sufficiently aware of the relevant mythological, literary, artistic and religious parallels, but that the significance of this material should not be entirely lost on the analysand. For the most part, however, these are observations which, although repeated by critics like Cox, Sykes and Zaehner,[3] have little to do with Jung's arguments and more to do with their presentation and the nature of Jung's clientele. For although the theory of archetypes does clearly require a degree of scholarship, it is also part of Jung's view that confirmation of the theory lies very much in the public domain, and that accordingly these validating cultural parallels can be drawn by Jungian and non-Jungian alike. The practical difficulties involved in establishing Jung's arguments are not therefore grounds for rejecting them.

What, then, of these arguments? The first thing to say about them is that they have been received with a bewildering variety of reactions. Jung has been variously accused of agnosticism and gnosticism, of mysticism and materialism, and much else besides. The Protestant theologian Max Frischknecht denounced him bluntly as an atheist,[4] while for Kathleen Raine Jung's impact within and outside the Church has been so immense 'that it seems that Zürich is once more the center of the Reformation.'[5] This will come as a shock to many Roman Catholics, particularly since, as Karl Stern points out in his review of Father Victor White's *God and the Unconscious* (1952), 'Catholic philosophers and psychologists seemed unwilling to touch Jung's Analytical Psychology with a ten-foot pole.'[6] But this state of affairs did not last for long. In 1957, the Jesuit theologian Raymond Hostie published his influential *Religion and the Psychology of Jung*, in which, despite many stringent criticisms, he concluded that Jung has 'rediscovered the religious and the sacred and got rid of an overweening rationalism.'[7] The Dominican priest, Antonio Moreno, was even more approving in his *Jung, Gods, and Modern Man* (1970). He writes that Jung's 'greatest contribution to theology' lies in proving 'that the symbols, dogmas, and images of Christianity are archetypal.'[8] Nor has Catholic interest in Jung abated, as a recent collection, *Catholicism and Jungian Psychology* (1994), illustrates.[9] Protestant theologians have also employed Jung to some effect. Wayne Rollins, in *Jung and the Bible* (1983), applies many Jungian terms in order to 'empathize' with the concerns of the biblical writers;[10] Gerald H. Slusser, in his book *From Jung to Jesus* (1986), appropriates Jung's account of the Hero-myth and applies it to the figure of Jesus;[11] Christopher Bryant, a member of an Anglican religious community, explores the implications of Jung's psychology for the Christian life;[12] and two episcopal priests, Morton Kelsey and John Sanford, both trained in Jungian psychotherapy, have explored the relation between individuation and Christian spirituality.[13] More significant still, Paul Tillich, in his *Theology of Culture* (1959) speaks of Jung as one 'who knows so much about the depths of the human soul and about the religious symbols,' although he is clearly uneasy about Jung's notion of revelation.[14]

More predictable, of course, are the reactions to Jung drawn along party lines. It comes as no surprise than a Jungian like Charles Hanna should claim that by studying Jung 'we can gain an insight into the ways by which men become aware of God,'[15] or that the Freudian Edward Glover should dismiss Jung's writings on religion as so much 'verbiage,' adding that

> so far from being religious in tendency, Jung's system is fundamentally irreligious. Nobody is to care whether God exists, Jung least of all. All that is necessary is to 'experience' an 'attitude' because it 'helps one to live'. Had Jung propounded this system in those Middle Ages, so dear to him because of their alchemical associations, he would certainly have been burned at the stake.[16]

As this quotation perhaps indicates, Glover's *Freud or Jung* (1950) is unparalleled in the whole history of anti-Jung literature. Others, however, of no apparent ideological predisposition, have been almost as vituperative as Glover. Richard Peters, the editor of George Brett's classic *History of*

Psychology, concludes that many of Jung's writings are 'so mysterious as to be almost undiscussable.'[17] Philip Rieff calls on

> both the authentically religious and the scientific to dismiss Jung's doctrine, as an unworthy amusement for the distraction of those who, by being thus entertained, confirm the nasty habit developed among cultivated moderns of thinking too seriously about themselves alone.[18]

As for Lydiard Horton, the only good thing to be said of Jung is that he presents criticisms of Freud that are 'concrete, positive and sensible, while just in scientific spirit.'[19] The title of Don McGowan's book, *What is Wrong with Jung*, indicates where he stands.[20] But for a more balanced view we should return to Father Victor White, whose opinion of Jung is altogether more cautious: 'I think that the friendliness of Jung presents a far more serious and radical challenge to religion as we know it than did ever the hostility of Freud.'[21] This view, which is also shared by the psychologist Erich Fromm,[22] is much nearer to my own. For the question now to ask of Jung is whether, in his campaign against Freud's materialistic determinism, he has not gone too far in the opposite direction and produced a reductionism of another kind, namely that of *psychologism* – of reducing religion to no more than a subjective phenomenon.

JUNG'S METHODOLOGY

Jung repeatedly insists that, 'although I have often been called a philosopher, I am an empiricist and adhere as such to the phenomenological standpoint.'[23] Phenomenology for Jung involved the fairly straightforward description of certain observable psychic 'facts,' among which could be included a much broader range of psychic phenomena than had hitherto been accepted. Thus the products of 'fantasy-thinking' – dreams, fantasies, visions, aesthetic experiences, beliefs, and so on – are not to be excluded because they require no correspondence with the outside world (as in 'directed-thinking') since indeed the imaging of reality by the psyche, even in its most pathological form, *remains the only reality for the individual who creates it*. Thus the subject-matter of the empiricist is subjective personal experience, and this experience is not to be denied merely because, say, it can be reduced to an Oedipal effect or because it is claimed to be a numinous response to a transcendental but unknowable reality. Repeatedly Jung stresses that psychology is only concerned with the facts of such experiences, and that accordingly any psychic experience, including therefore a religious experience, is 'true' in as much as it exists. For Jung, then, facts denote psychic phenomena, and they are correctly construed as facts because they provide the only immediate certainty we are capable of possessing, namely a knowledge of our own psychic world. This point is emphasized time and time again. 'All our knowledge consists of the stuff of the psyche which, because it alone is immediate, is superlatively real. Here, then, is a reality to which the psychologist can appeal – namely, psychic reality.'[24] Or again: 'Only psychic existence is immediately verifiable. To the extent that the world does not form a psychic image it is virtually non-existent.'[25]

Now while it is undoubtedly true that the catholicity of Jung's approach allows us to investigate a whole range of phenomena previously discarded by psychologists – making it entirely understandable that he should be lauded as a 'scientific pioneer'[26] – it is not the subject-matter thus included which causes concern but the so-called 'empirical method' which allows for its inclusion. Clearly Jung was aware of difficulties at this point. This is apparent from a fascinating correspondence with E. A. Bennet. Bennet argued that the hypothesis of archetypes had not been scientifically demonstrated. To this Jung responded by saying, first, that there was no such thing as an 'absolute proof,' and second, that accordingly all he could depend on was 'the observation of relevant facts.' When pressed by Bennet on whether this required 'something like a chemical or physical proof,' Jung replied that psychological evidence was more like legal evidence, operating on the basis of 'commensurability of evidence.' In his final letter, however, he shifts ground again, and agrees with Bennet that the objective observation of phenomena, with its method of classification, prediction and experimentation is 'exactly what I do and always have done' but he then concludes, rather confusingly, by distancing psychology from the Anglo-Saxon scientific tradition – which is based on 'physical, chemical, and mathematical evidence only' – and by placing it squarely in the European tradition where 'historical and comparative methods are scientific.'[27]

I shall have more to say about Jung's comparative and historical method when we come on to discuss the theory of archetypes. For the moment let us keep with his claim that we have no access to any world other than the psychic, and that accordingly empiricists, when investigating this world, cannot establish any facts about it which are not themselves psychic – the corollary of this being, of course, that neither can they provide any evidence that the world is not psychic. Roger Brooke is entirely correct to call this a 'fateful epistemological turn' in Jung's argument, 'the immediate effect of this self-enclosed position' being that the 'psyche lacks a definition that is not tautological.'[28] The tautology appears as follows: If, as Jung claims, it is true to say that 'Only the psychic world is verifiable,' then this statement precludes the possibility of its falsification, with the consequence that any investigation of the question, 'Is the world psychic or not?' will always have the same result. This, however, is to construe the proposition, 'The world is a psychic world,' not as an empirical proposition but as a *necessary* proposition, as one which, like the propositions of logic and mathematics, is essentially hypothetical and unrestrictive, being applicable to any state of affairs whatsoever. On this reasoning, therefore, it is not evidence which determines the claim but a particular *definition of the world* which precludes any denial of its truth. In that case, Jung's claim ceases to be empirical: it does not conform to the evidence but makes the evidence conform to it. This exposes the tautology. Describing 'the world' as psychical has added nothing that was not already implied in the definition of that term. Thus X is Y because by X we mean Y.

To clarify the point I am making here, let me refer to Friedrich Waismann's notion of 'open texture.'[29] Waismann contends that open texture is a fundamental characteristic of empirical concepts, and that it is this which prevents them from being verified conclusively. Open texture, that is, denotes the *essential incompleteness* of empirical descriptions, so that, however hard we may try, we can think of no definitions of open-textured terms that are not *always* corrigible or emendable.

> This has an important consequence. Phenomenalists have tried to translate what we mean by a material object statement into terms of sense experience. Now such a translation would be possible only if the terms of a material object statement were completely definable. For only then could we describe completely all the possible evidences which would make the statement true or false. As this condition is not fulfilled, the programme of phenomenalism falls flat. . . . Similar remarks apply to certain psychological statements such as 'He is an intelligent person'; here again it is due to the open texture of a term like 'intelligent' that the statement cannot be reduced to a conjunction or disjunction of statements which specify the way a man would behave in such-and-such circumstances.[30]

Waismann's position is, I believe, of particular relevance to Jung because it is precisely this that Jung denies. But this denial, following Waismann, leads Jung into an untenable position *as an empiricist*. For in saying that 'The world is a psychic world' he is claiming that men and women cannot see the world except psychically – that this psychic constraint is an essential and necessary quality of all human perception and cognition – and saying this removes the margin of uncertainty that belongs to statements about material objects, including human beings as material objects. Jung is thus forced into the uncomfortable position of having to affirm two things: first, that he has here completed a description of human beings which foresees completely all the possible circumstances in which that description is true and false; and second, that his own factual knowledge of human beings is complete to the point that nothing unforeseen can occur to upset or modify that description. This, however, is to assign to empirical knowledge an absolute or 'closed-textured' character it cannot possess.

These philosophical objections to Jung's notion of 'psychic facts' find an echo in Paul Kline's summary of attempts to validate Jung's research. Reviewing the central concepts of archetypes and the collective unconscious, Kline concludes that 'it is clear that in place of the Freudian theory which has empirical support to some extent at least and which *can* be tested, Jung has substituted two untestable hypotheses.'[31] Indeed, the only concepts that

Kline has any time for are those of extraversion and introversion, because these have achieved a measure of scientific support – Kline here mentions the two famous questionnaires measuring the two attitude-types, the Gray-Wheelwright Test (1946) and the Myers-Briggs Type Indicator (1962).[32] Similar criticisms of Jung at this point have been made by Vincent Brome, Philip Sherrard, Hall and Lindzey, and Hans Eysenck.[33]

Now while it is still true that most present-day Jungians hold to the primacy of 'psychic facts,' not all do, and it is interesting to note that many of the major modifications in Jungian theory in recent years have been to do with this greater need for scientific verification. In 1968, the co-founder of the C. G. Jung Institute in Zurich, C. A. Meier, called for 'a more scientific approach in Jungian psychology,'[34] a plea supported by one of Jung's most sympathetic commentators, Mary Ann Mattoon. She writes: 'My objection is that virtually all of the facts used in analytical psychology are inner facts regarding specific individuals. They are useful in the context of discovery, but not in the context of justification.'[35] Mattoon lists a good deal of supportive evidence for many of Jung's concepts – some of these I shall mention later – but perhaps her most telling point is that tests conducted among Jungian analysts revealed that the great majority of them were introverts, an attitude matched by an over-emphasis on the intuitive-function and a corresponding depreciation of the sensation-function – the function, significantly, which is primarily concerned with facts and things, that is, with the objective world. Her suggestion is, then, that Jungians have a natural tendency to overplay the 'non-rational aspects of our discipline' at the expense of scientific evidence. 'I recommend,' she concludes, 'that we explore, much more fully than we have, the possibilities of scientific method before we make pronouncements on its limitations.'[36] I take this as going some way towards recognizing the criticism I have just made, namely that Jung, despite all his protestations to the contrary, cannot claim to be an empiricist if he is not prepared to submit his findings to the scientific possibilities of verification and falsification.

I have laboured this point about Jung's method because, if the idea of the world as a 'psychic world' is the rock upon which he builds so many of his theories, it is also upon this, as we shall soon discover, that so much of his thinking about religion founders. Jung's method has, I hope, exposed his view about what constitutes a truth-claim: what is true is what is 'psychologically true.' What now needs to be repeated is that this statement implies an identification of what is known to be true with the particular psychological condition of the human subject. This explains why Jung dismisses meta-physical claims to truth. Metaphysics claims to know something that cannot in fact be known, and this is the case not because nothing exists to be known but because all such claims to knowledge involve an illegitimate extension of the psyche beyond itself. Now whether Jung is consistent in his rejection of metaphysics is, at this moment, beside the point. For what concerns us here is the proposition that the only thing that is known is an *inner psychological* state, and that accordingly, for Jung, the only question to ask is whether this state is a real state – that is, one actually being experienced by the subject – and certainly *not* the question of whether this psychological state has any grounding in a reality that can be distinguished apart from the subject concerned. Jung of course was well aware of metaphysical attempts to explain what is experienced by hypothesizing the existence of non-empirical and transcendent entities (e.g., Plato's Forms or Aristotle's Unmoved Mover) but tended to brush them aside by simply repeating his definition of the world as a psychic world. But this quite extraordinary rejection of the whole metaphysical tradition as epistemologically fruitless, with its correlative assertion of the primacy of psychic experience, leads Jung into difficulties of his own, not least because, as he sees it, this failure of metaphysics justifies his own position that no ontological warrant is required for a psychic experience to be accepted as a 'true' experience; or rather, that the truth of such an experience does not depend on whether it corresponds to reality but solely on whether it is 'felt' to be true.

Now it is this omission on Jung's part that bedevils his thinking on religion. For whether we are talking about his distinction between God as archetypal-form and as archetypal-contents, between the numen and the numinous, or between the symbolic language of religion and what it purports to express, the critical questions are: Is God to be regarded solely as part of the human psyche or as distinct from it? Does God exist as an ontological reality or only as a psychological reality? Or, to put the matter another way: Is religious experience essentially psychological, something generated by the psyche and certified by the psyche as true, or should it also be construed as a response to an objective deity, to something that exists apart from the psyche as an existential 'given' and which cannot therefore be equivalent to a psychological state?

THE THEORY OF ARCHETYPES

Jung's repudiation of the charge of psychologism is found in his theory of archetypes, and this I have examined in some detail in Chapter 8.[37] His defence is that, while it is certainly true that God exists only as psychic reality, the psychic reality with which God is being identified is archetypal – the archetypal God-form. Since, then, the archetypal God-form specifies an *a priori* mode of apprehension belonging to the collective unconscious, and which may be properly described as 'primordial' and 'eternal,' it makes absolutely no sense to claim that individual experiences can of themselves generate the God-form. These experiences will certainly determine how the God-form is presented in the symbolic images of the archetypal God-contents, but these images are themselves the perceptible effects of the God-form as an imperceptible and universal *cause*. In this argument, accordingly, the possibility of the completely subjective creation of all religious imagery –

including therefore images of God – is denied by reference to the objective, impersonal and unacquired status of the archetype which determines the form of the configurational process but not its contents.

Since, then, Jung's defence of his position depends on his general theory of archetypes, it is time to look at this theory and to consider the question of whether or not the supra-personal and collective status of archetypes can be established. Needless to say, this brings us to the most widely discussed aspect of Jung's psychology, not least because, as H. E. Barnes has correctly indicated, the validity of Jung's entire enterprise stands or falls with this hypothesis.[38] It is worth beginning with Jung's earliest notion of an archetype – that it is something akin to an 'instinct,' a biological norm or 'pattern of behaviour' that can be observed in, for example, the way a child sucks its thumb *in utero*. For Jungians there is considerable empirical support for this idea, in particular from ethnology, the study of animal behaviour. Fordham was the first to point to Niko Tinbergen's demonstration of 'innate release mechanisms' (IRMs) as evidence of archetype-like predispositions, and Stevens and Mattoon additionally refer to John Bowlby's 'goal-corrected behavioural systems,' and to the idea of 'imprinting' developed by the Austrian zoologist, Konrad Lorenz. Lorenz, indeed, assured Jung's disciple, Dr Marie-Louise von Franz, that 'he accepted Jung's theory of archetypes in principle.'[39] Stevens goes even further and cites further parallels in the field of genetics, seeing DNA as the 'replicable archetype of the species,' while Mattoon, admittedly with more misgivings, cites the neurological work of Rossi, who suggested that Jung's archetypes could be located in the right cerebral hemisphere.[40]

Whatever the merits of these researches, the question remains whether, in addition to these functional patterns of unlearned animal behaviour, we may posit also an archetypal disposition to construct images, myths or beliefs of a uniform type. Here, indeed, Stevens himself is taken to task by Marilyn Nagy for obscuring this aspect of the theory and for failing to see that Jung's subsequent shift away from a theory of instincts was because 'of his [Jung's] inability to accept the mechanistic assumptions which underlie ethnological theory.'[41] Indeed, according to his later view on archetypes, and clearly in order to distance himself from the accusation of Lamarckianism, Jung side-steps the question of the origin of mythological motifs altogether by simply saying that they are not to be naturalistically explained, as if equivalent to physical conditions, but that their appearance is coincident with the appearance of life itself. 'Empirically considered,' he writes, '. . . the archetype did not ever come into existence as a phenomenon of organic life, but entered into the picture with life itself.'[42] This, we remember, elevates the archetype to the level of the *a priori*: it becomes something innate rather than acquired, a 'mode of perception' known only through the images and ideas it engenders.[43]

Proceeding, then, as a phenomenologist, Jung collects these images and ideas and from them infers the form of the archetype. The most famous example of this procedure is the case of the young schizophrenic who imagined he saw the sun's phallus, and the similarity of his vision with Albrecht Dieterich's researches into Mithraism.[44] McGowan, never one to mince his words, thinks this case a fitting example of the fallacy of Jung's whole approach, wrong in method and wrong in fact. McGowan makes the point that it was entirely possible that this patient encountered this idea before, not least because, somewhat to the embarrassment of his editors, Jung incorrectly dates Dieterich's book and because the idea of a tube passing under the robes of the Virgin, being a common motif in European religious art of the Medieval and Renaissance, was one that this young man might well have come across, a fact which Jung conveniently omits to mention. All this uncovers the extreme subjectivity of Jung's method, in which evidence must conform to Jung's own convictions. But, as McGowan comments, quoting Karl Popper, 'a subjective feeling of the truth of an idea is no support for its being accepted as a hypothesis.'[45]

But even if we accept that this particular example of archetypal formation is unfortunate, there are plenty of others. What are we to make, for instance, of the archetypes of Shadow, Anima, Animus and Self, all of which are postulated on the basis of recurring motifs, or, moving to a more specific case, of the similarities between Miss Miller's 'Song of the Moth' and the visions of the Johannine Apocalypse? For Jung these are not coincidences but empirical evidences of the operation of the *a priori* category of the human psyche – the archetype itself – which is known only in these manifestations. Indeed, once we realize that an archetype is a *collective* concept, we can state as an axiomatic truth that, where these parallels exist, there exists an archetype; and, furthermore, that these parallels, being witnesses to the universality of a *specific* archetype, will be equally *specific* in their imagery and thus have a unity of meaning whenever and wherever they appear – such as we saw in the close affinity between Miss X and the alchemists or in the mythological analogies of the Trinity-archetype found in Babylonian and Egyptian thought.

There are, however, many serious problems with this theory. Some of these I shall refer to in other contexts, but for now three in particular should be noted:

1   The first and most obvious criticism of Jung at this point is that his theory of archetypes is a further exemplification of the inherent weakness of his empirical method, and thus of his more general tendency to rush to a definition having once established cogently similar information. Gardner Murphy makes this point as follows:

> Jung's method – it is no more than a friendly exaggeration to say this –
> is to argue that because A is somewhat like B and B can, under certain
> circumstances, share something with C, and C has been known on

occasion to have been suspected of being related to D, the conclusion in full-fledged logical form is that A = D. As the language of *science* this is meaningless.[46]

In fact, Jung goes even further than this, and compounds his error by making this definition the basis for another. For from this similarity of symbols, myths and dreams – assuming for the purposes of argument that they *are* similar – Jung also infers a universal characteristic of all men and women, the archetypal *a priori*. Thus, from the contingent appearance of such images Jung infers a necessary proposition about human beings in general, which will therefore be applicable *no matter what images they may construct*. This, however, is to assign to Jung's empirical knowledge of the human psyche the complete or 'closed-textured' knowledge of, say, geometry, in which, if I describe a triangle, I give a complete description in the sense that nothing can be added to it that is not included in, or at variance with, the data.

2   This philosophical objection has one important practical implication. Because the disposition to create archetypal images is said to be an *a priori* characteristic of all individuals, and because these images are themselves guaranteed as archetypal only by the immediate experience of these individuals, this means in effect that *any* image may be classified as archetypal. Certainly it is difficult to see how any image can be discounted as archetypal. If a person proposes that X is an archetypal image, then it is archetypal, for who can deny him his claim if the truth of an image is solely guaranteed by its psychological validity? This conclusion fits well with Jung's remarks about the inexhaustibility of archetypal symbols, and of the ever-present possibility of discarding one image for another if it ceases to be *perceived* as archetypal. He has made clear, however, that we can group these images into various distinct classes – for example, the archetypes of the Old Wise Man or the Earth Mother – and that these classes are determined by distinct parallels. But even within these groups, any change in the imagery, however dramatic, cannot dismiss it from membership of these particular classes because, to repeat, every person has an innate disposition to create archetypes, and so we cannot say that these changes are not instances of that disposition. These, then, are classes admitting of an almost limitless variation – indeed one class may even collapse into another, as we saw in the case of God-images and Self-images. The problem with this is that it runs the risk of rendering the term 'archetypal' virtually valueless as a means of distinguishing one image from another – to the point indeed where the statement 'This image is an archetypal image' may be rendered as the tautology 'This image is an image.' If this is the case, then we arrive at the unfortunate conclusion that Jung has provided us with no criterion by which to differentiate between, say, the religious myth of a believer and the myth of a delusional schizophrenic, and so no good reason why we should presume that it is only one of them who should be committed to hospital.

The point I am making here will be brought into sharper focus when we consider Jung's concept of individuation. For the non-Jungians, however, this lack of a criterion for distinguishing between images becomes immediately apparent when they seek empirical evidence for the operation of an archetype. John Fischer puts the matter well:

> The existence and working of the Jungian archetypes seems more difficult to demonstrate operationally: one can define objectively particular stimulus features or combinations of these, and can say whether or not they are present; but the Jungian archetypes have no clearly defined essential features by which their presence may be unequivocally established, and so many specific features are included as possible manifestations of one or another archetype that it is always possible to claim one is present.[47]

Of course, one response to this criticism is to claim that non-Jungians do not possess the practical experience necessary to recognize an archetype, as Jung himself does on occasions,[48] or that indeed they are insufficiently aware of those cross-cultural parallels which form the basis of the hypothesis. But this is a very weak defence. For saying that only those who believe in the theory of archetypes are capable of evaluating the material in its favour discounts the theory as empirical, and thus once again exposes the priority of theory over evidence. As Avis Dry remarks, 'either one remains outside and therefore insufficiently acquainted with the facts, or one moves inside and is cured of the desire to criticize.'[49]

3   But undoubtedly the most damaging criticism of Jung's theory of archetypes is that, in claiming that parallel images result from an archetypal human disposition – that these are the perceptible effects of an imperceptible cause – Jung has discounted the possibility that these *same* effects may be explicable in terms of a *different* cause. To make this point clearer, let us recall that Jung's reasoning here is inductive and analogical. On the basis of empirical observations of something that exists in the actual world – the existence of parallel images – he inductively infers that these images further resemble each other in a way that is not immediately observable, namely, that they all proceed from something that is in principle unknowable – the archetype itself or archetype-form. This, as he makes clear, does not demonstrate the existence of the archetype because all he is doing is postulating its existence as a *conceptual necessity* required to explain the patterns and repetitions of psychic phenomena.[50] But this assumption is by no means conclusive. That A resembles B in various ways does not in itself establish that it resembles B in another way; and to suppose that it does is to commit a well-known logical mistake, known as the fallacy of the 'affirmation of the consequent.' The logical form is as follows: A implies B; B is true; therefore A is true. Or: When Peter has had no sleep, he is irritable; Peter is irritable;

therefore Peter has had no sleep. The fallacy displayed here is fairly obvious. There may be a whole host of reasons, quite apart from insomnia, that account for Peter's irritability: he may have had a row with his wife or received an unpleasant letter from his bank manager. There may therefore be a great number of causes which have the same effect, or, put more technically, there may be more than one antecedent which leads to a particular consequent. Accordingly, that image A and image B resemble each other in possessing a particular characteristic – that, for instance, they are both 'Hero' images – is not in itself evidence that image A further resembles image B in possessing the additional property Y to account for that characteristic, namely, that both result from the deployment of the Hero-archetype. Thus the resemblance between effects does not establish a similarity in causes; and accordingly there may be more than one theory to account for the fact of parallel imagery. Or as Brown puts the matter: 'the hypothesis of the collective unconscious is . . . a quite unnecessary elaboration to explain certain observations which can be more simply explained in another way.'[51]

And several alternative explanations have been forthcoming. Not surprisingly, Freudians claim that the archetype concept is entirely explicable in terms of an individual's infantile history. Glover, for example, argues that myth formation can be easily accommodated by the 'forms of *individual* thinking, both conscious and unconscious, existing from the age of two onwards;'[52] and Nandor Fodor, analysing dream-theory, concludes that Jung's contribution is 'only verbal' and that there is nothing in the Jungian approach 'that the Freudian does not imply.'[53] Even less orthodox Freudians have no difficulty in rejecting the notion of a collective unconscious. For example, the Budapest anthropologist and psychoanalyst, Geza Róheim, who subscribed to Freud's primal horde theory but who rejected altogether any suggestion of a racial unconscious, had no trouble in explaining away Jung's archetypal phenomena in terms of shared human experiences, particularly those pertaining to infancy.[54] It is fairly obvious, he says, that human beings, irrespective of their various cultural situations, have certain experiences in common: all of us have parents, are born and die, and depend upon the sun and earth. What could be more natural, therefore, than to construct images and myths that express these universal themes: images of the Father, the Great Mother, the child, sun-gods, birth and rebirth, and so on? This point is echoed in the neo-Freudian school of Melanie Klein, which introduced the concept of 'internal objects' to account for archetypal phenomena. Following Klein, the construction of so-called archetypal images can be traced back to the child's earliest biological experiences, most notably feeding at the mother's breast. By a process of 'introjection,' these experiences, whether pleasurable or painful, are then internalized and incorporated into the infantile ego as internal objects, with the result that the infant lives in a world peopled by gods and devils.

In reality parents and child possess limited power of goodness and badness, wisdom and foolishness. The child's phantasy makes gods and demons and all those unearthly creatures of them which folklore and mythology, religious legends and artistic creation present to us in sublimated, and the imagination of the insane in more unsublimated, form. Moreover, the child places his self-created figures inside his own body and treats them as live entities alien to himself and beyond his control.[55]

One does not have to be a Freudian to agree with this critique. For example, the Harvard psychologist, Gordon Allport, although eschewing Freud's claim that religion is a thinly veiled sublimation of the repressed sexual impulse, and although having considerable sympathy for Jung's concern to locate religious belief at the centre of a forward-looking and developing ego, nevertheless denies altogether that mythological imagery cannot be acquired through acculturalization. For him, conformity to culture, especially during the period of childhood, is an important origin of the religious quest: a myth or ritual becomes accepted in order to cement the child's 'identification with those who provide him security, affection, approval.'[56] This explains why a child's earliest religious concepts are anthropomorphic – they are projections of the parents as powerful and loving agents – why religious-minded adults are invariably the products of parents who were themselves religious, and why a decline in the religious attitude is often coincident with the adolescent reaction against parental and cultural teaching. Religious systems are not therefore 'independent of the remaining portions of a culture, but are intimately integrated with them. For this reason the supplanting of one religion by another is not possible unless the culture is basically altered.'[57] At this point, however, it is not uncommon for Jungians to point to the writings of the structuralist, Jean Piaget, for confirmation of the archetypal hypothesis.[58] But, if anything, Piaget's work tends to support the criticism already expressed, that Jung's collective myths are more probably the consequence of common experience. Piaget's research into the cognitive development of children suggested that their progression through the stages of intuitive thinking, concrete thinking and abstract thinking were all levels of selecting, organizing and co-ordinating experience. The fact therefore that the infantile use of mythology and fairy-tales, which is a feature of the intuitive stage, gives way to something more realistic and then more conceptualized is an indication of the gradual differentiation of the self from external reality, and not, as Jung would have us believe, evidence of the unfolding of an archetype, of the activation of pre-formed images. This, as Piaget makes clear, is simply unfounded speculation:

Jung has an amazing capacity for construction, but a certain contempt for logic and rationality, which he contracted through daily contact with mythological and symbolic thought, has made him inclined to be content with too little in the way of proof. The better to understand the reality of which he speaks, he adopts an anti-rationalist attitude, and the surprising comparisons of which he has the secret cannot fail sometimes to disturb the critical reader.[59]

G. S. Kirk, who also quotes Piaget at this point, remarks that this view 'that Jung's general symbols could in theory be the result of common processes of symbolic assimilation in childhood, and in practice are, is going to take a great deal of refuting.'[60] It is worth mentioning here Kirk's own researches into the function of myth in ancient cultures. Kirk makes the valuable point that Jung's theory of archetypes presupposes a view of 'static symbolism'; in other words, that the significance of myths and symbols derives from duplicating an image or mythological motif already assumed to have a universal meaning because it proceeds from an archetype. Such a view, however, is 'largely erroneous.' For while it is certainly true that certain myths do contain static symbols of this kind – for example, recurrent subjects like ogres invariably carry with them the psychological associations of terror and revulsion – the great majority do not. Here, by contrast, the symbolic reference is 'dynamic and allegorical,' with whole episodes or situations being transposed into the form of the myth. Among these, Kirk mentions specifically those myths that embody responses to problems, with the needs of the community being reflected directly into mythical fantasy – this, Kirk claims, being particularly evident in extant Mesopotamian tales and in some relics of Greek mythology. These references to immediate social concerns make it very hard to accept 'the essentially romantic idea of myths as simply welling up directly out of the unconscious.'[61] Not surprisingly, Kirk concludes that Jung's theories are 'devoid of adequate evidential support.'[62] I should add here that the distinguished Oriental archeologist, Henri Frankfort, presents a criticism very similar to Kirk's. Frankfort tackles Jung directly by analysing the function of the Mother archetype in the religions of Ancient Egypt and Ancient Mesopotamia. He concludes that differences between them demonstrate that 'the archetypes are by no means universal and therefore obviously not necessary.' These differences can, however, be explained by the changing needs and problems of the community, such as the catastrophe of defeat or disastrous changes in the seasons. Jung's theory of archetypes accordingly 'leads him to misunderstand completely the historical life of symbols.'[63]

The main objection to Jung's theory is, then, that the existence of parallel images can be explained without having to make the further inductive inference that there exists in human beings an *a priori* disposition to form such images. This, needless to say, does not prove that Jung's hypothesis is false. This follows from the nature of inductive arguments. Since all inductive arguments deal with degrees of probability, all we can say is that, on the basis of the evidence before us, this hypothesis is improbable but not impossible. But here we should ask a further question. Even if we admit that myths, dreams, delusions and folklore do contain extraordinary similarities, and even if we were to admit for the moment that these similarities cannot be explained solely in terms of common human experiences, does this justify the inference that these similarities are *better* explained by postulating the existence of something even more extraordinary as their origin? Here we should do well to remember Hume's caution about the limitations of such arguments, namely, that they are incapable of leading to the discovery of any new and qualitatively different reality: that is, to a supra-empirical reality utterly distinct from those ordinary empirical experiences from which its existence was first inferred.[64] This is not to say that inductive reasoning cannot lead to the discovery of new information, but rather that the new facts discovered must be of the same general order as those which suggested the hypothesis in the first place. But that condition cannot be fulfilled in Jung's argument because here what is being inferred – the *a priori* existence of the archetypal-form, the archetype itself – is admitted to be outside our experience, unknowable and trans-empirical. This admission, it seems to me, is fatal to Jung's argument when he seeks to convince us that his explanation for the phenomenon of parallel imagery is preferable to any other. For the strength of the other arguments I have mentioned lies in the consistency they achieve between effects and causes: both lie within the fold of our common human experience, most notably our experience of the early years of life, and neither is explained by the invocation of another realm which is not directly accessible to us.

It is at this point that Jung, in reply, could well invoke Kant's moral argument.[65] For Kant, although sharing, and indeed being indebted to, Hume's most fundamental philosophical convictions about the purely speculative character of all metaphysical claims about supersensuous or supernatural reality, nevertheless proceeds, in his *Critique of Practical Reason*, to argue for God's existence as the *postulate* of the claims of morality upon us. That the existence of this reality cannot, strictly speaking, be known does not therefore mean that as moral agents, feeling the full force of moral obligation in the individual moral situation, we are not entitled to believe in it and to act *as if* our duties were divine commands. Like Jung, Kant thus stresses the personally experienced practical context in which this confession of belief is made: 'I must not even say, "*It is* morally certain that there is a God, etc.", but "*I am* morally certain, etc."'[66]

I am not the first critic, however, to point out that this invocation of Kant as a support for the theory of archetypes is by no means as straightforward as Jung thinks.[67] We should first record that Kant's moral argument, as many have noticed, sits uncomfortably with the anti-metaphysical conclusions of the main part of his *Critique*, and that indeed there are grounds for believing that Kant himself was uneasy about it.[68] More importantly, however, at no point in his argument does Kant claim that the system of moral rules *originates* in a transcendent reality, that these are the phenomenal effects of

180

an otherwise inaccessible cause, allowing us to move from laws to lawgiver. There are three reasons for this: first, we are incapable of obtaining any knowledge sufficient to support this claim; second, even if we could obtain it, the idea of God as the origin of moral obligation would destroy the autonomy of morals; and third, and most significantly, the existence or non-existence of God is not required for the determination of moral duty, it being a crucial feature of Kant's philosophy that the imperatives of duty can be and are generated by reason alone. Morality is not, accordingly, logically dependent on religion or God's existence. It is thus entirely contrary to Kant's central convictions to employ any immediate experience as the warrant for renewed speculative claims about the independent existence of something unknown but real as its cause. But this is precisely what Jung does, when specifying a supra-empirical reality – the eternal and imperceptible archetype – as the most appropriate explanation for the evident fact of parallel mythological imagery. Edward Casey puts this point well:

> Although Jung is granting with Kant that we can *know* appearances alone (in this case, imaginative appearances of presentations), he is asserting, in spite of a stated aversion to metaphysics, that the thing in itself can be characterized as real – that archetypes, as the ultimate metaphysical things in themselves, are metaphysically real because they are capable of producing certain 'effects.' Yet if Kant is right concerning the noumenal status of things in themselves, then we should not be able to say anything *at all* about them – not even that they are causally efficacious in some unknown way.... For even if the real is to be judged only by its effects, to assert the existence of these effects (as Jung explicitly does) is necessarily to presume the reality of their archetypal cause, and thus to indulge in metaphysics despite Kant's and Jung's own warnings.[69]

ARCHETYPES AND THE ARGUMENT FROM COMMON CONSENT

When we turn from Jung's general theory of archetypes to his concept of God as an archetype, we find the same inductive argument at work. Just as we may infer from the existence of images of the Great Mother or Wise Man an innate human disposition to form such images, so from the existence of innumerable God-images – the archetypal God-contents – we may likewise infer the *a priori* existence of the archetypal God-form. It is in these terms, says Jung, that we may properly speak of an 'instinct for God' in the sense that every individual possesses an impulse for religion as a psychic function. This same inference also forms the backbone of his account of religious experience. From the immediate and undeniable fact of having a 'numinous' experience in relation to a particular image of God, we may presume not just

181

that this image has been activated by an archetype but that this archetype is a 'numen,' that it has the qualities necessary to generate this experience, that is, that it is a 'revelation' of something that is 'holy' and of 'highest value,' of something that stands apart from the human recipient as the impersonal and eternal centre of his own existence. For Jung it is not enough, therefore, to say that in a religious experience one encounters only God-symbols. One must go further and say, as we just noted, that these symbols are phenomenal *effects*, mediating and disclosing an unknown, but nevertheless real and distinct, *cause*.

Once again there are very serious difficulties with this argument. The first, of course, arises from the fact that, since Jung is here using precisely the same inductive logic to establish the reality of the archetypal God-form as he deployed in his general theory of archetypes, this argument is subject to much the same objections, most notably that the alleged universality of God-images does not require the *a priori* capacity to create them. We can see this if we consider Jung's claim, often repeated, that human beings are by nature religious, that they have a religious impulse which they are born with. A newly born infant, we recall, is not a *tabula rasa*, but possesses at the deepest and collective level of its psyche an archetypal dimension, this dimension manifesting itself in the innate disposition to create images of a uniform type, amongst which we may count God-images. This ability, as we have seen, does not count as proof for the actual existence of God, but it does count as an argument for the *psychic reality* of God, of God as a self-evident and psychologically demonstrable factor in human experience.

This argument, as Paul Edwards points out, is a 'biological' variant of the so-called 'common consent' argument for the existence of God (the *argumentum e consensu gentium*): the universality of God-imagery is taken as evidence that men and women have an instinct for God, and it is then concluded that belief in God is psychologically true and so beyond dispute. In Jung's case, this argument is further supported by the claim that the denial of the religious instinct will have unfortunate consequences, namely, that it will invariably result in the onset of some psychological disturbance.[70]

There are, however, a number of well-rehearsed objections to The Argument from Common Consent, and these are, I submit, equally applicable to Jung's version of it. To begin with, it is worth recalling that John Locke, in the course of attacking the theory of innate ideas, rejects the notion of instinctive belief for two reasons: first, because the innateness of an idea or belief does not follow from its universality – after all, the ideas of the sun and heat are universal but are not 'natural impressions on the mind';[71] and second, because it can give no adequate reason why atheists are atheists or why there are 'whole nations among whom there was to be found no notion of a God.'[72] The first of these objections need not be developed since Locke is here repeating the criticism already advanced: that to move, as Jung does, from the universality of belief to the conclusion that this belief is innate appears to take no account of other possible explanations of belief's origin. It is worth mentioning here, however, that of modern philosophers the most persistent opponent of the Common Consent argument has been John Stuart Mill, and that in his *Three Essays on Religion* (1878) he offers several explanations for the universality of religious belief: that it is, for example, an extension of the natural tendency of the primitive mind to ascribe life and volition to inanimate objects; that, being considered indispensable for moral welfare, it will be inculcated in the young; and that it gratifies the common human desire to prolong life with the prospect of a future existence.[73] Again, whatever the merits of these arguments, reasons for rejecting them would have to be entered before inferring the innateness of belief in God from its universality.

To the second of Locke's objections, Jung has a ready response: both the denial of God and the absence of any idea of God indicate an ignorance of the actual composition of the collective unconscious, of which the archetypal God-form is a part. There may, of course, be a whole host of reasons why this is so, but the fact that people deny an archetype does not mean that they are right to deny it, that it does not in fact exist.

> Now religious ideas, as history shows, are charged with an extremely suggestive, emotional power. Among them I naturally reckon all *représentations collectives*, everything that we learn from the history of religion, and anything that has an '-ism' attached to it. The latter is only a modern variant of the denominational religions. A man may be convinced in all good faith that he has no religious ideas, but no one can fall so far away from humanity that he no longer has any dominating *représentation collective*. His very materialism, atheism, communism, socialism, liberalism, intellectualism, existentialism, or what not, testifies against his innocence. Somewhere or other, overtly or covertly, he is possessed by a supraordinate idea.[74]

Now what this extremely revealing passage seems to be saying is that, while manifestly the existence of belief does constitute part of the evidence for a religious instinct, the existence of unbelief constitutes another part – once of course we understand that any belief, even the belief that religious belief is wishful-thinking or the belief that there are no such things as archetypes, if worked up into an '-ism,' will provide evidence against itself. But frankly it is hard to be polite about this argument. Quite apart from exposing Jung's condescending attitude towards those 'innocents' who might disagree with him, it once more reveals the clear circularity of his own hypothesis. For by translating possible evidence against this hypothesis into evidence for it, the empirical status of his claim about the innateness of the God-archetype is elevated to the level of a necessary truth or definition, requiring no empirical confirmation. Thus what Jung seeks to establish has been already assumed.

What kind of observations would therefore be required to safeguard the empirical base of Jung's claim about instinctive belief? Well, at the very least we should require from him a more thorough investigation of those cases where a belief in God is not only denied but where its psychological benefits are at least questionable. There are, for example, people who not only do not believe but who do not wish to believe, who see religion, to quote Bertrand Russell, 'as a disease born of fear and as a source of untold misery to the human race.'[75] Then there are also those who do believe but who might well have been happier and more adjusted without belief – one thinks here of the eminent zoologist Philip Henry Gosse (1810-1888), whose son, Edmund, has movingly recorded his father's struggle with Darwinism in his masterpiece, *Father and Son*.[76] And then, of course, there is Darwin himself, whose rejection of religion was entirely rational and followed from its incompatibility with the theory of natural selection. Intending to become a clergyman, his first edition of *The Origin of Species* (1859) is an exercise in natural theology, with clear references to the power of the omniscient Creator; but by the sixth edition (1872) all such references have been deleted. By this time Darwin's religious position had developed into one of extreme agnosticism. In his own words, 'disbelief crept over me at a very slow rate, but was at last complete. The rate was so slow that I felt no distress, and have never since doubted even for a single second that my conclusion was correct.'[77] These cases, although not in themselves establishing that religious belief is not innate, do nevertheless stand as denials that it is, and for these to be discounted we need to be told more precisely why these are not genuine alternatives or why such denials are not also 'psychic facts' of equal legitimacy. But this Jung does not do. All we get is the repetition of the definition that human beings have this *a priori* disposition to construct God-images, a definition that renders the term 'religion' so broad in scope that it seems to cover any system of ideas whatsoever, thus making it virtually impossible for a human being not to be in some sense a believer *manqué*. What, then, are we to make of those religions which have no belief in God at all? As McGowan points out, it is perhaps not entirely fortuitous that Jung completely ignores the *nirguna* or atheistic strand of Hinduism, and that, when discussing Buddhism, he leans strongly towards the Mahayana tradition rather than Theravada Buddhism, the latter being non-theistic.[78]

ARCHETYPES AND REVELATION

There is, however, another aspect of Jung's discussion which is equally perplexing. This has to do with his concern to avoid the charge of psychologism by characterizing the *a priori* and archetypal God-form as a 'numen,' as that which is given and received as a 'revelation,' and thus as something distinguishable from the numinous experience that it generates. It is at this point that theologians have been most vocal in their objections. For while what is involved here may be *defined* as 'other' and of 'highest value,' it is difficult to see how this definition can be sustained once it is realized that, operating only at the empirical level and thus eschewing all discussion of whether God actually exists, Jung locates the archetypal God-form within the unconscious, albeit at its deepest level, and makes clear that ascribing meaning to a God-image involves a corresponding movement of the libido. Thus what may be defined as 'other' is unmasked as no more than an experience of Self, as an experience proceeding from the individual psyche and certified as significant by the psyche – hence the ease with which Jung can identify God-images as Self-images. This, so many theologians allege, is an illegitimate psychological reduction of the notion of God's transcendence, one which imposes a devastating limit on the scope of divine revelation. For while Jung may be correct to argue that God's transcendence should not be conceived as complete 'apartness' from the world, this same distinction allows us to safeguard God's sovereign activity upon the world without reducing it to the level of a psychic reality virtually indistinguishable from other subjective phenomena. This point has been made variously by such critics as Josef Goldbrunner, Thomas Altizer and Victor White,[79] and, most vociferous of all, by the distinguished Jewish theologian, Martin Buber, who characterizes Jung's 'new religion' as 'pseudoreligious' – as the 'religion of pure psychic immanence.'

> ... if religion is a relation to psychic events, which cannot mean anything other than to events of one's own soul, then it is implied by this that it is not a relation to a Being or Reality which, no matter how fully it may from time to time descend to the human soul, always remains transcendent to it. More precisely, it is not the relation of an I to a Thou. This is, however, the way in which the unmistakable religious of all ages have understood their religion even if they longed most intensely to let their I be mystically absorbed into that Thou.[80]

In his reply, Jung claims that Buber has here failed to understand what he means by the 'reality of the psyche.' By simply identifying a psychic fact as a subjective response, he has not observed that archetypes, while certainly requiring this response, have a dimension which is also autonomous and objective; and that it is precisely in being confronted with this level of his own psychic being that the individual does encounter a strange 'other,' and which may therefore be designated as a 'Thou.'[81] In part Jung's response is justified: Buber does ignore the distinction between the archetypal God-form and the archetypal God-contents, and this does allow him to make the easy assumption that the individual, in responding to God-images, is responding to nothing more than something of his own creation. But, as we have seen, Jung's argument is subtler than that, and he does make a determined effort to safeguard not just the immanent but also the transcendent character of these images, not least when classifying them as the perceptible effects of an imperceptible and eternal cause. But whether Jung is successful in this is another matter, and the question thus remains whether Buber is right in his conclusion that the theory of archetypes cannot accommodate any notion of revelation.

To clarify my own position, let me begin by recalling that the existence of the archetypal God-form is hypothesized on the basis that certain images have constellated into a clearly defined group, the God-images. If these images were not a clearly defined group we could not call them 'collective images' and could not then go on to say that their origin is supra-personal and that they are thus not subjective creations. Setting aside for the moment my earlier criticism that this grouping could be accounted for on the basis of common human experiences, and that accordingly it is unnecessary to postulate an archetype to account for them, it is worth enquiring further into the supposed link between what is known (the image) and what is unknown (the archetype). Now clearly there is something very odd with an argument that claims that X is unknown, and indeed will remain unknown, but yet has certain characteristics. This becomes doubly odd when we discover, first, that among the characteristics of this unknown X we may count its *distinctness* – that the God-archetype is impersonal and objective, that it acts upon its recipient as a 'numen,' that it is 'given' and 'received' in the situation of revelation; and second, that these particular properties are postulated on the basis of an *identity* between, on the one hand, the contents of God-images, and on the other, the archetypal contents of the psyche. Let me be clearer. Because God-images proceed from the collective unconscious, those archetypal elements which constitute the contents of the collective unconscious will be projected into the God-images. What, then, are these elements? They are, to name the principal ones, the archetypes of the Shadow, the Animus and Anima, and the Self; and we have seen on many occasions how these archetypes are incorporated directly into God-images. The presence of the Shadow archetype allows Jung to propose an evil side to God; Animus and Anima are absorbed into descriptions of the male and female attributes of deity; and the Self is presented in all those images of God that express wholeness and the union of opposites. The justification for this procedure is that *no other procedure is possible*. If God, in other words, is to be conceived only as a psychic reality, it is only through the medium of the psyche and its archetypal contents that he can be apprehended. Now one can certainly understand why Jung says this: it is at the centre of his concern to render statements about God meaningful and relevant to the human condition. For clearly if God is spoken of in terms that are not psychical, then God cannot be shown to be related to man's experience, given that, following Jung, the only experience human beings have is psychic experience. This allows Jung to restrict the human encounter with God to a solely psychic context, and thus to construe it as something which occurs only at the deepest level of the unconscious mind. The idea of God, as he says, has not dropped 'into man's lap from outside, straight down from heaven, as it were, but he contains all this *in nuce* within himself, and for this reason can produce it all out of himself.'[82]

But what is wrong with this? It is that, on this argument, no God-image can be constructed which is not already implicit within the human psychic structure, and that accordingly Jung cannot now speak of the giving-act of revelation as a distinct act if what is being given is no more than a duplicate of the contents of the psyche, if what is being received is already implied in the being of those who receive it. How, then, can we distinguish statements about God from statements about human psychic states? Or how are we to avoid the conclusion that a knowledge of God is no more than a form of psychological autobiography, in which we project into our notion of God no more than what we discern in ourselves? Jung does not resolve these questions; and this is because, having once allowed that God can only be understood psychically, he is bound to assert that we cannot speak of God except by reference to our own psychic condition, and that therefore God can be spoken of as being revealed *in* man but not as revealing himself *to* man, that is, apart from that condition. Indeed, at this point it is appropriate to ask whether there is not an implicit contradiction between Jung's concern to safeguard the archetype of God as something spontaneous and underived, and his subsequent derivation of the contents of this idea from psychological conclusions about the nature of the psyche. Here, then, I believe Buber is right. Having already defined 'God' as a 'synonym for the unconscious,'[83] it is hard to avoid the conclusion that for Jung the 'revelation of God' is another synonym for the revelation of man to himself.

ARCHETYPES AND INDIVIDUATION

These objections gather force when we turn to the final phase of Jung's discussion, to his concept of individuation. But let us first remind ourselves of what individuation involves. David Norton is, I believe, correct to set individuation within the tradition known as *eudaimonism*, which first achieved systematic formulation in the words of Socrates and in the writings of Plato and Aristotle.[84] 'Eudaimonia' is the name given to the process of living in harmony with one's daimon or innate potentiality, of actualizing that potential in such a way that one becomes a fully developed individual. Jung embraces this idea when he identifies the goal of individuation as the realization of Self – the 'coming to self-hood' or 'self-realization' – an identification which further characterizes individuation as an *archetypal process* and thus as something innate to human personality. All of us, in other words, however distinct and various our individual experiences, are travelling the same journey and are impelled by the same impulse towards Self-hood, that is, to unite the conscious and unconscious sides of the psyche. This allows Jung to make an important distinction between the personal contents of an individual life and its collective form, and so to conceive of each person's process towards Self-hood in terms of an archetypal ground-plan or life-cycle, which, we recall, is broadly divisible into the first and second stages of life. These two stages may be charted through the spontaneous images generated from the unconscious and they may be expressed in innumerable ways, through dreams, drawings, stories, myths, rituals, and so on. Amongst these we may count *images of God*, the archetypal God-contents. Because these images are empirically indistinguishable from images of Self, they may also stand as *symbols of individuation*, and it is for this reason that they have enormous psycho-therapeutic significance: they reveal the stage reached by the individuating personality and so, by implication, reveal to that personality what remains for Self-hood to be realized. When therefore Jung describes these images as 'religious' he is not saying this because their contents are recognizably religious – for example, that they depict the crucifixion of Jesus or the trials of Job – but because through them is opened up a specific dimension of psychic reality, the collective dimension, which transcends the individual even as he or she apprehends it. And by the same token, of course, we may have an image that is religious even though it deals with no overtly religious theme. For it is, to repeat, the archetypal validity of the image that makes it religious, and thus, for the individuating personality, any image of Self which reveals itself to be archetypal may be properly called 'religious.'

Jung's model of human development is fairly straightforward, and links up well with other 'stages of life' psychologies that have been devised in recent years. There is, for example, the extensive psycho-social model devised by the Danish-American psychoanalyst, Erik Erikson, in his 'The Eight Ages of Man'; the 'faith development' model proposed by the psychologist of religion, James Fowler; and Kohlberg's scheme of the six stages of 'moral development.'[85] Nor should we forget Freud's own famous description of psycho-sexual progression through the oral, anal, genital and latency stages – stages which, although admittedly confined to the period from infancy to adolescence, have been employed by the Dutch theologian, Heije Faber, to demarcate corresponding periods of religious belief.[86] Now whether these are or are not more appropriate schemes of development than Jung's it is not my business to decide here. For what matters now is not whether Jung has formulated a workable doctrine of stages but whether the progression through these stages to Self-hood, together with the images that it generates, may be properly characterized as religious.

Let me begin with an image that can without dispute be classified as religious: the image of the Christ. For Jung this is religious because it is a pre-eminent symbol of individuation, and for the more orthodox Christian it is religious because it attests to the supreme instance of specific revelation, the divine manifestation of God in history. But Jung is not interested in the man Jesus of Nazareth, and thus in the question of whether there are historical warrants to support these claims about him, but only in the psychic experience witnessed to by the title 'Christ.' This experience is described in the terminology of individuation. Jesus is the exemplification of an archetype, so that what confirms the biblical image as an image of the Christ is that it expresses the archetype of Self, or rather, to be more exact, that it expresses in pre-eminent fashion a fundamental and *a priori* human need, and this is the need for wholeness.[87]

Here Jung posits two Christs: there is the past-historical Christ who is the subject of the gospel story, but who can never be known through historical research; and there is the present-immediate Christ who is made known here and now through psychic encounter. The fact that Jung could be accused of the heresy of dividing Christ's person would have troubled Jung not at all, and it is not difficult to see why he should argue in this way. For this is yet another demonstration of his laudable intention to render meaningful what many may regard as an otherwise inaccessible historical story, and to do this by exposing the psychic significance of the central event it describes. It is not, accordingly, the figure of Jesus of Nazareth that makes the biblical picture of him significant, but rather the perception that this picture has *archetypal content*. Present faith, that is, in confessing that this biblical image *is* of the Christ, bears witness to its own reception of this image as a *psychic reality*: it is, as it were, doing no more than stating as a *psychic fact* that, through the medium of this image, it has had an immediate experience of a collective and primordial nature. And this experience is quite irrefutable because, being psychic, it operates solely as an internal activity and is thus recognized only by the individual who has it. Once again, then, Jung is operating as a phenomenologist, and as such making no metaphysical claims to know that Jesus *was* the Christ. All he is doing is inductively inferring that the biblical picture is archetypal on the basis of the direct and empirical evidence of its effect. While faith cannot therefore guarantee the historical accuracy of this image, it can, by this means, say *that the Self-archetype is presented there*. This indeed is faith's only access to Christ; but it is sufficient for the Christ-figure to be recognized as belonging to the collective foundations of the psyche and thus in this sense to everybody *a priori*.

Now while Jung is undoubtedly right in refusing to see the past-historical figure of Jesus as any substitute for the Christ of faith – the historical memory of this man being evidently incommensurate with a contemporary awareness of his presence – serious problems arise when we look closer at Jung's presuppositions when establishing this distinction. Once again his assumption is that, if we are to speak of the gospel image as significant, this image must be revealed as 'psychologically significant,' by which Jung means two things: 1) that this image has an archetypal content; and 2) that the validity of this content is guaranteed by its psychic effects.

My first objection to Jung's argument he could well disregard as being purely parochial but it is, I think, one worth making if it exposes a basic misrepresentation of the very religion he is seeking to render more accessible. Most Christians believe not only that God's act of salvation occurred uniquely in a past-historical event but also that their belief is supported by the historical evidence of the gospels. If they were shown that such support was invalid, their faith would be weakened and in all probability destroyed. Jung avoids this possibility by denying that historical evidence can ever reveal the Christ that is known by faith. And the reason for his denial is illuminating. It is because Jung considers *the history itself relatively unimportant*, because what we find in the drama of this individual life is not something unique to it but rather the distillation of a generalized truth about the human psychic condition – the archetypal disposition towards the realization of Self – which could just as easily be presented in other images, such as images of the Buddha or Purusha or Tao. Every Christ-image may thus be translated without remainder into statements which describe the common psychic process of individuation; and that being the case, the exclusivity of, say, the idea that 'No man cometh to the Father but by Me' (John 14: 6) becomes quite inadmissible. Nothing, indeed, can be given in the act of revelation which is particular to that act because, as Jung sees it, to make that act intelligible it must be set within the ordinary psychological mode of explanation by which we attempt to account for other things, most notably the innate human desire for Self-hood. As Jung makes clear: 'Since Christ never meant more to me than what I could understand of him, and since this understanding coincides with my empirical knowledge of the self, I have to admit that I mean the self in dealing with the idea of Christ.'[88]

The result of this argument is plain: it ends by abolishing the distinctly Christian conception of revelation altogether. For what we are being given here, in place of an objective and miraculous revelation of the divine nature, is an indeterminate (and indeterminable) historical figure whose appearance is not in a class of one but in a class of many, the class of Self. To this extent, what Christ makes known the psychologist is capable of knowing already and by other means. In the light of this conclusion it comes as no surprise to learn that one of the most frequent criticisms of Jung at this point – one made by critics like White, Buber and the Buberian scholar, Maurice Friedman[89] – is that, in trying to make the historical Jesus contemporary by assimilating him to our psychic existence, he has repeated the heresy of the Gnostics who equated Christ with the divine essence latent in the human soul.

But even if we set aside this objection as one that Jung would not perhaps deny – the relativization of the figure of Jesus being a necessary consequence of its collective interpretation – his treatment of the historical content of Christianity remains nevertheless instructive because it is a paradigm of the way in which, by failing to distinguish a God-image from a Self-image, *any* religion that claims to possess a unique body of knowledge (e.g., that known by divine revelation) will find that claim discarded; and this by virtue of the fact that this claim must, under the exigencies of Jung's own apologetic method, be interpreted archetypally, as a collective claim, and thus as one which can be replaced by any other claim, so long as it too expresses the inherent human disposition movement towards Self-realization. Because Jung disbars any notion of God acting outside archetypal reality, he is bound to assert, once again, that the only revelation that is possible is through an encounter with the archetypes, and thus with what is already latent within the psychic personality; and, that said, he must refuse to consider that self-understanding could be mediated in any other ways, and that these ways might require the employment of other images – for example, images of miraculous events or sacramental action – whose meaning consists precisely in the fact that they cannot be construed as no more than satellites of the psychic order.

There is, however, another element of Jung's discussion of Christianity which is equally perplexing and which also points to a more general problem to do with individuation. As we have seen, Jung, although decrying the possibility of ever obtaining accurate information about the man Jesus of Nazareth, still wishes to assert that Jesus is the exemplification of the Self-archetype. But how can he say this if no historical evidence can ever confirm (or disconfirm) this assertion? His answer is that archetypal images are validated by their *psychic effects*, and that accordingly the fact that people have a numinous experience in relation to the gospel-image is evidence of the presence of an archetype in that image. This is true not just of images of Jesus: it is true of any Self-image and so, as its sub-set, of any God-image, whether incorporated in a dogma, rite, myth or dream. And, by the same token, the absence of any such experience indicates the absence of the archetype. An image, however venerable, becomes redundant once it ceases to evoke this response; and, conversely, an image that does provoke such a response, however bizarre others might think it, must be counted as archetypal. Jung gives many examples of this happening – the schizoid delusions of Miss Miller, the belief in UFOs – and here is another:

> I vividly recall the case of a professor who had had a sudden vision and thought he was insane. He came to see me in a state of complete panic. I simply took a 400-year-old book from the shelf and showed him an old woodcut depicting his very vision. 'There's no reason for you to believe that you're insane,' I said to him. 'They knew about your vision 400 years ago.' Whereupon he sat down entirely deflated, but once more normal.[90]

This is a good example of Jung's procedure: the claim that we are here dealing with an archetype is based not just on the amplificatory fact of parallel imagery but on the empirical and publicly attested psychological fact that the presence of the archetype has produced beneficial therapeutic results. But of all the elements that make up Jung's theory of archetypes, this is the weakest, based as it is on a kind of crude pragmatism: *something is real if it works.* Presumably if the professor had replied, 'The person who had that vision was as mad as I,' Jung could not have made the inference from healing experience to archetype, from effect to cause, because the experience was lacking and because, far from healing him, Jung's information had confirmed the professor's own diagnosis. But this argument lays Jung open once more to the charge of subjectivism. For it is clearly not the case that a statement is true simply because someone is convinced it is, however beneficial that conviction may be. A proposition like 'A is certain that B exists' may be true in so far as it tells us something of the psychological disposition of A when he or she claims to know of B's existence; but the truth of the assertion that A was certain in this respect does not entail that he or she was correct in their knowledge of B, that it does in fact exist. Subjective certainty, in other words, is not the measure of objective truth, nor is it a sufficient condition for the truth of an existential claim. This holds true not only for the Christ-image – in the absence of historical evidence to the contrary, how can we dismiss the possibility that the story of Jesus is not a fiction? – but also for Self-images in general. That I may experience a particular sensation through the medium of an image does not of itself justify the conclusion that there exists something distinct from that sensation as its cause, which is itself collective in origin and which I may thus discount as a product of the creative imagination: it does not, in other words, establish that the archetypal form of the image is categorically distinct from its personal content. Nor will it do for Jung to reply that the persistence of such images throughout the centuries, whether in the guise of God-images or not, provides corroborative evidence of their archetypal and impersonal origin. For this, it seems to me, is to fall back once more on the Argument from Common Consent, to which there is a fairly obvious objection. As Paul Edwards puts it: 'There is, on the face of it, no reason why the whole of mankind should not have been as wrong on a speculative topic as it has been on some more empirical questions on which, history teaches, it has been mistaken.'[91]

There is, however, a final difficulty to be mentioned. There remains the question of whether Jung is right to claim that individuation is a religious process, and right to claim in consequence that adopting a 'religious outlook on life' is necessary for the fulfilment of Self. Now if, following the criticisms just mentioned, Jung cannot justifiably infer the presence of an archetype from the experience of transformation, these claims cannot, under the terms of his own theory, be sustained. But rather than repeat this point, let us, for the purposes of argument, disregard these criticisms and accept for the moment that Jung is right to say that 'something is real if it works.' Does this, then, justify his claims? It does not, and for two reasons.

1   I should here recall my earlier criticism of the general theory of archetypes, namely, that Jung provides us with no criterion by which to distinguish one archetypal image from another. This is so because, applying the principle that 'from effect we may infer reality,' all images that have such an effect will be equally valid.[92] This applies also to the distinction between religious and non-religious images, and becomes particularly acute when we remember how these images function within individuation. This process is charted

through the only empirical evidence available to us, that is, through Self-images. These images (when they work) must be considered genuine psychic products, and amongst them we may count subordinate God-images (when they work). God-images are subordinate to Self-images because a) God-images are particular instances of the more general archetypal disposition towards Self; and because b) Self-images constitute a class to which may be admitted images that do not employ overtly religious subject-matter. That being the case, the description of individuation as a 'religious' process is not dependent on the analysis of certain images that can be distinguished as religious – distinguished, that is, in the sense that I can say of them, when reviewing their content, that they are religious and others are not – but on *the prior definition that all Self-images are religious*. This implies that any evidence from so-called 'non-religious' images will be discounted and taken as a further support for the definition. So comprehensive, indeed, has the class of Self-images become that it is now impossible to debar any image from membership (so long as it works). We have returned, in other words, to the tautology that stands at the heart of Jung's method, of which this is a variant: The claim that 'Self-images are religious' cannot be falsified because by religious images *we mean* Self-images. Under these terms, we might say, all distinctions between the sacred and secular have been eradicated: the sacred has collapsed into the secular and the secular into the sacred. Why, then, should we describe individuation as 'religious' at all if the term describes nothing which is not applicable to Self, if nothing is added by that term that is not already implied within the process?

2   The perception that Self-images are religious images is part and parcel of the 'religious outlook on life' that Jung claims is necessary for individuation. But this outlook also has a moral dimension. For in responding to the archetype mediated through the Self-image, the personality experiences also what needs to be done for Self-hood to be realized. All images of Self – and so all God-images – have, in other words, an *ethical function*. This follows from the fact that individuation is not an inevitable consequence of living out the life-cycle. What is archetypal is the impulse and the goal, the life-work, but not the attainment of the goal. This, as Jung makes clear, imposes upon us a moral responsibility to achieve psychic balance and wholeness, and requires making decisions which may or may not further that end. Risk is thus attendant upon the process. But here the archetypes themselves come to our aid, providing, through the power of their symbolic and collective imagery (e.g., Christ, quaternity, mandala, fish) vital information about what is required for balance to be achieved – whether, for example, it lies in the adjustment of Shadow, of Anima and Animus, and so on. Self-images, in this sense, function as moral guides, revealing to us what we are and by implication what we ought to be. Thus we can say that having a 'religious outlook on life'

is not simply a matter of perceiving that we have an archetypal Self, but determining our lives in accordance with that perception.

This seems straightforward enough, but it becomes much less so when we ask more precisely about the moral actions that are being commended here. Under the rubric that only what works is real, any image that has health-giving properties will be deemed to be archetypal. If, at time T1, a person experiences transformation through an image, that image is archetypal; but if, at time T2, transformation has not occurred, then that image has ceased to be archetypal. Similarly, if two people look at the same image at the same time, and one experiences transformation and the other does not, that image is simultaneously archetypal and not archetypal. An image, it would seem, is 'real' because it is *my* image and had *worked for me*. The upshot of this is that whatever action the image might commend as appropriate for the 'religious outlook,' and thus for the purposes of my Self-actualization, this action will be appropriate for me but not necessarily for anybody else. Indeed, because the ethical principle of individuation is that moral action should be a Self-directed activity, any moral command to act other than for my Self would offend that principle. That being the case, Don Browning is right when he says that Jung's theory of moral obligation appears to be a form of *ethical egoism* dressed up in religious clothes, and that consequently it cannot provide us with any means of deciding between competing moral claims.[93] What happens, for example, in situations of moral conflict, where my need, say, to activate my Anima may conflict with another's need to activate theirs? If the answer is that I ought here to apply a 'religious outlook' and listen to my archetypes, then this hardly helps since the advice will be the same in both cases – that each of us should act to individuate, and that *any* action for Self-hood that either of us may perform will be dignified as religious (so long as it works). This, I need hardly say, renders Jung's use of the term 'religious' quite meaningless in distinguishing one action from another, and so quite irrelevant to the promotion of any particular way of life. Nor is this conclusion unexpected. For if a religious image cannot at the empirical level be separated from a Self-image, then neither can its commendation to act be separated from the more general injunction to achieve Self-hood. This makes it hard to see why Jung should say that the 'religious attitude' is necessary for individuation when religion advocates nothing which is not already implied with the archetypal desire to individuate, no matter how much that process may vary from person to person.

CONCLUSION

Following these criticisms, my earlier agreement with Victor White that we should be cautious about accepting Jung as a 'friend' of religion, will come as no surprise. To agree with Jung is to adopt a conception of God as an innate human disposition, indistinguishable as anything other than a particular psychic state, and 'existing' only in the sense that anything that 'works' for the psyche will be 'real.' The circularity of this idea is quite apparent – what proceeds from the psyche is validated by the psyche – and provided for Jung, as he took it, with a certain degree of immunity from attack. For clearly it is difficult to impinge upon any psychological condition which believes that the only world that exists is its own world, a psychic world, and that the only certainty to be had is the immediate certainty of its own experiences.

The trouble with this is that, by setting God within this circle, Jung opens himself up to the charge of 'psychologism,' namely, that God has thereby been reduced to nothing more than a subjective experience, on a par with any other experience that one might have and for which one might require treatment, and guaranteed as such in much the same way as, say, a belief in flying saucers. As my own remarks will have indicated, I believe this criticism justified, although not, I should add, for the reason sometimes adduced (for example, by Glover) that Jung's argument is no more than an unsophisticated psychologizing of God. Jung is much more interesting than that and indeed, as we have seen many times, he makes strenuous efforts to refute the charge – his central distinction between the archetypal God-form and the archetypal God-contents is, after all, designed expressly for that purpose. Jung's psychologism proceeds, then, not from any failure to see the criticism but from the failure of his own arguments to deal with it.

Because this book has been about Freud and Jung, it is appropriate at this stage to allow Freud a final appearance. The focus of Freud's attack was belief in the objective reality of God: that there is indeed a transcendent Father, living, concrete and personified, who exists external to the psyche and who reveals himself to us through the images and rituals of religion. Freud's response was to convert the metaphysical claims of religion into meta-psychology, and to do this by unmasking these images and rituals as no more than psychic products, as the outward projections of our own Oedipal and obsessional desires. The impact upon Jung of this psychoanalytic demolition of religion was immense: at first he agreed with Freud, then he resisted him, and finally he rejected him altogether. His reply to Freud is to shift the focus. Nothing can be known of an objective God and so there is no metaphysical question to be answered about whether such a being exists. Consequently he directs our attention to the psychic product alone, to the image of God internal to the psyche, now evaluated not as an infantile fantasy but as a collective and archetypal substrate of the unconscious. We thus have the juxtaposition of two conflicting God-images: the God-image that Freud attacks and the God-image that Jung defends. But the fact that Jung is in the defensive position, and the fact that his defence is certainly justified in highlighting the one-sidedness of Freud's sexual theory, should not blind us to the inadequacy of Jung's own image, not least because it requires, as I have tried to show, a retreat into a self-justifying psychic world, in which the validity of God's image is established by its psychic effect, this effect making it indistinguishable from any other image having the same transforming power. This argument may certainly help us to avoid the hazard of elevating the notion of God's transcendence to the point where this idea cannot be correlated with any inner psychological experience; but this argument has, by the same token, so radicalized the notion of God's immanence as an exclusively psychic reality that it becomes equally questionable whether anything has been left of God at all, and thus whether anything distinctive is meant when we speak of religion. Many will regard this as too heavy a price to pay; but it is perhaps the inevitable cost of discarding all questions of metaphysical truth in favour of psychological truth.

NOTES

PART I: FREUD

1 Introduction

1 'An Autobiographical Study' (1925) in *The Penguin Freud Library*, translated from the German under the general editorship of James Strachey, London, Penguin Books, 1986, vol. 15, p. 200. This edition hereafter cited as *PFL*. I shall use this edition in conjunction with *The Standard Edition of the Complete Psychological Works of Sigmund Freud*, translated and edited by James Strachey in collaboration with Anna Freud, London, The Hogarth Press. Hereafter cited as *SE*.

2 *Studies on Hysteria*, (1895) *PFL* (1991) 3: 56.

3 'Sigmund Freud: A Sketch of his Life and Ideas,' *PFL* (1979) 10: 17.

4 Ernest Jones, *Sigmund Freud: Life and Work*, London, Hogarth Press, 1953, vol. I, p. 22.

5 Letter of 6 May 1926 in *Letters of Sigmund Freud*, ed. Ernest L. Freud and trans. Tania and James Stern, New York, Basic Books, 1960, p. 366.

6 For what follows I am indebted to Reuben M. Rainey, *Freud as Student of Religion: Perspectives on the Background and Development of his Thought*, Missoula, Montana, American Academy of Religion & Scholars Press, Dissertation Series 7, 1975.

7 Given by Rainey, *op.cit.* note 6, pp. 43–4.

8 Cf. 'The Moses of Michelangelo' (1914) *PFL* (1985) 14: 251–82. Freud clearly identified himself with the figure of Moses, particularly in relation to Jung, whom he called his 'Joshua.' Cf. Jones, *Life and Work, op. cit.* note 4, vol. 2, p. 37.

9 Jones, *op.cit.* note 4, p. 21. The influence of the nanny is dealt with in detail by Paul C. Vitz, *Sigmund Freud's Christian Unconscious*, London and New York, The Guilford Press, 1988, pp. 3–30. Vitz's thesis is that Freud had a powerful attraction to Christianity, largely derived from his nanny and connected to the hope of her return and also to the hope of salvation. This view is supported by E. Velikovsky, 'The Dreams Freud Dreamed,' *Psychoanalytic Review* (1943) 30: 487–511. Cf. also Gregor Zilboorg, *Psychoanalysis and Religion*, ed. Margaret Stone Zilboorg (1967) p. 139; and his *Freud and Religion*, London, Geoffrey Chapman, 1958, pp. 58–9.

10 So Paul Roazen implies that Freud's feelings for religion were more ambivalent that he realized. 'Whenever Freud sounds intolerant, it is likely that something in him was threatened and he may have been more involved with the problem of

religion than he cared to know.' *Freud and his Followers*, New York, Knopf, 1975, p. 251.

11 *Letters of Sigmund Freud, op. cit.* note 5, p. 22.

12 'The Resistances to Psychoanalysis' (1925) *PFL* (1986) 15: 273. In the same article Freud suggests that the initial hostility to psychoanalysis was a form of anti-semitism directed against himself.

13 Peter Gay, *Freud: A Life for Our Time*, New York, W. W. Norton, 1988, p. 10.

14 Yosef Yerushalmi, *Freud's Moses: Judaism Terminable and Interminable*, New Haven and London, Yale University Press, 1991, p. 116.

15 'Interpretations of Freud's Jewishness, 1924–1974,' *Journal of the History of the Behavioral Sciences* 18: 357–74.

16 Quoted by Siegfried Bernfeld, 'Freud's Earliest Theories and the School of Helmholtz,' *The Psychoanalytic Quarterly* (1944), 13: 341–62.

17 Peter Gay, *A Godless Jew: Freud, Atheism, and the Making of Psychoanalysis*, New Haven and London, Yale University Press, 1987, p. 60. Jones explains further: 'Freud's emancipation from this influence [Brücke's] consisted not in renouncing the principles, but in becoming able to apply them empirically to mental phenomena while dispensing with any anatomical basis.... Brücke would have been astonished, to put it mildly, had he known that one of his favourite pupils, one apparently a convert to the strict faith, was later, in his famous wish theory of the mind, to bring back into science the ideas of "purpose," "intention," and "aim" which had just been abolished from the universe. We know, however, that when Freud did bring them back he was able to reconcile them with the principles in which he had been brought up; he never abandoned determinism for teleology.' *Op.cit.* note 4, vol. 1, p. 292.

18 *PFL* (1991) 2: 191.

19 *Ibid.*, pp. 206–7.

20 *Ibid.*, p. 193.

21 *Ibid.*, p. 208.

22 So Emil Ludwig condemns Freud: 'Thousands of the healthy are declared sick because one man was sick, and believed that the gloomy symptoms rising out of his childhood were common to all. The world is sexualized, every motive is perverted at source, because a stubborn nature managed to impose its pathological visions on people made of less stern stuff.' *Doctor Freud*, New York, Manor Books, 1973, p. 282.

23 *PFL* (1901) 5: 223. This example was included in the enlarged edition of 1919. In the same book Freud reports two other attempts to influence the course of events by a sacrifical act: he averts an evil by breaking an Egyptian figurine (p. 223); and he brings good luck to his daughter by breaking glass and china in the days preceding her wedding (p. 227). Ernest Jones reports another: that in 1925, while awaiting his daughter's arrival by train, Freud lost his pince-nez, thinking that this would somehow protect her from accident (*op.cit.* note 4, vol. 3, p. 409).

24 Jones, *op. cit.* note 4, vol. 3, p. 418.

25 'The Uncanny', *SE* XVII: 240–1.

26 Jones, *op.cit.* note 4, vol. 3, p. 408.

27 'On the History of the Psychoanalytic Movement' (1914) *PFL* (1986) 15: 85. Note also Jung's own comments: 'I can still recall vividly how Freud said to me, "My dear Jung, promise me never to abandon the sexual theory. That is the most essential thing of all. You see, we must make a dogma of it, an unshakable bulwark." ... In some astonishment I asked him, "A bulwark – against what?" To which he replied, "Against the black tide of mud" – and here he hesitated for a moment, then added – "of occultism." *Memories, Dreams, Reflections*, ed. Aniela

Jaffé, trans. Richard and Clara Winston, New York, Pantheon Books, 1963, p. 150. See also below, pp. 90–1.

28 *Freudiana, Including Unpublished Letters from Freud, Havelock Ellis, Pavlov, Bernard Shaw, Romain Rolland, et alii*, Cambridge, Mass., Sci-Art Publishers, 1957, p. 25.

29 'Reminiscences of Freud and Jung,' *Freud and the 20th Century*, ed. Benjamin Nelson, Cleveland and New York, The World Publishing Company, 1957, p. 67.

30 In 'New Introductory Lectures on Psychoanalysis,' (1933) *PFL* (1973) 2: 60–87.

31 These have been collected by Rainey, *op.cit.* note 6, pp.129–50.

32 *PFL* (1991) 5: 321–22.

33 *PFL* (1985) 13: 40. In *A Short Account of Psychoanalysis* (1924) Freud writes: '. . . it is impossible to escape the impression of the perfect correspondence which can be discovered between the obsessive actions of certain obsessional patients and the religious observances of believers all over the world. Some cases of obsessional neurosis actually behave like a caricature of a private religion, so that it is tempting to liken the official religions to an obsessional neurosis that has been mitigated by becoming universalized. This comparison, which is no doubt highly objectionable to all believers, has nevertheless proved most fruitfully psychological. For psychoanalysis soon discovered in the case of obsessional neurosis what the forces are that struggle with one another in it till their conflicts find a remarkable expression in the ceremonial of obsessive actions. Nothing similar was suspected in the case of religious ceremonial until, by tracing back religious feeling to the relation with the father as its deepest root, it became possible to point to an analogous dynamic situation in that case too.' *PFL* 15: 178–9.

34 *Ibid.*, p. 31.

35 *Ibid.*, p. 216.

36 *PFL* (1990) 14: 216.

37 *Studies on Hysteria*, *PFL* (1991) 3: 58.

38 The most famous being Breuer's (1895): the case of Anna O. See *Ibid.*, pp. 73–102; and above, p. 4.

39 'On the History of the Psychoanalytic Movement' (1914) *PFL* (1986) 15: 73.

40 'The Aetiology of Hysteria,' (1896) *SE*, III: 203.

41 'An Outline of Psychoanalysis' (1940) *PFL* (1986) 15: 423–4.

2 Totem and Taboo

1 *PFL* (1990) 13: 43–224.

2 *Ibid.*, p. 49.

3 *Ibid.*, p. 79.

4 *Ibid.*, p. 85.

5 *Ibid.*, p. 88.

6 Freud cites three examples of taboos in which the phenomenon of ambivalence is evident: in the taboos attaching to the treatment of enemies, in which the slain are also ceremonially appeased for fear of their ghosts; in the taboos concerning rulers, who must be both guarded and guarded against; and in the taboos upon the dead, which supposes that a relative on dying changes into a hostile demon. In each of these cases, Freud argues, an ambivalent attitude is present, expressing the conflicting emotions of pain and satisfaction.

7 Most notably in his *Primitive Culture*, London, Murray, 1871.

8 The case appears as 'Notes upon a Case of Obsessional Neurosis' (1909) *PFL* (1990) 9: 33–128.

9 *Ibid.*, pp.143–4.
10 *Ibid.*, p. 135.
11 *Ibid.*, p. 136.
12 *Ibid.*, p. 141.
13 The case appears in *PFL* (1990) 8: 167–305.
14 *Ibid.*, p. 189.
15 *Ibid.*, p. 190.
16 *Ibid.*, pp. 204–5.
17 *Ibid.*, p. 206.
18 *Ibid.*, pp. 210–11.
19 *Ibid.*, p. 217.
20 *Ibid.*, p. 222.
21 *Ibid.*, p. 224. 'Im Anfang war die Tat' – a quotation from Goethe's *Faust*, Part 1,
    Scene 3. In his Preface to the first volume of Reik's *Probleme der Religions-
    psychologie* (1919) Freud summarizes the thesis of *Totem and Taboo* with an
    'unexpectedly precise conclusion: namely that God the Father once walked upon
    the earth in bodily form and exercised his sovereignty as chieftain of the primal
    human horde until his sons united to slay him. It emerged further that this crime
    of liberation and the reactions to it had as their result the appearance of the first
    social ties, the basic moral restrictions and the oldest form of religion – totemism.
    But the later religions too have the same content, and on the one hand they are
    concerned with obliterating the traces of that crime or with expiating it by bringing
    forward other solutions of the struggle between father and sons, while on the other
    hand they cannot avoid repeating once more the elimination of the father.' Quoted
    by Ernest Jones, *Sigmund Freud: Life and Work*, vol. 3, p. 380.
22 *A Phylogenetic Fantasy*, ed. Ilse Grubrich-Simitis, trans. Axel Hoffer and Peter
    T. Hoffer, Cambridge, Mass., The Belknap Press of Harvard University Press,
    1987, p. 7.
23 See Wittels, *Alles um Liebe; Eine Urweltdichtung*, Berlin, E. Fleischl, 1912; and
    Ferenczi, 'Stages in the Development of the Sense of Reality' (1913) in *First
    Contributions to Psycho-Analysis*, trans. Ernest Jones, London, Hogarth Press,
    1952, pp. 213–39.
24 *Op.cit.*, p. 13.
25 *Ibid.*, p. 14.
26 *Ibid.*, pp. 15–16 (my emphasis).
27 *Ibid.*, p. 18.
28 *PFL* (1985) 12: 93–178.
29 *Ibid.*, p. 123.
30 *Ibid.*
31 *Ibid.*, p. 155.
32 *Ibid.*, p. 123.
33 *Ibid.*, p. 157.
34 In the Preface to the third edition of *Three Essays on the Theory of Sexuality*, Freud
    clarifies this point: 'Ontogenesis may be regarded as a recapitulation of phylo-
    genesis, in so far as the latter has not been modified by more recent experience.
    The phylogenetic disposition can be seen at work behind the ontogenetic process.
    But disposition is ultimately the precipitate of earlier experience of the species to
    which the more recent experience of the individual, as the sum of the accidental
    factors, is super-added.' *PFL* (1991) 7: 40.
35 *Op.cit.*, p. 146.
36 *Ibid.*, p. 148.

3 Religion and illusion

1 *PFL* (1985) 12: 179–241.
2 Famously, Freud makes no distinction between culture and civilization: 'I scorn to distinguish between culture and civilization.' *Ibid.*, p. 184.
3 *PFL* (1985) 12: 245–340.
4 See above, pp. 28–9.
5 *Civilization and its Discontents*, (1930) *PFL*, 12: 213.
6 *Ibid.*
7 *Ibid.*, p. 208.
8 *Ibid.*, p. 195.
9 *Ibid.*, p. 196.
10 *Ibid.*, pp.198–9.
11 '"Civilized" Sexual Morality and Modern Nervous Illness' (1908) *PFL* (1991): 12: 29–55.
12 *PFL* (1985) 12: 251–2.
13 *Ibid.*, p. 260.
14 *Ibid.*, p. 290.
15 The first indication that the aggressive instinct is distinct from the sexual one comes in his paper, 'Instincts and their Vicissitudes' (1915) *PFL* 11: 105. Prior to this Freud had classified aggression as a sadistic aspect of the sexual instinct.
16 *Civilization and its Discontents*, (1930) *PFL*, 12: 284.
17 *Ibid.*, pp. 315–16.
18 *The Future of an Illusion*, (1927) *PFL*, 12: 204–5.
19 *Ibid.*, p. 261.
20 Various criticisms are collected in Norman Kiell's *Freud without Hindsight*, Madison, Connecticut, International Universities Press, 1988, pp. 623–54. Tertius Chandler is almost alone is praising Freud unreservedly in 'Ikhanaton and Moses,' *American Imago*, 1966, vol. 19 pp. 127–39. Compare this, for example, with S. Baron's review in *American Journal of Sociology* (1939) 45: 471–7. There is also a fascinating psychoanalysis of Akhenaten – who, it is alleged, was suffering from passive homosexuality towards his father, rather like Judge Schreber – by James Strachey in his 'Preliminary Notes upon the Problem of Akhenaten,' *International Journal of Psycho-Analysis* (1939) 20: 33–42.
21 See W. F. Albright, *From the Stone Age to Christianity*, Baltimore, The Johns Hopkins Press, 1946, pp. 166–7, 194–6. It is not surprising that Albright condemns *Moses and Monotheism* as 'totally devoid of serious historical method,' dealing with 'historical data even more cavalierly than with the data of introspective and experimental psychology' (*ibid.*, p. 75).
22 *Moses and Monotheism*, (1939) *PFL* (1985) 13: 322–3.
23 *Ibid.*, p. 356.
24 *Ibid.*, p. 357.
25 *Ibid.*, pp. 369–70.
26 *Ibid.*, pp. 384–5.
27 *Ibid.*, p. 386.
28 *Ibid.*, p. 347.
29 *Ibid.*, p. 381.
30 *Ibid.*, p. 378.
31 So religion, as an illusion, has no 'material' truth, which is not the same as saying it has no 'historical' truth. This point is clarified in a letter to Lou Andreas-Salomé on 1 June, 1935: 'Religions owe their compulsive power to the *return of the repressed*; they are reawakened memories of very ancient, forgotten, highly emotional episodes of human history. I have already said this in *Totem and Taboo*.

I express it now in the formula: the strength of religion lies not in its *material* but in its *historical* truth.' *Letters*, ed. Ernst Pfeiffer, trans. William and Elaine Robson-Scott, New York, Harcourt Brace Jovanovich, 1972, p. 205.

32 Meissner makes a strong case for saying that Freud's imaginary opponent is in fact his close friend and advocate of psychoanalysis, Oskar Pfister, who also happened to be a Lutheran pastor. In 1928 Pfister published his counterargument, 'The Illusion of the Future' in the journal *Imago*, and a lengthy correspondence with Freud ensued. See Heinrich Meng and Ernst Freud (eds), *Psychoanalysis and Faith: The Letters of Sigmund Freud and Oskar Pfister*, trans. Eric Mosbacher, London, The Hogarth Press, 1963. Cf. also W. Meissner, *Psychoanalysis and Religious Experience*, New Haven and London, Yale University Press, 1984, pp. 73–103.

33 *The Future of an Illusion*, (1927) *PFL* 12: 216–17.

34 *Ibid.*, p. 217. In 'Group Psychology and the Analysis of the Ego' (1921) Freud writes: 'Even those who do not regret the disappearance of religious illusions from the civilized world of to-day will admit that so long as they were in force they offered those who were bound by them the most powerful protection against the danger of neurosis.' *PFL* 12:176.

35 *Ibid.*, p. 220.

36 *Ibid.*, pp. 224–5.

37 *Ibid.*, p. 233.

38 *Ibid.*

39 *Ibid.*, pp. 226–7.

4 Forms of religious neurosis

1 Translated from the second German edition of *Probleme der Religionspsychologie* by Douglas Bryan, with a Preface by Sigmund Freud, London, Hogarth Press and The Institute of Psycho-Analysis, 1931.

2 *Ibid.*, p. 16.

3 *Ibid.*, p. 17.

4 London, 1910, vol. 4, p. 248.

5 Reik *op.cit.* note 1, p. 59.

6 *Ibid.*, p. 50.

7 *Ibid.*, p. 65.

8 *Ibid.*, p. 80.

9 *Ibid.*, pp. 75–6.

10 These six are included in two volumes: *PFL* 8 and 9.

11 Published as 'From the History of an Infantile Neurosis' (1918). See *PFL* (1990) 9: 227–366. Of particular interest is *The Wolf Man and Sigmund Freud*, ed. Muriel Gardiner, London, The Hogarth Press, 1972. This includes not only the continuation of the analysis by one of Freud's pupils, Dr Ruth Mack Brunswick, but also the Wolf Man's own account of what it was like being psychoanalysed by Freud. See also Karin Obholzer, *The Wolf-Man: Sixty Years Later*, London, Routledge & Kegan Paul, 1982. This describes the subsequent medical history of Freud's most famous patient.

12 *PFL* 9: 259.

13 *Ibid.*, p. 269.

14 *Ibid.*, p. 280.

15 *Ibid.*, pp. 244–5.

16 *Ibid.*, p. 299.

17 *Ibid.*, p. 301.

18 *Ibid.*, p. 357.

19 'Inhibitions, Symptoms and Anxiety' (1926) *PFL* (1993) 10: 256–7. This essay contains useful summaries of both the Little Hans and Wolf Man cases.

20 *Ibid.*, p. 337. Although Freud does not mention the primal horde directly, this reference is clearly intended.

21 *Ibid.*, p. 338.

22 Published as *Denkwürdigkeiten eines Nervenkranken*, Leipzig, Oswald Mutze, 1903. Freud's analysis appeared in 1911 as 'Psychoanalytic Notes on an Auto-biographical Account of a Case of Paranoia (Dementia Paranoides)'. See *PFL* (1990) 9: 131–223.

23 *Ibid.*, p. 188.

24 More spectacularly, the same was true of the American President, Woodrow Wilson. According to Freud Wilson's God was in fact his father, the Reverend Joseph Ruggles Wilson. This identification led Wilson to identify himself as a Christ-figure, with a messianic need to save the world. See Freud (co-authored with William Bullitt) *Thomas Woodrow Wilson*, London, Weidenfeld & Nicolson, 1967. I have not included this work in the list of case-studies because there is considerable doubt about the extent of Freud's involvement. For further details of this somewhat embarrassing publication, see Peter Gay, *Freud: A Life for our Time*, London, Macmillan, 1989, pp. 553–62, 775–6.

5 A critical appraisal

1 'A Difficulty in the Path of Psycho-Analysis,' *SE* (1917) 19: 140–1.

2 Bruno Bettelheim, *The Uses of Enchantment: The Meaning and Importance of Fairy Tales*, London, Thames & Hudson, 1976.

3 Hume, 'The Natural History of Religion' in *David Hume on Religion*, ed. A. Wayne Culver and John Valdimir Price, Oxford, The Clarendon Press, p. 32.

4 Quoted by J.C.A. Gaskin (ed.) in *Varieties of Unbelief*, London, Macmillan, 1989, p. 149.

5 *The Future of an Illusion*, (1927) *PFL* 12: 217–18.

6 See above, p. 42.

7 A.L. Kroeber, 'Totem and Taboo: An Ethnologic Psychoanalysis,' *American Anthropologist* (1920) 22 (1): 51; E. E. Evans-Pritchard, *Theories of Primitive Religion*, Oxford, Clarendon Press, 1965, p. 42. Cf. also Claude Lévi-Strauss, *Totemism*, trans. Rodney Needham, London, Merlin Press, 1964, pp. 69–70.

8 For what follows I am indebted to Edwin R. Wallace, *Freud and Anthropology*, New York, International Universities Press, 1983, pp. 200–2.

9 *The Social Primates*, New York, Harper & Row, 1974, pp. 162–3.

10 S. Zuckerman, *The Social Life of Monkeys and Apes*, New York, Harcourt & Brace, 1932, p. 24.

11 Jane Goodall, 'Life and Death at Gombe,' *National Geographic* (1979) 155: 593–621.

12 *The Origin and Growth of Religion*, trans. H. J. Rose, London, Methuen & Co., 1931, p. 114. Schmidt's conclusion is worth repeating: 'The picture which we thus get of the earliest men is certainly very different from that which Freud constructs in his theory. To bring such men into connexion with modern sex-ridden neurotics, as he would have us do, and from this connexion to deduce the alleged fact that all thought and feeling, especially subliminal, is founded on and saturated with sex, must remain lost labour. Thus Freud's hypothesis loses its last hope ever to corroborate or establish any single part of itself, for every part collapses in ruin' (p. 115).

13 *Totemism and Exogamy*, London, Macmillan, 1910, vol. 4, p. 27.

14 *Totem and Taboo*, (1913) *PFL* 13: 52. Two other criticisms are worth mentioning. The anthropologist A. L. Kroeber, as early as 1920, reported that 'Robertson Smith's allegation that blood sacrifice is central in ancient cults holds chiefly or only for the Mediterranoid cultures of a certain period – say the last two thousand years B.C. – and cultures then or subsequently influenced by them. It does not apply to regions outside the sphere of affection by these cultures.' *American Anthropologist* (1920) 22 (1): 50. Kroeber also makes the valid point that 'the fact that a child sometimes displaces its father-hatred upon an animal . . . is no proof that the sons did so' (*ibid.*) Claude Lévi-Strauss makes the equally pertinent point that the relation between clan members and their totem does not always involve an identification of the totem with a forefather or ancestor. See *Totemism*, Boston, Beacon Press, 1963; and 'The Family,' in *Man, Culture and Society*, ed. Henry L. Shapiro, New York, Oxford University Press, 1960, pp. 261–85.

15 *Moses and Monotheism*, (1939) *PFL* 13: 380.

16 In his biography of Freud, *Sigmund Freud: Life and Work*, vol. 3, p. 310, Jones laments Freud's persistent Lamarckism 'as an extraordinary part of the story, which provides us with a baffling problem in the study of the development of Freud's ideas, and also in that of his personality.' Anna Freud remembers 'very well how imperturbed my father was by everybody's criticism to his neo-Lamarckianism. He was quite sure that he was on safe ground.' Quoted by Lucille B. Ritvo on the frontispiece of *Darwin's Influence on Freud*, New Haven and London, Yale University Press, 1990. For further details on this aspect of Freud's theory, see: Henry Edelheit, 'On the Biology of Language: Darwinian/Lamarckian Homology in Human Inheritance (with some thoughts about the Lamarckism of Freud),' *Psychiatry and the Humanities* (1978) 3: pp. 45–74; Sydney Margolin, 'Freud's Concept of Constitution in Psychoanalysis' in *Psychoanalysis and Current Biological Thought*, ed. Norman S. Greenfield and William C. Lewis, Madison and Milwaukee, The University of Wisconsin Press, 1965, pp. 125–49; and Jerome Neu, 'Genetic Explanation in *Totem and Taboo*' in *Freud*, ed. Richard Wollheim, New York, Doubleday, 1974, pp. 366–93.

17 *Moses and Monotheism*, (1939) *PFL* 13: 345.

18 New York, Social Science Research Council, Bulletin No. 31, p. 136.

19 See S. M. Friedman, 'An Empirical Study of the Castration and Oedipus Complexes,' *Genetic Psychology Monographs* (1952) 46: 61–130; and C. S. Hall, 'Strangers in Dreams: An Empirical Confirmation of the Oedipus Complex,' *Journal of Personality* (1963) 31: 336–45.

20 *Fact and Fantasy in Freudian Theory*, London, Methuen, 1972, p. 348. A more recent survey, conducted by Fisher and Greenberg, reaches a similar conclusion: 'Freud's attempt to construct a grand theory that would explain within one framework many of the multiple developmental events involved in achieving sexual and moral identities does not hold up well to empirical investigation. It is doubtful that any theory will ever be devised capable of convincingly pulling together such diverse components.' Seymour Fisher and Roger P. Greenberg, *Freud Scientifically Reappraised*, New York, John Wiley and Sons, 1996, p. 169.

21 For example Geza Roheim, who was a committed Freudian, in his *Psycho-Analysis and Anthropology*, New York, International Universities Press, 1950.

22 Cf. also A. Parsons, 'Is the Oedipus Complex Universal?' *The Psychoanalytic Study of Society*, ed. W. Muensterberger and S. Axelrad, New York, International Universities Press, 1969, pp. 278–328.

23 London, Routledge & Kegan Paul. Cf. also M. Fortes, 'Malinowski and Freud,' *Psychoanalysis and the Psychoanalytic Review* (1958–59) 45: 120–45.

24 *Ibid.*, p. 31.
25 *Ibid.*, pp. 80–1.
26 *Ibid.*, p. 165.
27 *Ibid.*, p. 164.
28 *Ibid.*, p. 166.
29 *Ibid.*, p. 251.
30 *Ibid.*, p. 261.
31 Malinowski's conclusions are supported within the psychoanalytic tradition by Erich Fromm, who adopts a remarkably similar argument. See his *The Fear of Freedom*, London, Routledge & Kegan Paul, 1942; *Man for Himself*, London, Routledge & Kegan Paul, 1949; and 'The Oedipus Complex and the Oedipus Myth,' in R. N. Anshen, *The Family: its Function and Destiny*, vol. 5, New York, Harper & Row, 1948, pp. 334–58.
32 I must add here that the general agreement with Malinowski's critique of Freud has been challenged in a most stimulating way by Melford E. Spiro, *Oedipus in the Trobriands*, New Brunswick and London, Transaction Publishers, 1993.
33 *Metaphorical Theology: Models of God in Religious Language*, London, SCM Press, 1982, p. 216. For other feminist critiques of God as father see: Mary Daly, *Beyond God the Father: Toward a Philosophy of Women's Liberation*, Boston, Beacon Press, 1973; Naomi R. Goldenberg, *Changing of the Gods: Feminism and the End of Traditional Religions*, Boston, Beacon Press, 1979; Rita Gross (ed.), *Beyond Androcentrism: New Essays on Women and Religion*, Missoula, Mont., Scholars Press, 1977; Rosemary Ruether (ed.), *Religion and Sexism: Images of Women in the Jewish and Christian Traditions*, New York, Simon & Schuster, 1974; and Phyllis Trible, *God and the Rhetoric of Sexuality*, Philadelphia, Fortress Press, 1978.
34 See Rank, *The Trauma of Birth* (1924); edition used: New York, Dover, 1993; Karen Horney, 'On the Genesis of the Castration Complex in Women' and 'The Flight from Womanhood: The Masculinity-Complex in Women as Viewed by Men and Women' in *Feminine Psychology* , ed. Harold Kelman, London & New York, Norton, 1967, pp. 37–53, 54–70; Ernest Jones, 'Early Female Sexuality' in *Papers on Psycho-Analysis*, London, Ernest Benn (4th edn), 1938, pp. 605–16. For further on Freud's attitude towards women, see Juliet Mitchell, *Psychoanalysis and Feminism*, London, Allen Lane, 1974.
35 Peter Gay, *Freud: A Life for our Time*, London, Macmillan, 1989, p. 507
36 *Ibid.*, p. 3. An interesting piece of research has been undertaken by Antoine Vergote, Director of the Laboratory of Religious Psychology in the Catholic University of Louvain. By questioning nearly 400 students, Vergote concluded that, while the image of God is more paternal than maternal, it is not exclusively so. Indeed, the child's desire for protection, providence and care – all of which, according to Freud, are projected into the notion of God the Father – are in fact maternal values. See 'Concept of God and Parental Images,' *Journal of the Scientific Study of Religion* (1969) 8: 79–87; and 'Parental Images and Representations of God,' *Social Compass* (1972–3) 19: 431–44. Cf. also C. G. Schoenfeld, 'God the Father – and Mother: Study and Extension of Freud's Conception of God as an Exalted Father,' *American Imago* (1960) 19: 213–34.
37 *Civilization and its Discontents* (1930), *PFL* 12: 269. The only illusion which has an important role in society is art, but even artistic satisfactions, which are accessible to only a few, 'cannot give complete protection from suffering' (*ibid.*, p. 267).
38 Donald Winnicott, *Playing and Reality*, New York, Routledge, 1971. Cf. also *The Maturational Process and the Facilitating Envirnoment*, New York, International Universities Press, 1965.
39 *Ibid.*, p. 2.

40 W. Meissner, *Psychoanalysis and Religious Experience*, New Haven and London, Yale University Press, 1984, p. 177.

41 *Op.cit.* note 38, p. 2.

42 A.-M. Rizzuto, *The Birth of the Living God*, Chicago and London, University of Chicago Press, 1979, p. 209.

43 *Ibid.*, p. 179.

44 *Ibid.*, p. 202. In the most fascinating part of her book, Rizzuto quotes four extensive case-studies to substantiate this claim. In each the representation of God changes as the relation to the primary object changes and as new experiences, pleasant and unpleasant, occur. She also presents an elaborate chart detailing the successive recreations of God as a transitional object and as they evolve in relation to the individual's sense of self (pp. 206–7).

45 *Ibid.*, p. 209. A similar challenge to Freud's notion of 'illusion' has come from the Dutch-born clinical psychologist, Paul Pruyser (1916–1987). Similarly indebted to Winnicott's theory of transitional phenomena, Pruyser places illusion in an intermediate area of experience, which he calls the 'illusionistic world.' This is the world of play, of creative imagination, and pre-eminently of cultural development, in which skills and talents are used to their utmost. See Pruyser, *Between Belief and Unbelief*, New York, Harper & Row, 1974; 'The Seamy Side of Current Religious Beliefs,' *Bulletin of the Menninger Clinic* (1977) 41: 329–48; and *The Play of the Imagination: Towards a Psychoanalysis of Culture*, New York, International Universities Press, 1983. For further discussions of object-relations theory, particularly as it applies to religion, see the following: James W. Jones, *Contemporary Psychoanalysis and Religion*, New Haven and London, Yale University Press, 1991; Hans Loewald, *Sublimation*, New Haven and London, Yale University Press, 1988; John McDargh, *Psychoanalytic Object Relations Theory and the Study of Religion*, New York and London, Lanham, 1984); and W. W. Meissner, *op.cit.* Cf. also Moshe Halevi Spero, *Religious Objects as Psychological Structures*, Chicago and London, University of Chicago Press, 1992.

46 *The Future of an Illusion*, (1927) *PFL* 12: 220.

47 London, Victor Gollancz, 1936; edition used, Penguin Books, 1987, p. 158.

48 *Op.cit.* note 46, p. 239.

49 *Ibid.*, p. 241.

50 For further discussions see I. G. Barbour (ed.) *Science and Religion*, SCM Press, 1968, and *Issues in Science and Religion*, Englewood Cliffs, N.J., Prentice-Hall, 1966; Thomas Kuhn, *The Structure of Scientific Revolutions*, Chicago, University of Chicago Press, 1962; Harold Schilling, *Science and Religion*, New York, Charles Scribner's Sons, 1962; and Stephen Toulmin, *The Philosophy of Science*, New York, Harper & Row, 1960.

51 Quoted in Meissner, *op.cit.*, p. 96.

52 *Ibid.*, p. 98.

53 *Psycho-Analysis and Faith: The Letters of Sigmund Freud & Oskar Pfister*, ed. Heinrich Meng and Ernst L. Freud, trans. Eric Mosbacher, London, The Hogarth Press, 1963, p. 114.

54 Richard Purtill, *Thinking about Religion*, Englewood Cliffs, New Jersey, Prentice-Hall, 1978, p. 7.

55 See Wittgenstein, *Philosophical Investigations*, trans. G.E.M. Anscombe, New York, Macmillan, 1958. A useful summary of Wittgenstein's position is given by Dan R. Stiver in *The Philosophy of Language*, Oxford, Blackwell, pp. 59–68.

56 *The Future of an Illusion* (1927), *PFL* 12: 215.

57 *Ibid.*

58 *Ibid.*, p. 237.

PART II: JUNG

6 Introduction

1 Barbara Hannah, *Jung: His Life and Work*, New York, G.P. Putnam's Sons, 1976, p. 27.
2 *Memories, Dreams, Reflections* (1962), recorded and ed. Aniela Jaffé, trans. Richard and Clara Winston, London, Fontana Press, 1993, p. 27. Hereafter cited as *MDR*.
3 *Ibid.*, p. 28.
4 *Ibid.*, p. 25.
5 *Ibid.*, p. 26.
6 *Ibid.*, p. 56.
7 *On Jung*, London, Penguin Books, 1990, p. 136.
8 Laurens van der Post, *Jung and the Story of Our Time*, London, Penguin Books, 1978, pp.106–7.
9 *MDR*, p. 74.
10 An expanded version is included in the first volume of the *Collected Works of C. G. Jung*, London, Routledge & Kegan Paul, 1957 (2nd edn) 1970, pp. 3–88. Hereafter cited as *CW*.
11 *MDR*, p. 130.
12 *Ibid.*, p. 135.
13 The most informative source is, of course, the correspondence between Freud and Jung: *The Freud/Jung Letters: The Correspondence between Sigmund Freud and C. G. Jung*, ed. William McGuire, trans. Ralph Manheim and R.F.C. Hull, Princeton, Princeton University Press, 1974; abridged, Penguin, 1979. For an interesting commentary on these exchanges, see Leonard Shengold, 'The Freud/ Jung Letters: The Correspondence between Sigmund Freud and C. G. Jung,' *Journal of the American Psychoanalytical Association* (1976) 24: 669–83. Not surprisingly, Ernest Jones, in his biography of Freud, takes Freud's side in the debate (*Sigmund Freud: Life and Work*, vol. 2, pp. 155–71), as does Edward Glover in *Freud or Jung*, London, George Allen & Unwin, 1950. For a discussion more favourable to Jung, see Paul Stepansky, 'The Empiricist as Rebel: Jung, Freud and the Burdens of Discipleship,' *Journal of the History of the Behavioral Sciences*, (1976) 12: 216–39. For further details, see Peter Gay, *Freud*, London, Macmillan, 1988, pp. 225–43 and E. A. Bennet, *C. G. Jung*, London, Barrie & Rockliff, 1961, pp. 33–62.
14 *Op.cit.* note 13, vol. 2, p. 77. In a letter to Abraham (3 May 1908) Freud writes: 'Only his [Jung's] appearance has saved psychoanalysis from becoming a Jewish national concern.' *A Psycho-Analytic Dialogue: The Letters of Sigmund Freud and Karl Abraham, 1907–1926*, ed. Hilda C. Abraham and Ernst L. Freud, trans. Bernard Marsh and Hilda C. Abraham, New York, Basic Books, 1965, p. 34.
15 *The Freud/Jung Letters*, op cit. note 13, p. 100.
16 *MDR*, pp. 181–2.
17 As in the BBC television 'Face to Face' interview with John Freeman in 1959.
18 *MDR*, p. 173. For a full discussion of what Jung means by 'numinous,' see the section 'The Nature of Religious Experience' in Chapter 8.
19 See above p. 198, n. 27.
20 *MDR*, p. 173.
21 *Ibid.*
22 *Ibid.*, pp.174–5.
23 See above, pp. 9–10.

24 'Freud and Jung: Contrasts' (1929) *CW* 4: 336.

7 The structure of the psyche

1 This is apparent, for example, in the series of five articles written between 1908 and 1911: 'Psychic Conflicts in a Child' (1910) *CW* 17: 1–35; 'The Significance of the Father in the Destiny of the Individual' (1909) *CW* 4: 301–23; 'A Contribution to the Psychology of Rumour' (1910–11) *CW* 4: 35–47; 'On the Significance of Number Dreams' (1910–11) *CW* 4: 48–55; and 'The Content of the Psychoses' (1908) *CW* 3: 155–78. Jung's gradual departure from Freud in this series is discussed by Avis M. Dry, *The Psychology of Jung*, London, Methuen, 1961.

2 *The Freud/Jung Letters*, ed. William McGuire, translated by Ralph Manheim and R.F.C. Hull, abridged by Alan McGlashan, London, Penguin Books, 1979, pp. 44–5. Throughout the correspondence the references to Aschaffenburg are highly uncomplimentary.

3 'Freud's Theory of Hysteria: A Reply to Aschaffenburg' (1906) *CW* 4: 4. In his correspondence with Freud a year later, Jung is much less complimentary about Aschaffenburg, complaining that 'he still hasn't understood anything.' (Preface in *The Freud/Jung Letters*, Penguin, p. 59).

4 'The Freudian Theory of Hysteria' (1908) *CW* 4: 23.

5 *CW* 3: 4.

6 The two parts first appeared in the *Jahrbuch*, the first part in the same volume with Freud's paper on the Schreber case. The first English translation, *The Psychology of the Unconscious*, was by Beatrice Hinkle in 1916 and has recently been republished by Routledge (1993). The translation in *CW* 5 is an extensive revision, first published in 1952. All extracts will be taken from this later edition.

7 *The Freud/Jung Letters*, op. cit. note 2, p. 244.

8 *MDR*, p. 191.

9 *Ibid*. There are, however, some remarkable letters from Emma Jung to Freud in which she underlines Jung's difficulties over completing Part II because of his 'constant worry over what you would say about it.' Less tactfully she also takes Freud to task over the treatment of his own children. *The Freud/Jung Letters*, op. cit. note 2, pp. 241–7.

10 *Ibid.*, pp. 277–8.

11 *PFL* (1986) 15: 128.

12 Originally published in French under the title 'Quelques fait d'imagination créatrice subconsciente,' *Archieves de psychologie* (Geneva) (1906) 5: 36–51.

13 *Symbols of Transformation*, p. 48.

14 *Ibid.*, p. 460.

15 *Ibid.*, p. 11.

16 *Ibid.*, pp.17–18.

17 *Moses and Monotheism* (1939), *PFL* 13: 345.

18 *Symbols of Transformation*, pp. 27–8.

19 *Ibid.*, p. 109.

20 *Ibid.*, p. 101. Some other references to this case are in 'The Significance of Constitution and Heredity in Psychology' (1929) *CW* 8: 111; and in 'The Structure of the Psyche' (1927/1931) *CW* 8: 150. To confuse matters, in the original 1912 version of *Symbols of Transformation*, Jung states that it was not he who saw the patient but his colleague, Johann Jakob Honegger.

21 Quoted by Jung. Jung subsequently discovered that Dieterich's *Eine Mithras-liturgie* was first published in Leipzig in 1903 and not 1910 as he originally thought. The patient mentioned had, however, been committed some years before 1903.

22 *Ibid.*, p. 102. Jung first uses the term 'archetype' (*Archetypus*) in his essay 'Instinct and the Unconscious' (1919) *CW* 8: 133. In *Symbols of Transformation* the equivalent term is 'primordial image' (*Urbild*).

23 Jung provides an elaborate analysis of how these adjustments occur. Primarily consciousness develops through the application of four mental functions – thinking, feeling, sensing and intuiting. These functions are not activated in equal proportion and this determines character. Thus we get four function-types: thinking types, feeling types and so on. In addition to these four functions, there are also two further, and mutually exclusive, 'attitudes' – extraversion and introversion – the first orientating consciousness towards the external and objective world, the second towards the inner and subjective world. According to Jung, attitudes are much more dependent on our biological make-up than functions and are therefore more clearly determined from birth. The subsequent combination of function and attitude provide eight behavioural patterns – extraverted thinking type, introverted thinking type etc. – and each of these has a tendency to develop a particular form of neurosis or psychosis. Cf. *Psychological Types* (1921) *CW*, 6: 330–407.

24 'On the Psychology of the Unconscious' (1917) *CW* 7: 66.

25 'The Concept of the Collective Unconscious' (1936) *CW* 9 (1): 48.

26 'Foreword to Harding: "Woman's Mysteries"' (1949) *CW* 18: 518.

27 'The Concept of the Collective Unconscious,' *CW* 9 (1): 44.

28 'Psychological Aspects of the Mother Archetype' (1938) *CW* 9 (1): 79.

29 Stevens, *On Jung*, London, Penguin, 1990, p. 38.

30 *The Ego and the Id* (1923) *PFL* 11: 378.

31 *Symbols of Transformation*, pp. 134–5.

32 *Ibid.*, pp.144–5.

33 *Religion and the Psychology of Jung*, trans. G. R. Lamb, London and New York, Sheed & Ward, 1957, p. 30.

34 The following account is based on Jung's essay 'On Psychic Energy' *CW* 8: 3–66. Although published in 1928, this article was completed shortly after *Symbols of Transformation*.

35 'The Theory of Psychoanalysis' (1913) *CW* 4: 124.

36 Cf. Garfield Tourney, 'Empedocles and Freud, Heraclitus and Jung,' *Bulletin of the History of Medicine*, (1956) 30 (1): 109–23.

37 'On Psychic Energy,' *CW* 8: 9.

38 *Ibid.*, p. 18.

39 *Ibid.*, p. 26.

40 *Ibid*.

41 *Ibid.*, p. 34.

42 'Freud and Jung: Contrasts' (1929) *CW* 4: 334.

43 *Symbols of Transformation*, p. 136.

44 'The Relations between the Ego and the Unconscious' (1928) in *Two Essays on Analytical Psychology* (1928, 1943) *CW* 7: 215–16.

45 See above, n. 23.

46 *Symbols of Transformation*, p. 135. Here Jung makes the point that if every relationship was a sexual one, the 'idea of sexuality would become so nebulous that the very word "sexuality" would be deprived of all meaning.'

47 See above, p. 17.

8 God as archetype of the collective unconscious

1 *The Freud/Jung Letters*, p. 236.

2 *CW* 4: 320. Significantly this passage is deleted in later editions.

3 'Concerning the Archetypes, with Special Reference to the Anima Concept' (1936) *CW* 9: 66.
4 See above, p. 97.
5 *CW* 7: 66.
6 *CW* 8: 133.
7 'Archetypes of the collective unconscious' (1934) *CW* 9 (1): 4–5.
8 'A Study in the Process of Individuation' (1950) *CW* 9: 351.
9 'Archaic Man,' (1931) *CW* 10: 51.
10 See June K. Singer, 'Religion and the Collective Unconscious: Common Ground of Psychology and Religion,' *Zygon* (1969) 4: 315–32; and Ira Progoff, *Jung's Psychology and its Social Meaning*, London, Routledge & Kegan Paul, 1953, p. 70–1.
11 'Psychological Aspects of the Mother Archetype' (1938) *CW* 9 (1): 81.
12 'The Psychology of the Child Archetype' (1941) *CW* 9 (1): 158–60.
13 The Jungian anthropologist, Jennette Jones, organizes and extends Jung's list of archetypes into four groups: 1) geometric figures, like the mandala and tetrahedron; 2) patterns, like the spiral, and natural forms, like the sun; 3) the personifications already given by Jung; and 4) the alchemical processes. Quoted by Mary Ann Mattoon, *Jungian Psychology in Perspective*, London and New York, The Free Press, 1981, pp. 41–2.
14 'Pyschological Aspects of the Mother Archetype' (1938) *CW* 9 (1): 79–80.
15 *Psychological Types* (1921) *CW* 6: 400.
16 'Psychological Aspects of the Mother Archetype' (1938) *CW* 9 (1): 78.
17 *The Psychology of C. G. Jung*, London, Routledge & Kegan Paul, 1962, p. 45.
18 'Psychological Aspects of the Mother Archetype' (1938) *CW* 9 (1):101.
19 *Psychology and Alchemy* (1944) *CW* 12: 211.
20 For the influence of Kant on Jung, see Marian L. Pauson, *Jung the Philosopher*, New York, Peter Lang, 1988, pp. 13–27; James W. Heisig, *Imago Dei: A Study of C. G. Jung's Psychology of Religion*, Lewisburg, Penn., Bucknell University Press, 1978, pp.196–8; and J. Harley Chapman, *Jung's Three Theories of Religious Experience*, Lewiston, Ontario, The Edwin Mellen Press, 1988, pp. 37–8, 136–8.
21 'The Role of the Unconscious' (1918) *CW* 10: 10–11.
22 *Aion* (1951) *CW* 9 (2): 179.
23 'The Concept of the Collective Unconscious' (1936) *CW* 9 (1): 48.
24 'Instinct and the Unconscious' (1919) *CW* 8:137–8.
25 'On the Nature of the Psyche' (1947) *CW* 8: 214.
26 *Ibid.*, p. 228.
27 The most detailed analysis of these archetypes is given in Edward C. Whitmont, *The Symbolic Quest*, Princeton, NJ, Princeton University Press, 1969, pp. 156–230.
28 *Two Essays on Analytical Psychology* (1928, 1943) *CW* 7: 192. There is some debate among commentators about whether the Persona is an archetype. For the purposes of this exposition I shall follow Whitmont, Calvin Hall and others in claiming that it is an archetype, not least because it regulates typical forms of behaviour, albeit in this instance behaviour primarily dependent on social expectation.
29 *Ibid.*, p. 194.
30 Cf. Whitmont, *op.cit.* note 27, p. 158.
31 'Conscious, Unconscious, and Individuation' (1939) *CW* 9 (1): 284–5.
32 In 'Problems of Modern Psychotherapy' (1929) Freud himself becomes an instance of the shadow. 'The result of the Freudian method of elucidation is a minute elaboration of man's shadow-side unexampled in any previous age. It is the most effective antidote imaginable to all idealistic illusions about the nature of man; and it is therefore no wonder that there arose on all sides the most violent opposition to Freud and his school.' *CW* 16: 63–4.

33 Cf. *Two Essays on Analytical Psychology* (1928, 1943) *CW* 7: 188–211.
34 See above, pp. 104–6.
35 *Two Essays on Analytical Psychology* (1928, 1943) *CW* 7: 240.
36 *Ibid.*, p. 238.
37 Cf. 'The Psychological Aspects of the Kore' (1951) *CW* 9 (1): 187.
38 *Psychology and Religion* (1938) *CW* 11: 73.
39 'Concerning Mandala Symbolism' (1950) *CW* 9 (1): 357.
40 *CW* 12. Two other volumes of the collected edition are devoted to alchemy: *Alchemical Studies* (*CW* 13) and *Mysterium Coniunctionis* (*CW* 14).
41 *Two Essays on Analytical Psychology* (1928, 1943) *CW* 7: 220. For further details on Jung's discussion of alchemy, see Allison Coudert, *Alchemy: The Philosopher's Stone*, Boulder, Col., Shambhala Publications, 1980; Edward Edinger, *Anatomy of the Psyche: Alchemical Symbolism in Psychotherapy*, LaSalle, Ill., Open Court Publishing Co., 1985; Mircea Eliade, *The Forge and the Crucible: The Origins and Structure of Alchemy*, New York, Harper & Row, 1962; Marie-Louise von Franz, *Alchemical Active Imagination*, Irving, Texas, Spring Publications, 1979; and Michael Fordham, 'The Relevance of Analytical Theory to Alchemy, Mysticism, and Theology,' *Journal of Analytical Psychology* (1960) 5 (2): 113–28.
42 'A Psychological Approach to the Dogma of the Trinity' (1942) *CW* 11: 148–9.
43 *Psychology and Alchemy* (1944) *CW* 12: 14.
44 Quoted by H. L. Philp, *Jung and the Problem of Evil*, London, Rockliff, 1958, pp. 15–16. Also given in *The Symbolic Life* (1976) *CW* 18: 706–7.
45 John Macquarrie, *20th Century Religious Thought*, London, SCM Press, 1971, p. 109.
46 *MDR*, p. 384.
47 *Ibid.*, p. 385.
48 Letter to Robert C. Smith (dated 29 June 1960). *C. G. Jung Letters*, ed. G. Adler, with A. Jaffé, Princeton, Princeton University Press, 1973 and 1975, vol. 2 (1951–1961), p. 570.
49 W. McGuire and R. F. Hull, *C. G. Jung Speaking*, Princeton, Princeton University Press, 1977, p. 428. Jung makes the same point in an earlier interview (1955): 'All that I have learned has led me step by step to an unshakeable conviction of the existence of God. I only believe what I know. And that eliminates believing. Therefore I do not take his existence on belief – I *know* that He exists.' (*Ibid.*, p. 251).
50 *Psychology and Religion* (1938) *CW* 11: 104–5.
51 'The Psychology of the Unconscious' (1917) *CW* 7: 66. In *Answer to Job* (1952) Jung writes: The archetypes of the collective unconscious 'are spontaneous phenomena which are not subject to our will, and we are therefore justified in ascribing to them a certain autonomy. They are to be regarded not only as objects but as subjects with laws of their own.' *CW* 11: 362.
52 *God and the Unconscious*, London, Fontana Books, 1960, p. 78.
53 One exception is Don McGowan in *What is Wrong with Jung*, Buffalo, New York, Prometheus Books, 1994.
54 *CW* 6: 473–81.
55 *Ibid.*, p. 474.
56 *Ibid.*, p. 475.
57 *Ibid.*, p. 476.
58 See above, p. 110.
59 *Two Essays on Analytical Psychology* (1928, 1943) *CW* 7: 132.
60 *Ibid.*, p. 137.
61 *Psychological Types* (1921) *CW* 6: 475.
62 'A Psychological Approach to the Dogma of the Trinity' (1948) *CW* 11: 110.

63 *Aion* (1951) *CW*, 9 (2): 178.

64 'A Psychological Approach to the Dogma of the Trinity' *CW* 11: 130.

65 This explains why the doctrine of the Trinity can provoke a religious experience. Here Jung cites the case of Brother Nicholas of Flüe. Cf. *CW* 9 (1): 8–12; and 'Brother Klaus' (1933) *CW* 11: 316–23.

66 See 'Transformation Symbolism in the Mass' (1942; revised 1954) *CW* 11: 296–448.

67 'A Psychological Approach to the Dogma of the Trinity' *CW* 11: 153.

68 'Jung and Religious Belief,' *The Symbolic Life*, *CW*, 18: 737.

69 'A Psychological Approach to the Dogma of the Trinity' *CW* 11: 154–5.

70 See above, p. 121.

71 *Aion* (1951) *CW* 9 (2): 37.

72 *Ibid.*, p. 33.

73 For the most detailed analysis, see J. Harley Chapman, *op.cit.* note 20.

74 *Psychology and Religion*, pp. 98, 104.

75 In *Das Heilige* (1917). English trans., *The Idea of the Holy*, Oxford: Oxford University Press, 1923.

76 *Psychology and Religion* (1938) *CW* 11: 7.

77 'On the Nature of the Psyche' *CW* 8: 221.

78 See above, pp. 102–8.

79 'A Psychological Approach to the Dogma of the Trinity' *CW* 11: 152.

80 Letter to H. Haberlandt (dated 23 April 1952). *C.G. Jung Letters*, ed. G. Adler, with A. Jaffé, Princeton, Princeton University Press, 1973 and 1975, (1951–1961) vol. 2 pp. 53–5. Jung makes the same point in his 'Religion and Psychology: A Reply to Martin Buber' (1952): 'It should not be overlooked that what I am concerned with are psychic phenomena which can be proved empirically to be the bases of metaphysical concepts, and that when, for example, I speak of "God" I am unable to refer to anything beyond these demonstrable psychic models which, we have to admit, have shown themselves to be devastatingly real. To anyone who finds their reality incredible I would recommend a reflective tour through a lunatic asylum.' *CW* 18: 666.

9 God and individuation

1 *MDR*, p. 235.

2 *The Future of an Illusion* (1927) *PFL* 12 (1991): 227.

3 See above, p. 92.

4 'Pyschotherapists or the Clergy' (1932) *CW* 11: 334.

5 'Conscious, Unconscious and Individuation' (1939) *CW* 9 (1): 275.

6 *Two Essays on Analytical Psychology* (1928, 1943) *CW* 7: 173.

7 *Ibid.*, pp. 239–40.

8 See above, pp. 120–2.

9 Levinson cites Nietzsche, Dylan Thomas, Scott Fitzgerald and van Gogh as examples for whom the individuating process was destructive, and Dante, Hesse, Mann, Frank Lloyd Wright and Bertrand Russell as examples for whom it was creative. He also includes Freud and Jung in the latter group. See D. Levinson (with C. N. Darrow, E.B. Klein, M.H. Levinson, and B. McKee), *The Seasons of a Man's Life*, New York, Knopf, 1978. Quoted by Anthony Stevens, *op.cit.*, p. 200.

10 C. A. Meier, co-founder of the C. G. Jung Institute in Zurich, has given an admirably clear and succinct account of the process, citing many amplificatory parallels, in his *Personality* (1977), trans. D. N. Roscoe, Einsiedeln, Switzerland, Daimon, 1995.

11 See above, p. 107.

12 'A Study in the Process of Individuation' (1934; revised 1950) *CW* 9 (1): 291.
13 *Ibid.*, p. 352.
14 *Ibid.*, p. 348.
15 In his 'Concerning Mandala Symbolism' Jung gives no fewer than fifty-four examples of mandalas. *CW* 91 (1): 355–84.
16 'A Study in the Process of Individuation' *CW* 9: 305.
17 *Ibid.*, p. 304.
18 Because of this it is a moot point for Jung whether the very young child can be included within the individuation process. However, for some Jungians individuation does begin in infancy. See Michael Fordham, *New Developments in Analytical Psychology*, London, Routledge & Kegan Paul, 1957.
19 'The Stages of Life' (1930–31) *CW* 8: 392.
20 *Ibid.*, p. 125.
21 Quoted by Henri Ellenberger, *The Discovery of the Unconscious*, New York, Basic Books, 1970, p. 712.
22 Edward F. Edinger, *Ego and Archetype*, Boston and London, Shambhala, 1992, p. 186.
23 *Ibid.*, pp. 3–104.
24 Cf. M. Esther Harding, *Journey into Self: An Interpretation of Bunyan's Pilgrim's Progress*, London and New York, Longmans, Green, 1956; Barbara Hannah, *Striving Towards Wholeness*, New York, G. P. Putnam's Sons, 1971; Daryl L. Sharp, *The Secret Raven: Conflict and Transformation in the Life of Franz Kafka*, Toronto, Inner City Books, 1980; Liliane Frey-Rohn, *Friedrich Nietzsche: A Psychological Approach to His Life and Work*, ed. R. Hinshaw and L. Fischli, Zurich, Daimon Verlag, 1984; John A. Sanford, *King Saul, the Tragic Hero: A Study in Individuation*, New York and Mahwah, NJ, Paulist Press, 1985; and Timothy R. O'Neill, *The Individuated Hobbit: Jung, Tolkien, and the Archetypes of Middle-Earth*, London, Thames & Hudson, 1980.
25 See above, pp. 137–41.
26 *CW* 14: 546.
27 'Flying Saucers: A Modern Myth' (1958) *CW* 10: 339.
28 *Ibid.*
29 *Aion* (1951) *CW* 9 (2): 268.
30 Quoted by Frei in Victor White, *God and the Unconscious*, London, Fontana Books, 1960, p. 258.
31 *Ibid.*, p. 267. A different translation appears in *Letters*, vol.1, pp. 486–7.
32 *The Myth of Meaning*, trans. R. F. C. Hull, London, Penguin Books, 1975, p. 113.
33 *Ibid.*, p. 266.
34 *Aion* (1951) *CW* 9 (2): 22.
35 *Ibid.*, p. 183.
36 *Ibid.*, p. 171.
37 'Flying Saucers: A Modern Myth' (1958) *CW* 10: 424.
38 *Aion* (1951), *CW*, 9 (2): 206.
39 *Ibid.*, p. 31.
40 *Psychological Types* (1921) *CW* 6: 243.
41 *Ibid.*, p.248.
42 See above, p. 128.
43 *Answer to Job* (1952) *CW* 11: 405.
44 *Religious Thought and the Modern Psychologies*, Philadelphia, Fortress Press, 1987, p. 193.
45 'A Psychological View of Conscience' (1958) *CW* 10: 458.
46 As H. L. Philp claims in *Jung and the Problem of Evil*, London, Rockliff, 1958 pp. 31–43.

47 The same argument requires the inclusion of the feminine (the 'anima') within the Godhead. This explains why Jung welcomed the dogma of the Assumption of the Virgin, which was proclaimed by Pope Pius XII in 1950. This added a fourth and feminine principle to the masculine Trinity, thereby presenting another unifying symbol of totality. Cf. *Answer to Job* (1952) *CW* 11: 398–9. Jung's most important discussion of the problem of evil is found in 'Christ, a Symbol of the Self,' *Aion* (1951) *CW* 9 (2): 36–71. As with any religious symbol, the image of Christ is 'an archetype of the self' (p. 37); but without its 'shadow-side' this image is not a totality. For this image to be a complete symbol of wholeness, however, a fourth must be included: hence the importance of the Devil in the divine drama of redemption as the adversary of Christ. Cf. also 'A Psychological Approach to the Dogma of the Trinity', which contains an elaborate account of the Devil as the 'aping shadow of God.' *CW* 11: 168–80.

48 Other accounts of the stages are to be found in *MDR*, pp. 359–60; and in 'On Psychic Energy' (1928) *CW* 8: 54–6.

49 *CW* 11: 287.

50 I am particularly indebted at this point to Stanley Riukas' detailed exposition of the three stages in his unpublished doctoral dissertation, God: Myth, Symbol, and Reality – A Study of Jung's Psychology, New York University, 1967, pp. 99–144.

51 'A Psychological Approach to the Dogma of the Trinity' *CW* 11: 181.

52 *Ibid.*, p. 134.

53 *Ibid.*, p. 133.

54 *Ibid.*, p. 182.

55 *Ibid.*, p. 134.

56 *Ibid.*

57 *Ibid.*, p. 182.

58 *Ibid.*, pp. 183, 185.

59 *Ibid.*, p. 136.

60 *Answer to Job* (1952) *CW* 11: 413.

61 *Ibid.*

62 'A Psychological Approach to the Dogma of the Trinity' *CW* 11: 110.

63 There is a problem of interpretation here. If the symbolism of the Trinity expresses the final stage of the individuation process, why does Jung also argue that any representation of the deity must employ a fourth element if it is to include evil and a feminine element, that is, God's 'shadow' and 'anima'? Are therefore quaternity or mandala symbols more appropriate for the expression of wholeness? Edinger argues that trinitarian symbols express the 'dynamic' and 'developmental' aspect of individuation, whereas quarternity symbols express a static and completed 'goal.' So, speaking of the mandalas of Tibetan Buddhism, he writes: 'They are instruments of meditation which convey to consciousness a sense of peace and calm as though one were grounded in the eternal structural substance and protected from the disrupting dangers of change.' I think this interpretation is correct because it accepts that the goal of individuation is never completely realized. The three-fold process thus becomes the process of life in seeking the unobtainable. (*Ibid.*, pp. 182, 192).

64 'The Undiscovered Self' (1957) *CW* 10: 265.

65 'The Spiritual Problem of Modern Man' (1928/1931) *CW* 10: 75.

66 'The Soul and Death' (1934) *CW* 8: 409.

67 'The Spiritual Problem of Modern Man' *CW* 10: 83.

68 *Psychology and Religion* (1938) *CW* 11: 95.

69 'Flying Saucers: A Modern Myth' (1958) *CW* 10: 327.

70 'Foreword' to Werblowsky's 'Lucifer and Prometheus' (1952) *CW* 11: 315.

71 *Two Essays on Analytical Psychology* (1928, 1943) *CW* 7: 143.

72 *Ibid.*
73 *Ibid.*, p. 144.
74 'The Spiritual Problem of Modern Man' *CW* 10: 77.
75 *Psychology and Alchemy* (1944) *CW* 12: 461.
76 'The Spiritual Problem of Modern Man' *CW* 10: 88.
77 'Beyond the Pleasure Principle' (1920) *PFL* 11: 314.

10 A critical appraisal

1 Quoted in *FL* 13: 47.
2 *Jung*, London, Fontana, 1986 p. 117. James Heisig gives a valuable critique of Jung's style in *Imago Dei: A Study of C. G. Jung's Psychology of Religion*, Lewisburg, Penn., Bucknell University Press, 1978, pp. 104–10.
3 Cf. David Cox, *Jung and St. Paul*, New York, Association Press, 1959; Gerald Sykes, *The Hidden Remnant*, New York, Harper & Row, 1962; and R. C. Zaehner, 'A New Buddha and a New Tao,' *The Concise Encyclopaedia of Living Faiths*, New York, Hawthorn Books, 1959, pp. 402–12.
4 In *Die Religion in der Psychologie C. G. Jungs*, Berne, 1945. Quoted by Victor White, in *God and the Unconscious*, p. 267.
5 Kathleen Raine, 'A Major Influence in Western Thought,' *New Republic*, May 18, 1953.
6 'Jung and the Christians,' *Commonweal* (1953) 58 (9): 229–31.
7 London and New York, Sheed and Ward, 1957, p. 222.
8 London, Sheldon Press, 1970, p. 252.
9 Tempe, Arizona, New Falcon Publications, 1994.
10 Atlanta, John Knox Press, 1983.
11 Atlanta, John Knox Press, 1986.
12 *Jung and the Christian Way*, Minneapolis, Seabury Press, 1983.
13 See Kelsey, *God, Dreams, and Revelations*, Minneapolis, Augsburg Publishing House, 1974; and Sanford, *Dreams: God's Forgotten Language*, Philadelphia, J. B. Lippincott, 1968. For the connection between Jung and contemporary spirituality, see also *Carl Jung and Christian Spirituality*, ed. Robert Moore, Mahwah, N. J.: Paulist Press, 1988.
14 Edition used: New York, Oxford University Press, 1964, p. 122.
15 *The Face of the Deep: The Religious Ideas of C. G. Jung*, Philadelphia, Westminster Press, 1967 p. 20.
16 *Freud or Jung*, London, George Allen & Unwin, 1950; edition used: Evanston, Illinois, Northwestern University Press, 1991, p. 163. Another good example of Freudian criticism is Nandor Fodor's *Freud, Jung, and Occultism*, New York, New Hyde Park, University Books, 1971.
17 *Brett's History of Psychology* (revised edn), London, George Allen & Unwin, 1962.
18 'C. G. Jung's Confession', *Encounter* (1964) 22: 47.
19 'A Critique of Contributions to Analytical Psychology,' *The Journal of Abnormal and Social Psychology* (1929–30) 24: 441–52.
20 Buffalo, NY, Prometheus Books, 1994.
21 'Challenges to Religion,' *Commonweal* (1952) 55 (23): 561–2.
22 See 'Freud and Jung,' *Pastoral Psychology*, (1950) 1: 11–15.
23 *Psychology and Religion* (1938) *CW* 11: 5.
24 'Basic Postulates of Analytical Psychology' (1931) *CW* 8: 353.
23 'Psychological commentary on "The Tibetan Book of the Great Liberation"' (1954) *CW* 11: 480–1.
26 Mattoon, *Jungian Psychology in Perspective*, New York, The Free Press and

London, Collier Macmillan, 1981 p. 281.

27 Jung, *Letters*, vol. 1, ed. G. Adler in collaboration with A. Jaffé, trans. R. Hull, London, Routledge & Kegan Paul, 1973, pp. 558–67. This correspondence is also published in Bennet, *C. G. Jung*, London, Barrie & Rockliff, 1961, pp. 95–103.

28 *Jung and Phenomenology*, London, Routledge, 1991, p. 64.

29 'Verifiability,' *The Theory of Meaning*, ed. G. H. R. Parkinson, Oxford, Oxford University Press, 1968, p. 37.

30 *Ibid.*, p. 39.

31 *Fact and Fantasy in Freudian Theory*, London and New York, Methuen, 1972, p. 411.

32 See H. Gray and J.B. Wheelwright, 'Jung's Psychological Types, Their Frequency of Occurrence,' *Journal of General Psychology* (1946) 34: 3–17; and I. B. Myers, *Manual: The Myers-Briggs Type Indicator*, Princeton, Educational Testing Service, 1962.

33 See Brome, *Jung: Man and Myth*, New York, Atheneum, 1978; Sherrard, 'An Introduction to the Religious Thought of C. G. Jung,' *Studies in Comparative Religion* (1969) 111: 33–49; and C. S. Hall and G. Lindzey, *Theories of Personality*, (3rd edn), New York, John Wiley & Sons, 1978. Eysenck's remarks are particularly pertinent: 'Jung is but one of a large number of analysts who consciously reject scientific methodology in favour of subjectivity, intuition, and unconscious "understanding". There can be no argument here; those who look for religion, faith, beauty, or other non-scientific values need fear no scientific criticism. Neither, on the other hand, should they make any claims to having established scientific truths; they cannot reject the methods of science and yet claim the results. This desire to have the best of both worlds is very frequent among analysts, but it would be difficult to proffer any logical argument in its defence.' *Uses and Abuses of Psychology*, London, Penguin Books, 1953, pp. 226–7.

34 'Psychological Types and Individuation: A Plea for a More Scientific Approach in Jungian Psychology,' in *The Analytic Process*, ed. J. B. Wheelwright, New York, Putnam's, 1971, pp. 276–89.

35 'The Neglected Function of Analytical Psychology,' *Journal of Analytical Psychology*, (1977) 22 (1): 22.

36 *Ibid.*, p. 19.

37 See above, pp. 123–8.

38 'Neo-Platonism and Analytical Psychology,' *Philosophical Review* (1945) 54: 558–77.

39 See Fordham, 'Biological Theory and the Concept of Archetypes,' *New Developments in Analytical Psychology*, London, Routledge & Kegan Paul, 1957; Anthony Stevens, *Archetype: A Natural History of the Self*, London, Routledge & Kegan Paul, 1982; Mattoon, *op.cit.* note 26, pp.25–6.

40 Stevens, *op.cit.* note 39, p. 73; and E. Rossi, 'The Cerebral Hemispheres in Analytical Psychology,' *Journal of Analytical Psychology* (1977) 22: 32–58.

41 Marilyn Nagy, *Philosophical Issues in the Psychology of C. G. Jung*, Albany, State University of New York Press, 1991, p. 174.

42 'A Psychological Approach to the Dogma of the Trinity' *CW* 11: 149, note 2.

43 See above, p. 127.

44 See above, p. 98.

45 McGowan, *op.cit.* note 20, p. 67. Cf. Karl Popper, *The Logic of Scientific Discovery*, 1934; reprint: New York, Science Editions, 1961, p. 47.

46 *Personality: A Biosocial Approach to Origins and Structure*, New York, Harper, 1947. Quoted by J. A. C. Brown, *Freud and the Post-Freudians*, Harmondsworth, Penguin, 1961, p. 45.

47 John L. Fischer, 'The Sociopsychological Analysis of Folktales,' *Current Anthropology* (1963) 4: 256.

48 As Jung does in a letter to Stephen Abrams, 5 March 1959. *Letters*, vol. 2, p. 490.
49 Avis Dry, *The Psychology of Jung*, London, Methuen, 1961, p. xiii.
50 See above, p. 118.
51 *Ibid.*
52 Glover, *op.cit.*, note 16 p. 37.
53 *Freud, Jung, and Occultism*, New Hyde Park, New York, University Books, 1971, pp. 177, 182.
54 Cited by Brown, *op.cit.* note 46, p. 47.
55 Paula Heimann, 'Some Notes on the Psycho-analytic Concept of Introjected Objects,' *British Journal of Medical Psychology* (1949) 22: 14. Quoted by Walter A. Shelburne, *Mythos and Logos in the Thought of Carl Jung*, Albany, State University of New York Press, 1988, p. 72.
56 Allport, *The Individual and His Religion*, New York, Macmillan, 1960, p. 24.
57 *Ibid.*
58 Cf. Robin Robertson, *Jungian Archetypes*, York Beach, Maine, Nicolas-Hays, 1995, p. 105.
59 *Play, Dreams and Imitation in Childhood*, trans. C. Gattegno and F. M. Hodgson, London, W. Heinemann, 1951, p. 196. For further on Piaget's theories, see J. L. Phillips, *The Origins of Intellect*, New York, W. H. Freeman, 1975.
60 *Myth: Its Meaning and Functions in Ancient and Other Cultures*, Cambridge, Cambridge University Press, 1970, p. 276.
61 *Ibid.* p. 283.
62 *Ibid.*, p. 245.
63 'The Archetype in Analytical Psychology and the History of Religion', *Journal of the Warburg and Courtauld Institutes* (1954) 21: 166–78.
64 See David Hume, *Enquiry Concerning Human Understanding* (1748) ed. L. A. Selby-Bigge, (3rd edn) revised by P. H. Nidditch, Oxford, Clarendon Press, 1975, p. 148.
65 See above, p. 125.
66 *Critique of Pure Reason*, trans. Norman Kemp Smith, London, Macmillan, 1929, p. 650.
67 See Heisig, *op.cit.* note 1, pp. 196–8; and Chapman, *Jung's Three Theories of Religious Experience*, Lewiston, NY, The Edwin Mellen Press, 1988 pp.136–9.
68 See, for example, Roger J. Sullivan, *Immanuel Kant's Moral Theory*, Cambridge, Cambridge University Press, 1989, pp. 261–75, and W. H. Walsh, *Kant's Criticism of Metaphysics*, Edinburgh, Edinburgh University Press, 1975, pp. 229–41. Whether or not Kant had abandoned his moral argument altogether by the time he wrote his *Opus Postumum*, is discussed in detail, and rejected, by G. A. Schrader in his 'Kant's Presumed Repudiation of the "Moral Argument" in the Opus Postumum,' *Philosophy* (1951) 26: 228–41. Cf. also Erich Adickes, *Kant's Opus postumum dargestellt und beurteilt*, Berlin, Ergänzungsheft der Kant-Studien, 1920.
69 'Toward an Archetypal Imagination,' *Spring* (1974) p. 29. Quoted by Chapman, *op.cit.* note 67, pp.137–8.
70 Paul Edwards, 'Common Consent Arguments for the Existence of God,' 'Encyclopedia of Philosophy' 98., New York, Macmillan, 1967, vol. 2, p. 148.
71 'Essay Concerning Human Understanding', Ch. 2, sec. 2, abridged and ed. A. S. Pringle-Pattinson, Oxford, Clarendon Press.
72 *Ibid.*, Ch. 2, sec. 4.
73 *Three Essays on Religion*, edition used: Bristol, Thoemmes Press, 1993, pp. 96, 101, 119.

74 'Concerning the Archetypes with Special Reference to the Anima Concept' (1936) *CW* 9 (1): 62.
75 *Why I am Not a Christian* (1957), edition used: London, George Allen & Unwin, 1975, p. 27.
76 London, Heinemann, 1907.
77 Cambridge MSS. Quoted by Gertrude Himmelfarb, *Darwin and the Darwinian Revolution*, London, Chatto & Windus, 1959, p. 315.
78 *Op.cit.* note 45, p. 23.
79 See Goldbrunner, *Individuation: A Study of the Depth Psychology of Carl Gustav Jung*, Notre Dame, University of Notre Dame Press, 1964, p. 172; Altizer, 'A Critical Analysis of C. G. Jung's Understanding of Religion', unpublished PhD thesis, University of Chicago, 1955, p. 266; and White, *op.cit.* note 4, p. 94.
80 Buber, *Eclipse of God: Studies in the Relation between Religion and Philosophy*, London, Victor Gollancz, 1953, pp.105–6.
81 'Religion and Psychology: A Reply to Martin Buber' (1952) *CW* 18: 665. For extensions of the Jung/Buber debate, see Maurice Friedman, 'Religion and Psychology: The Limits of the Psyche as Touchstone of Reality,' *Quaker Religious Thought* (1970) 12: 2–28; Edward Whitmont, 'Prefatory remarks to Jung's "Reply to Buber",' *Spring* (1973) pp.188–95; and John P. Dourley, 'In the Shadow of the Monotheisms: Jung's Conversations with Buber and White' in *Jung and the Monotheisms*, ed. Joel Ryce-Menuhin, London and New York, Routledge, 1994, pp.125–45.
82 'General Aspects of Dream Psychology' (1916/1948) *CW* 8: 278.
83 *MDR* p. 369.
84 *Personal Destinies*, Princeton, Princeton University Press, 1976, pp. 3–5, 161–5.
85 See Erikson, *Childhood and Society*, London, Penguin Books, 1965; Fowler, *Stages of Faith: The Psychology of Human Development and the Quest for Meaning*, San Francisco, Harper & Row, 1981; and L. Kohlberg, *The Philosophy of Moral Development*, San Francisco, Harper & Row, 1981. For a summary of these, see Michael Jacobs, *Living Illusions*, London, SPCK, 1993.
86 See Faber, *Psychology of Religion*, London, SCM Press, 1976.
87 See above, p. 135.
88 'Jung and Religious Belief,' *The Symbolic Life*, *CW* 18: 737.
89 See White, *op.cit.* note 4, pp. 219–27; Buber, *op.cit.* note 80, p. 112–13; and Friedman, *To Deny Our Nothingness*, Chicago, The University of Chicago Press, 1978. For a defence of Jung see Gilles Quispel, 'C. G. Jung und die Gnosis', translated in *The Gnostic Jung*, selected and introduced by Robert A. Segal, London, Routledge, 1992, pp. 219–38. Segal provides a valuable overview of this discussion (*ibid.*, pp. 4–52).
90 *Man and His Symbols*, New York, Dell, 1964, p. 58.
91 Edwards, 'Common Consent Arguments for the Existence of God,' *Encyclopedia of Philosophy*, New York, Macmillan, vol. 2, p. 148.
92 See above, p. 175.
93 *Religious Thought and the Modern Psychologies*, Philadelphia, Fortress Press, 1987, p. 184.

BIBLIOGRAPHY

SIGMUND FREUD

Albright, W. F. *From the Stone Age to Christianity*, Baltimore, The John Hopkins Press, 1946.

Aron, Willy. 'Notes on Sigmund Freud's Ancestry and Jewish Contacts,' *YIVO Annual of Jewish Social Sciences* (1956–7) 9: 286–95.

Atkinson, James J. *Primal Law*, London, Longmans, Green & Co., 1903.

Ayer, A. J. *Language, Truth and Logic*, London, Victor Gollancz, 1936.

Badcock, C.R. *The Psychoanalysis of Culture*, Oxford, Basil Blackwell, 1980.

Bakan, David. *Sigmund Freud and the Jewish Mystical Tradition*, Princeton, NJ, D. van Nostrand Co., 1958.

Banks, Robert. 'Religion as Projection: A Re-appraisal of Freud's Theory,' *Religious Studies* (1973) 9: 401–26.

Barbour, I. G. *Issues in Science and Religion*, Englewood Cliffs, NJ, Prentice-Hall, 1966.

——. (ed.) *Science and Religion*, SCM Press, 1968.

Baron, S. 'Review' of *Moses and Monotheism* in *American Journal of Sociology* (1939) 55: 471–7.

Bergmann, M. S. 'Moses and the Evolution of Freud's Jewish Identity,' in *Judaism and Psychoanalysis*, ed. Mortimer Ostow, New York, Ktav Publishing House, Inc., 1982.

Bettelheim, Bruno. *The Uses of Enchantment: The Meaning and Importance of Fairy Tales*, New York, Random House, 1976.

Bernfeld, Siegfried. 'Freud's Earliest Theories and the School of Helmholtz,' *The Psychoanalytic Quarterly* (1944) 13: 341–62.

Browning, Don S. *Religious Thought and the Modern Psychologies*, Philadelphia, Fortress Press, 1987.

Casey, R. P. 'Oedipus Motivation in Religious Thought and Fantasy,' *Psychiatry* (1942) 5: 219–28.

Chandler, Tertius. 'Ikhanaton and Moses,' *American Imago* (1966) 19: 127–39.

Clark, David Stafford. *What Freud Really Said*, London, Penguin, 1965.

Daly, Mary. *Beyond God the Father: Toward a Philosophy of Women's Liberation*, Boston, Beacon Press, 1973.

Darwin, Charles. *The Descent of Man*, London, John Murray, 1871.

Diller, Jerry V. *Freud's Jewish Identity – a Case Study in the Impact of Ethnicity*, London and Toronto, Associated University Press, 1991.

Edelheit, Henry. 'On the Biology of Language: Darwinian/Lamarckian Homology in Human Inheritance (with some thoughts about the Lamarckism of Freud),' *Psychiatry and the Humanities* (1978) 3: 45–74.

219

Evans-Pritchard, E. E. *Theories of Primitive Religion*, Oxford, The Clarendon Press, 1965.

Feuerbach, Ludwig. *The Essence of Christianity* (1841), trans. George Eliot, London, John Chapman, 1854.

Fine, Reuben. *The Development of Freud's Thought*, New York, Jason Aronson, Inc., 1973.

Fisher, Seymour and Roger P. Greenberg. *Freud Scientifically Reappraised*, New York, John Wiley and Sons, 1996.

Fliegel, Zenia Odes. 'Feminine Psychosexual Development in Freudian Theory: A Historical Reconstruction,' *Psychoanalytic Quarterly* (1973) 42: 385–408.

——. 'Half a Century Later: Current Status of Freud's Controversial Views on Women,' *Psychoanalytic Review* (1982) 69: 7–28.

Fortes, M. 'Malinowski and Freud,' *Psychoanalysis and the Psychoanalytic Review* (1958–59) 45: 120–45.

Frazer, J. G. *The Golden Bough*, London, Macmillan, 1890.

——. *Totemism and Exogamy*, London, Macmillan, 1910.

Freud, Sigmund. *Collected Works*. Editions used: 1) *The Penguin Freud Library*, translated under the general editorship of James Strachey, London, Penguin Books, and cited in this work as *PFL*; and 2) *The Standard Edition of the Complete Psychological Works of Sigmund Freud*, trans. and ed. James Strachey in collaboration with Anna Freud, London, The Hogarth Press, 1953–74, and cited in this work as *SE*.

——. *Letters of Sigmund Freud*, ed. Ernest L. Freud, trans. Tania and James Stern, London, The Hogarth Press, 1961.

——. *Psycho-Analysis and Faith: The Letters of Sigmund Freud and Oskar Pfister*, trans. Eric Mosbacher, London, The Hogarth Press, 1963.

——. (with William Bullitt). *Thomas Woodrow Wilson*, Boston, Houghton Mifflin Co., 1967.

—— (with Lou Andreas-Salomé). *Letters*, ed. Ernst Pfeiffer, trans. William and Elaine Robson-Scott, New York, Harcourt Brace Jovanovich, 1972.

Frieden, Ken. *Freud's Dream of Interpretation*, New York, Suny Press, 1990.

Friedman, S. M. 'An Empirical Study of the Castration and Oedipus Complexes,' *Genetic Psychology Monographs* (1952) 46: 61–130.

Fromm, Erich. *The Fear of Freedom*, London, Routledge & Kegan Paul, 1942.

——. 'The Oedipus Complex and the Oedipus Myth,' in *The Family: Its Function and Destiny*, ed. R. N. Anshen, New York, Harper, 1948.

——. *Man for Himself*, London, Routledge & Kegan Paul, 1949.

——. *Psychoanalysis and Religion*, New Haven, Yale University Press, 1950.

——. *Beyond the Chains of Illusion: My Encounter with Marx and Freud*, London, Abacus, 1986.

Gardiner, Muriel (ed.) *The Wolf Man and Sigmund Freud*, London, The Hogarth Press, 1972.

Gay, Peter, *Freud, Jews and Other Germans*, New York, Oxford University Press, 1978.

——. 'Six Names in Search of an Interpretation: A Contribution to the Debate over Sigmund Freud's Jewishness,' *Hebrew Union College Annual* (1982) 53: 295–307. Also available in *Reading Freud*, ed. Peter Gay, New Haven, Yale University Press, 1990.

——. *A Godless Jew: Freud, Atheism, and the Making of Psychoanalysis* New Haven and London, Yale University Press, 1987.

——. *Freud: A Life for Our Time*, New York, W. W. Norton, 1988.

Gay, Volney P. *Freud on Ritual – Reconstruction and Technique*, Missoula, Mont.: Scholars Press, 1979.

Goldenberg, Naomi. *Changing of the Gods: Feminism and the End of Traditional Religions*, Boston, Beacon Press, 1979.

Goldstein, Bluma. 'From Rome to Egypt: Freud's Mosaic Transformations,' in *Reinscribing Moses*, Cambridge, Mass., Harvard University Press, 1992.

Goodall, Jane. 'Life and Death at Gombe,' *National Geographic* (1979) 155: 593–621.

Gross, Rita (ed.) *Beyond Androcentrism: New Essays on Women and Religion*, Missoula, Mont., Scholars Press, 1977.

Grünbaum, Adolf. *The Foundation of Psychoanalysis*, Berkeley, University of California Press, 1984.

——. 'Psychoanalysis and Theism,' *The Monist* (1987) 70: 152–92.

Hall, C. S. 'Strangers in Dreams: An Empirical Confirmation of the Oedipus Complex,' *Journal of Personality* (1963) 31: 336–45.

Holt, Robert R. 'A Review of Some of Freud's Biological Assumptions and their Influence on his Theories,' in *Psychoanalysis and Current Biological Thought*, ed. Norman S. Greenfield and William C. Lewis, Madison and Milwaukee, University of Wisconsin Press, 1965, pp.93–123.

Homans, Peter. *Theology after Freud*, Indianapolis, Bobbs-Merrill Company, 1970.

Horney, Karen. *Feminine Psychology*, ed. Harold Kelman, London, Routledge & Kegan Paul, 1967.

Hume, David. *The Natural History of Religion* (1757) in *David Hume on Religion*, ed. A. Wayne Colver and John Valdimir Price, Oxford, The Clarendon Press, 1976, pp. 25–95.

Jacobs, Michael. *Living Illusions*, London, SPCK, 1993.

Jones, Ernest. 'Early Female Sexuality,' *Papers on Psycho-Analysis*, London, Baillière, Tindall & Cox (4th edn), 1938, pp. 605–16.

——. *Sigmund Freud: Life and Work*, London, Hogarth Press, 1953–57.

Jones, James W. *Contemporary Psychoanalysis and Religion*, New Haven and London, Yale University Press, 1991.

Jung, C. G. *Memories, Dreams, Reflections*, ed. Aniela Jaffé, trans. Richard and Clara Winston, New York, Pantheon Books, 1963.

Kiell, Norman. *Freud Without Hindsight*, Madison, Connecticut, International Universities Press, 1988.

Klein, Dennis B. *Jewish Origins of the Psychoanalytic Movement*, Chicago and London, University of Chicago Press, 1985.

Kline, Paul. *Fact and Fantasy in Freudian Theory*, London, Methuen, 1972.

Kroeber, A. L. 'Totem and Taboo: An Ethnologic Psychoanalysis,' *American Anthropologist* (1920) 22: 48–55.

——. 'Totem and Taboo in Retrospect,' *American Journal of Sociology* (1939) 40: 446–51.

Kuhn, Thomas. *The Structure of Scientific Revolutions*, Chicago, University of Chicago Press, 1962.

Kung, Hans. *Freud and the Problem of God*, New Haven, Yale University Press, 1979. Also contained in *Does God Exist?* trans. Edward Quinn, London, SCM Press, 1991, pp. 262–339.

Lambert, Kenneth. 'Some Religious Implications of the Work of Freud, Jung, and Winnicott,' *Winnicott Studies*, vol. 2 (1987) pp. 49–70.

Lee, R. S. *Freud and Christianity*, London, James Clarke & Co., 1948.

Leeuw, P.J. Van der. 'The Pre-Oedipal Phase of the Male,' *Psychoanalytic Study of the Child*, vol.13 (1958) pp. 352–374.

Lévi-Strauss, Claude. 'The Family' in *Man, Culture and Society*, ed. Henry L. Shapiro, New York, Oxford University Press, 1960, pp. 261–85.

——. *Totemism*, trans. Rodney Needham, London, Merlin Press, 1964.

Lewis, Theodore. 'Freud, the Jews and Judaism,' *The Jewish Spectator* (1958): 11–14.

Loewald, Hans. *Sublimation*, New Haven and London, Yale University Press, 1988.

Lorand, S. 'Psychoanalytic Therapy of Religious Devotees: A Theoretical and Technical Contribution,' *International Journal of Psycho-Analysis* (1962) 43: 50–5.

Ludwig, Emil. *Doctor Freud*, 1947; edition used: New York, Manor Books, 1973.

Malinowski, B. *Sex and Repression in Savage Society*, London, Routledge & Kegan Paul, 1927.

Margolin, Sydney. 'Freud's Constitution in Psychoanalysis' in *Psychoanalysis and Current Biological Thought*, ed. Norman S. Greenfield and William C. Lewis, Madison and Milwaukee, University of Wisconsin Press, 1965, pp.125–149.

McDargh, John. *Psychoanalytic Object Relations Theory and the Study of Religion* New York and London, Lanham, 1984.

McFague, Sallie. *Metaphorical Theology: Models of God in Religious Language* London, SCM Press, 1982.

Meissner, William. *Psychoanalysis and Religious Experience*, New Haven and London, Yale University Press, 1984.

Miller, Justin. 'Interpretations of Freud's Jewishness, 1924–1974,' *Journal of the History of the Behavioral Sciences* 17: 357–74.

Mitchell, Juliet. *Psychoanalysis and Feminism*, Harmondsworth, Penguin Books, 1974.

Morris, Brian. *Anthropological Studies of Religion*, Cambridge, Cambridge University Press, 1987.

Mullahy, Patrick. *Oedipus: Myth and Complex*, with an Introduction by Erich Fromm, New York, Hermitage Press, 1948.

Neu, Jerome. 'Genetic Explanation in *Totem and Taboo*' in *Freud*, ed. Richard Wollheim, New York, Doubleday, 1974, pp. 366–93.

Obholzer, Karin. *The Wolf-Man: Sixty Years Later*, London, Routledge & Kegan Paul, 1982.

Olsen, O. A. (with Simo Køppe). *Freud's Theory of Psychoanalysis*, trans. Jean-Christian Delay and Carl Pedersen, New York and London, New York University Press, 1988.

Ostow, Mortimer. *Judaism and Psychoanalysis*, New York, KTAV, 1982.

Parsons, A. 'Is the Oedipus Complex Universal?' in *The Psychoanalytic Study of Society*, ed. W. Muensterberger and S. Axelrad, New York, International Universities Press, 1969, pp. 278–328.

Philp, Howard. *Freud and Religious Belief*, London, Greenwood Press, 1956.

Pruyser, Paul. *Between Belief and Unbelief*, New York, Harper & Row, 1974.

——. 'The Seamy Side of Current Religious Beliefs,' *Bulletin of the Menninger Clinic* (1977) 41: 329–48.

——. *The Play of the Imagination: Towards a Psychoanalysis of Culture*, New York, International Universities Press, 1983.

Purtill, Richard. *Thinking about Religion*, Englewood Cliffs, NJ, Prentice-Hall, 1978.

Racker, Heinrich. 'On Freud's Position Towards Religion,' *American Imago* (1956) 13: 97–121.

Rainey, Reuben M. *Freud as Student of Religion: Perspectives on the Background and Development of his Thought*, Missoula, Mont., American Academy of Religion & Scholars Press, Dissertation Series 7, 1975.

Rank, Otto. *The Trauma of Birth*, New York, Harcourt and Brace, 1929.

Reik, Theodor. *Ritual: Psycho-Analytic Studies*, translated from the second German edition of *Probleme der Religionspsychologie* by Douglas Bryan, with a Preface by Sigmund Freud, London, The Hogarth Press and The Institute of Psycho-Analysis, 1931.

Rice, E. 'The Jewish Fathers of Psychoanalysis,' *Judaism: A Quarterly Journal of Jewish Life and Thought* (1987) 36: 109–15.

——. *Freud and Moses – The Long Journey Home*, Albany, State University of New York Press, 1990.

Richards, Barry. *Images of Freud*, London, J. M. Dent & Sons, 1989.

Ricoeur, Paul. *Freud and Philosophy*, trans. Denis Savage, New Haven and London, Yale University Press, 1970.

Rieff, Philip. *Freud: The Mind of the Moralist*, London, Victor Gollancz, 1959.

——. *The Triumph of the Therapeutic*, London, Chatto & Windus, 1966.

Ritvo, Lucille B. *Darwin's Influence on Freud*, New Haven and London, Yale University Press, 1990.

Rizzuto, Ana-Maria. *The Birth of the Living God*, Chicago and London, University of Chicago Press, 1979.

Roazen, Paul. *Freud and his Followers*, New York, Knopf, 1975.

Robert, Marthe. *From Oedipus to Moses – Freud's Jewish Identity*, London, Routledge & Kegan Paul, 1977.

Roheim, Geza. *Psycho-Analysis and Anthropology*, New York, International Universities Press, 1950.

Rosmarin-Weiss, T. *The Hebrew Moses: An Answer to Sigmund Freud*, New York, The Jewish Book Club, 1939.

Rubenstein, R.L. 'A Note on the Research Lag in Psychoanalytic Studies of Religion,' *Jewish Social Studies* (1963) 25: 133–44.

——. 'The Significance of Castration Anxiety in Rabbinic Mythology,' *Psychoanalytic Review* (1963–64) 50: 289–99.

Ruether, Rosemary (ed.) *Religion and Sexism: Images of Women in the Jewish and Christian Traditions*, New York, Simon & Schuster, 1974.

Saffady, William. 'New Developments in the Psychoanalytic Study of Religion: A Bibliographic Review of the Literature since 1960,' *Psychoanalytic Review* (1976) 63: 291–9.

Sanders, B. G. *Christianity after Freud*, London, Geoffrey Bles, 1949.

Schilling, Harold. *Science and Religion*, New York, Charles Scribner's Sons, 1962.

Schlossmann, H. 'God the Father and His Sons,' *American Imago* (1972) 8: 35–51.

Schmidt, W. *The Origin and Growth of Religion*, trans. H. J. Rose, London, Methuen & Co., 1931.

Schoenfeld, C. G. 'God the Father – and Mother: Study and Extension of Freud's Conception of God as an Exalted Father,' *American Imago* (1960) 19: 213–34.

Schreber, Daniel Paul. *Denkwürdigkeiten eines Nervenkranken*, Leipzig, Oswald Mutze, 1903.

Sears, R. R. *Survey of Objective Studies of Psychoanalytic Concepts*, New York, Social Science Research Council, Bulletin No. 31, 1943.

Simon, Ernst. 'Sigmund Freud, the Jew,' *Leo Baeck International Yearbook* (1957) vol. 2 pp. 270–302.

Simonds, Paul. *The Social Primates*, New York, Harper & Row, 1974.

Smith, W. Robertson. *Lectures on the Religion of the Semites*, London, A. & C. Black, 1889.

Spero, Moshe Halevi. *Religious Objects as Psychological Structures*, Chicago and London, University of Chicago Press, 1992.

Spiro, Melford E. *Oedipus in the Trobriands*, New Brunswick and London, Transaction Publishers, 1993.

Stiver, Dan R. *The Philosophy of Language*, Oxford, Blackwell, 1996.

Storr, Anthony. *Freud*, Oxford and New York, Oxford University Press, 1989.

Strachey, James. 'Sigmund Freud: A Sketch of his Life and Ideas,' *PFL*, 10: 11–23.

——. 'Preliminary Notes upon the Problem of Akhenaten,' *International Journal of Psycho-Analysis* (1939) 20: 33–42.

Sulloway, Frank J. *Freud: Biologist of the Mind*, London, Fontana, 1980.

Toulmin, Stephen. *The Philosophy of Science*, New York, Harper & Row, 1960.

Trible, Phyllis. *God and the Rhetoric of Sexuality*, Philadelphia, Fortress Press, 1978.

Tylor, Edward. *Primitive Culture*, London, Murray, 1871.

Velikovsky, E. 'The Dreams Freud Dreamed,' *Psychoanalytic Review* (1943) 30: 487–511.

Vergote, Antoine (with Catherine Aubert). 'Parental Images and Representations of God,' *Social Compass* (1972–73) 19: 431–44.

Vergote, Antoine (with Alvaro Tamayo, Luiz Pasquali, Michael Bonami, Marie-Rose Pattyn and Anne Gusters). 'Concept of God and Parental Images,' *Journal of the Scientific Study of Religion* (1969) 8: 79–87.

Vitz, Paul C. *Sigmund Freud's Christian Unconscious*, London and New York, The Guilford Press, 1988.

Wallace, Edwin R. *Freud and Anthropology*, New York, International Universities Press, 1983.

Ward, Ivan (ed.) *Is Psychoanalysis another Religion?* London, Freud Museum Publications, 1993.

Weizsaecker, Viktor von. 'Reminiscences of Freud and Jung,' *Freud and the 20th Century*, ed. Benjamin Nelson, Cleveland and New York: The World Publishing Company, 1957.

Winnicott, D. *The Maturational Process and the Facilitating Environment*, New York, International Universities Press, 1965.

——. *Playing and Reality*, New York, Routledge, 1971.

Wittgenstein, Ludwig. *Philosophical Investigations*, trans. G.E.M. Anscombe, New York, Macmillan, 1958.

Wollheim, Richard. *Sigmund Freud*, London, Fontana, 1971.

Yerushalmi, Yosef. *Freud's Moses: Judaism Terminable and Interminable*, New Haven and London, Yale University Press, 1991.

Zilboorg, Gregor. *Freud and Religion*, London, Geoffrey Chapman, 1958.

——. *Psychoanalysis and Religion*, ed. Margaret Stone Zilboorg, New York, Farrar, Straus & Cudahy, 1967.

Zuckerman, S. *The Social Life of Monkeys and Apes*, New York, Harcourt & Brace, 1932.

CARL GUSTAV JUNG

Adickes, Erich. *Kant's Opus postumum dargestellt und beurteilt*, Berlin, Ergänzungsheft der Kant-Studien, 1920.

Adler, Gerhard. *Studies in Analytical Psychology*, London, Routledge & Kegan Paul, 1948.

Allport, Gordon. *Becoming*, New Haven, Yale University Press, 1955.

——. *The Individual and his Religion*, New York, Macmillan, 1960.

Altizer, Thomas. A Critical Analysis of C. G. Jung's Understanding of Religion, unpublished PhD thesis, University of Chicago, 1955.

Baynes, H. G. 'Freud *versus* Jung,' *The British Journal of Medical Psychology* (1928) 8 (1): 14–43.

Bennet, E. A. *C. G. Jung*, London, Barrie & Rockliff, 1961.

Bertine, Eleanor. 'Jung's Psychology and Religion,' *Religion in Life* (1959) 28: 365–75.

Bonime, Walter. 'The Psychic Energy of Freud and Jung,' *American Journal of Psychiatry* (1955) 112: 372–4.

Borelli, John. 'Dreams, Myths, and Religious Symbolism,' *Thought* (1975) 50: 56–66.

Boss, Medard. *The Analysis of Dreams*, London, Rider & Co., 1957.

Browning, Don S. *Religious Thought and the Modern Psychologies*, Philadelphia, Fortress Press, 1987.

Bryant, Christopher. *Jung and the Christian Way*, Minneapolis, Seabury Press, 1983.

Buber, Martin. *Eclipse of God: Studies in the Relation between Religion and Philosophy*, New York, Harper & Row, 1952.

Burchard, Edward. 'Mystical and Scientific Aspects of the Psychoanalytic Theories of Freud, Adler, and Jung,' *American Journal of Psychotherapy* (1961) 14: 289–307.

Bychowski, Gustav. 'Freud and Jung: An Encounter,' *The Israel Annals of Psychiatry and Related Disciplines* (1964) 2: 129–43.

Carlsson, Allan. 'Jung on Meaning and Symbols in Religion,' *The Journal of General Education* (1970) 22: 29–40.

Chapman, J. Harley. *Jung's Three Theories of Religious Experience*, Lewiston, NY, The Edwin Mellen Press, 1988.

Clark, Robert A. 'Jung and Freud: A Chapter in Psychoanalytic History,' *American Journal of Psychotherapy* (1955) 9: 605–11.

Coudert, Allison. *Alchemy: The Philosopher's Stone*, Boulder, Colorado, Shambhala Publications, 1980.

Cox, David. *Jung and St. Paul*, New York, Association Press, 1959.

Crowley, T. 'Jung and Religion,' *Irish Theological Quarterly* (1956) 23: 73–9.

Curtis, Monica. 'Jung's Essay on the Transformation Symbol in the Mass,' *Spring* (1952): 1–22.

Dourley, John P. 'In the Shadow of the Monotheisms: Jung's Conversations with Buber and White' in *Jung and the Monotheisms*, ed. Joel Ryce-Menuhin, London and New York, Routledge, 1994, pp. 125–45.

Douglas, William. 'The Influence of Jung's Work: A Critical Comment,' *Journal of Religion and Health* (1962) 1: 260–72.

Dry, Avis M. *The Psychology of Jung*, London, Methuen, 1961.

Dyer, Donald R. *Cross-currents of Jungian Thought*, Boston, Mass., Shambhala Publications, 1991.

Edinger, Edward. *Anatomy of the Psyche: Alchemical Symbolism in Psychotherapy*, LaSalle, Ill., Open Court Publishing Co., 1985.

——. *Ego and Archetype*, Boston and London, Shambhala Publications, 1992.

Edwards, Paul (ed.). 'Common Consent Arguments for the Existence of God,' *Encyclopedia of Philosophy*, New York, Macmillan, vol. 2, pp. 147–55.

Eliade, Mircea. *The Forge and the Crucible: The Origins and Structure of Alchemy*, New York, Harper & Row, 1962.

Ellenberger, Henri. *The Discovery of the Unconscious*, New York, Basic Books, 1970.

Erikson, E. *Childhood and Society*, London, Penguin Books, 1965.

Faber, Heije. *Psychology of Religion*, London, SCM Press, 1976.

Fischer, John L. 'The Sociopsychological Analysis of Folktales,' *Current Anthropology* (1963) 4: 235–95.

Fodor, Nandor. *Freud, Jung, and Occultism*, New Hyde Park, New York, University Books, 1971.

Fordham, Frieda. *An Introduction to Jung's Psychology*, London, Penguin Books, 1953.

Fordham, Michael (with Robert Moody). 'Symposium on Jung's Contribution to Analytical Thought and Practice,' *The British Journal of Medical Psychology* (1956) 29: 3–14.

——. *New Developments in Analytical Psychology*, with a Foreword by C. G. Jung, London, Routledge & Kegan Paul, 1957.

——. 'The Relevance of Analytical Theory to Alchemy, Mysticism, and Theology,' *Journal of Analytical Psychology* (1960) 5: 113–29.

Fowler, James W. *Stages of Faith: The Psychology of Human Development and the Quest for Meaning*, San Francisco, Harper & Row, 1981.

Frankfort, Henri. 'The Archetype in Analytical Psychology and the History of Religion,' *Journal of the Warburg and Courtauld Institutes* (1954) 21: 166–78.

Franz, Marie-Louise von. *Alchemical Active Imagination*, Irving, Tx, Spring Publications, 1979.

Frey, Liliane. 'Evil from the Psychological Point of View,' *Spring* (1965) 5–48.

Frey-Rohn, Liliane. *Friedrich Nietzsche: A Psychological Approach to His Life and Work*, ed. R. Hinshaw and L. Fischli, Zurich, Daimon Verlag, 1984.

Friedmann, Maurice. 'Religion and Psychology: The Limits of the Psyche as Touchstone of Reality,' *Quaker Religious Thought* (1970) 12: 2–48.

——. *To Deny Our Nothingness*, Chicago, The University of Chicago Press, 1978.

Fromm, Erich. 'Freud and Jung,' *Pastoral Psychology, Vol. I* (1950): 9–15.

Galdston, Iago. 'Job, Jung and Freud: An Essay on the Meaning of Life,' *Bulletin of the New York Academy of Medicine* (1958) 34 (12): 770–83.

Glover, Edward. *Freud or Jung*, London, George Allen & Unwin, 1950.

Goldbrunner, Josef. *Individuation: A Study of the Depth Psychology of Carl Gustav Jung*, Notre Dame, University of Notre Dame Press, 1964.

Gosse, Edmund. *Father and Son*, London, Heinemann, 1907.

Hall, Calvin S. (with Vernon Nordby). *A Primer of Jungian Psychology*, London, Croom Helm, 1974.

—— (with G. Lindzey). *Theories of Personality* (3rd edn), New York, John Wiley & Sons, 1978.

Hanna, Charles B. *The Face of the Deep: The Religious Ideas of C. G. Jung*, Philadelphia, Westminster Press, 1967.

Hannah, Barbara. *Striving Towards Wholeness*, New York, G. P. Putnam's Sons, 1971.

——. *Jung: His Life and Work*, New York, G. P. Putnam's Sons, 1976.

Harding, Esther. *Journey into Self: An Interpretation of Bunyan's Pilgrim's Progress*, London and New York, Longmans, Green, 1956.

Heimann, Paula. 'Some Notes on the Psycho-analytic Concept of Introjected Objects,' *British Journal of Medical Psychology* (1949) 22: 8–15.

Heisig, James W. *Imago Dei: A Study of C. G. Jung's Psychology of Religion*, Lewisburg, Penn., Bucknell University Press, 1978.

Himmelfarb, Gertrude. *Darwin and the Darwinian Revolution*, London, Chatto & Windus, 1959.

Hostie, Raymond. *Religion and the Psychology of Jung*, London and New York, Sheed and Ward, 1957.

Jacobi, Jolande. *The Way of Individuation*, trans. R. F. C. Hull, London, Hodder and Stoughton, 1967.

Jaffé, Aniela. *The Myth of Meaning*, trans. R. F. C. Hull, London, Penguin Books, 1975.

Jung, C. G. *The Collected Works of C. G. Jung*, ed. Sir Herbert Read, Michael Fordham and Gerhard Adler; exec. ed. William McGuire, trans. R.F.C. Hull, London, Routledge & Kegan Paul, 1953–79. Cited in this work as *CW*.

——. *Man and His Symbols*, New York, Dell, 1964.

——. 'Religionless Christianity: A Letter by Carl G. Jung', trans. Mrs Stephen Benko, *Journal of the American Association of Religion* (1971) 39: 43–7.

——. *C. G. Jung Letters*, ed. G. Adler, with A. Jaffé, Princeton, Princeton University Press, 1973 and 1975.

——. *Selected Writings*, selected and introduced Anthony Storr, London, Fontana Press, 1983.

——. *The Gnostic Jung*, selected and introduced Robert A. Segal, London, Routledge, 1992.

——. *Memories, Dreams, Reflections*, London, Fontana Press, 1993. Cited in this work as *MDR*.

Kant, Immanuel. *Critique of Pure Reason* (1781) trans. Norman Kemp Smith, London, Macmillan, 1929.

Kelsey, Morton T. *God, Dreams, and Revelations*, Minneapolis, Augsburg Publishing House, 1974.

Kirk, G. S. *Myth: Its Meaning and Functions in Ancient and Other Cultures*, Cambridge, Cambridge University Press, 1970.

Levinson, D. (with C. N. Darrow, E. B. Klein, M. H. Levinson and B. McKee). *The Seasons of a Man's Life*, New York, Knopf, 1978.

Locke, John. *Essay Concerning Human Understanding* (1690), abr. and ed. A. S. Pringle-Pattison, Oxford, Clarendon Press, 1956.

Macquarrie, John. *20th Century Religious Thought*, London, SCM Press, 1971.

McGowan, Don. *What is Wrong with Jung*, Buffalo, NY, Prometheus Books, 1994.

McGuire, W. (with R. F. Hull). *C. G. Jung Speaking*, Princeton, Princeton University Press, 1977.

Martin, Luther H. (ed. with James Goss). *Essays on Jung and the Study of Religion*, London, University Press of America, 1985.

Mattoon, Mary Ann. *Jungian Psychology in Perspective*, New York, The Free Press, and London, Collier Macmillan, 1981.

Meier, C. A. *Personality*, trans. D. N. Roscoe, Einsiedeln, Switzerland, Daimon, 1995.

Moore, R. L. (ed.). *Carl Jung and Christian Spirituality*, Mahwah, NJ, Paulist Press, 1988.

Moreno, Antonio. *Jung, Gods, and Modern Man*, London, Sheldon Press, 1970.

Nagy, Marilyn. *Philosophical Issues in the Psychology of C. G. Jung*, Albany, State University of New York Press, 1991.

O'Neill, Timothy. *The Individuated Hobbit: Jung, Tolkien, and the Archetypes of Middle-Earth*, London, Thames & Hudson, 1980.

Otto, Rudolf. *Das Heilige* (1917). English trans., *The Idea of the Holy*, Oxford, Oxford University Press, 1923.

Pauson, Marion L. *Jung the Philosopher*, New York, Peter Lang, 1988.

Perry, John. 'A Jungian Formulation of Schizophrenia,' *American Journal of Psychotherapy* (1956) 10: 54–65.

Peters, R. S. (ed.). *Brett's History of Psychology* (revised edn) London, George Allen & Unwin, 1962.

Phillips, J. L. *The Origins of Intellect*, New York, W. H. Freeman, 1975.

Philp, H. L. *Jung and the Problem of Evil*, London, Rockliff, 1958.

Piaget, J. *Play, Dreams and Imitation in Childhood*, trans. C. Gattegno and F. M. Hodgson, London, W. Heinemann, 1951.

Post, L. van der. *Jung and the Story of Our Time*, London, Penguin Books, 1978.

Postle, Beatrice. 'Religion in the Psychologies of Jung and Freud,' *Ohio State Medical Journal* (1947) 43: 947–50.

Progoff, Ira. *Jung's Psychology and Its Social Meaning*, with an Introduction by Goodwin Watson, London, Routledge & Kegan Paul, 1953.

Quispel, Gilles. 'C. G. Jung und die Gnosis' (1968), trans. *The Gnostic Jung*, selected and introduced Robert C. Segal, London, Routledge, 1992, pp. 219–38.

Rieff, Philip. 'C. G. Jung's Confession,' *Encounter* (1964) 22: 45–50.

Ricketts, M. L. 'The Nature and Extent of Eliade's "Jungianism",' *Union Seminary Quarterly Review* (1970) 25: 211–34.

Riukas, Stanley. God: Myth, Symbol, and Reality: A Study of Jung's Psychology, unpublished PhD thesis, New York University, 1967.

Robertson, Robin. *Jungian Archetypes*, York Beach, Maine, Nicolas-Hays, 1995.

Russell, Bertrand. *Why I am Not a Christian* (1957), edition used: London, George Allen & Unwin, 1975.

Sanford, John A. *Dreams: God's Forgotten Language*, Philadelphia, J. B. Lippincott, 1968.

——. *King Saul, the Tragic Hero: A Study in Individuation*, New York and Mahwah, NJ, Paulist Press, 1985.

Schaer, Hans. *Religion and the Cure of Souls in Jung's Psychology*, trans. R.F. C. Hull, London, Routledge & Kegan Paul, 1951.

Schrader, G. A. 'Kant's Presumed Repudiation of the "Moral Argument" in the Opus Postumum,' *Philosophy* (1951) 26: 228–41.

Segal, Robert A. 'Introduction: The Gnostic Jung,' *The Gnostic Jung*, selected and introduced Robert A. Segal, London, Routledge, 1992, pp. 3–52.

Sharp, Daryl L. *The Secret Raven: Conflict and Transformation in the Life of Franz Kafka*, Toronto, Inner City Books, 1980.

Shelburne, Walter A. *Mythos and Logos in the Thought of Carl Jung*, Albany, State University of New York Press, 1988.

Shengold, Leonard. 'The Freud/Jung Letters: The Correspondence between Sigmund Freud and C. G. Jung,' *Journal of the American Psychoanalytical Association* (1976) 24: 669–83.

Sherrard, Philip. 'An Introduction to the Religious Thought of C. G. Jung,' *Studies in Comparative Religion* (1969) 111: 33–49.

Singer, June K. 'Religion and the Collective Unconscious: Common Ground of Psychology and Religion,' *Zygon* (1969) 4: 315–31.

Slusser, Gerald. *From Jung to Jesus*, Atlanta, John Knox Press, 1986.

Sobosan, Jeffery. 'Kierkegaard and Jung on the Self,' *Journal of Psychology and Theology* (1975) 3: 31–5.

Spiegelman, J. M. (ed.) *Catholicism and Jungian Psychology*, Arizona, New Falcon Publications, 1994.

Stein, Murray (ed., with Robert L. Moore). *Jung's Challenge to Contemporary Religion*, Wilmette, Ill., Chiron Publications, 1987.

Stepansky, Paul. 'The Empiricist as Rebel: Jung, Freud and the Burdens of Discipleship,' *Journal of the History of the Behavioral Sciences* (1976) 12: 216–39.

Stevens, Anthony. *On Jung*, London, Penguin Books, 1990.

Storr, Anthony. *Jung*, London, Fontana 'Modern Masters' Series, 1986.

Strunk, Orlo. 'Psychology, Religion, and C. G. Jung: A Review of Periodical Literature,' *Journal of Bible and Religion* (1956) 24: 106–13.

Sullivan, Roger J. *Immanuel Kant's Moral Theory*, Cambridge, Cambridge University Press, 1989.

Sykes, Gerald. *The Hidden Remnant*, New York, Harper & Row, 1962.

Tourney, Garfield. 'Empedocles and Freud, Heraclitus and Jung,' *Bulletin of the History of Medicine* (1956) 30: 109–23.

Ulanov, Barry. *Jung and the Outside World*, Wilmette, Ill., Chiron Publications, 1992.

Vandermeersch, P. 'The Archetypes: A New Way to Holiness?' *Cistercian Studies* (1975) 10: 3–21.

Walsh, W. H. *Kant's Criticism of Metaphysics*, Edinburgh, Edinburgh University Press, 1975.

White, Victor. *God and the Unconscious*, London, Fontana Books, 1960.

Whitmont, Edward. *The Symbolic Quest: Basic Concepts of Analytical Psychology*, Princeton, NJ, Princeton University Press, 1969.

——. 'Prefatory Remarks to Jung's "Reply to Buber",' *Spring* (1973): 188–95.

Zaehner, R. C. 'A New Buddha and a New Tao,' *The Concise Encyclopaedia of Living Faiths*, New York, Hawthorn Books, pp. 402–12.

INDEX OF NAMES

INDEX OF
SUBJECTS:
FREUD

INDEX OF
SUBJECTS:
JUNG